READING
the WORLD,
the GLOBE,
and the COSMOS

GLOBAL
STUDIES IN
EDUCATION

A.C. (Tina) Besley, Michael A. Peters,
Cameron McCarthy, Fazal Rizvi
General Editors

Vol. 28

The Global Studies in Education series is part of the Peter Lang Education list.
Every volume is peer reviewed and meets
the highest quality standards for content and production.

PETER LANG
New York • Washington, D.C./Baltimore • Bern
Frankfurt • Berlin • Brussels • Vienna • Oxford

SUZANNE S. CHOO

READING
the WORLD,
the GLOBE,
and the COSMOS

Approaches to Teaching Literature
for the Twenty-First Century

PETER LANG
New York • Washington, D.C./Baltimore • Bern
Frankfurt • Berlin • Brussels • Vienna • Oxford

Library of Congress Cataloging-in-Publication Data

Choo, Suzanne S.
Reading the world, the globe, and the cosmos: approaches
to teaching literature for the twenty-first century / Suzanne S. Choo.
pages cm. — (Global studies in education; v. 28)
Includes bibliographical references and index.
1. Literature—Study and teaching. 2. Literature—Cross-cultural studies.
3. Citizenship—Cross-cultural studies. 4. World citizenship.
5. Education and globalization. I. Title.
PN61.C46   807.1—dc23   2013012999
ISBN 978-1-4331-2178-4 (hardcover)
ISBN 978-1-4331-2177-7 (paperback)
ISBN 978-1-4539-1153-2 (e-book)
ISSN 2153-330X

Bibliographic information published by **Die Deutsche Nationalbibliothek.**
Die Deutsche Nationalbibliothek lists this publication in the "Deutsche
Nationalbibliografie"; detailed bibliographic data is available
on the Internet at http://dnb.d-nb.de/.

Cover image by Pia Stern
www.piastern.com

The paper in this book meets the guidelines for permanence and durability
of the Committee on Production Guidelines for Book Longevity
of the Council of Library Resources.

© 2013 Peter Lang Publishing, Inc., New York
29 Broadway, 18th floor, New York, NY 10006
www.peterlang.com

Printed in the United States of America

Contents

List of Figures

List of Tables

Series Editor's Foreword:
A Riposte to Globalization

The concept of time-space compression remains curiously unexamined. In particular, it is a concept which often remains without much social content (Doreen Massey, 1993 p. 59).

All our ventures and exploits, all our acts and dreams, are bridges designed to overcome . . . separation and reunite us with the world and our fellow beings (Octavio Paz, 1990, p. 11).

In recent years, no term has more stirred up critical and mainstream social science scholarship than the insistent term "globalization." The invocation of globalization has not rendered conceptual closure on the processes to which the term points: the heightened interconnectivity between and among individuals, groups and institutions that characterizes our late-modern world. It has, instead, provoked ceaseless formulation and reformulation. Thus there are those, for instance, who see globalization as linked to expanding economic and cultural transactions across national borders — the so-called flat world of Thomas Freidman (1999, 2005). There are those who use the term, pessimistically, theorizing globalization as an extension of imperialism in its latest phase and pointing to the neoliberal expansion of the West into the third world as somehow more efficiently capturing surplus value (Ritzer, 2010; Waters, 2010). On this view, neoliberal globalization is no more than a kind of McDonaldization of those countries struggling to break out of colonial pasts. There are yet those who seem completely taken by the technological scale of recent globalizing developments that have sparked what David Harvey and Anthony Giddens call *time-space compression*, which in turn has allowed for the revolution in financial services and other peer-to-peer transactions that have made the state virtually irrelevant (Castells, 2009, 2012). This investment in globalization, in a manner that leaves the term itself unmarked and unquestioned, actually characterizes the scholarly approaches of both mainstream and critical theorists. This is a kind of contemporary positivism on the global. This is what Norman Fairclough correctly calls "globalism" — a kind of unreflexive, objectivist invocation of the global and its capacities to alter the world (Fairclough, 2006, p. 7).

In reaction to this tendency to deploy a flat, monolithic invocation of globalization, an insurgent group of feminist critical scholars such as Doreen Massey (1993, 2007), Aihwa Ong (1999, 2006), and Saskia Sassen (2008) has called for closer reading and more careful research attention to variability, nuance, discontinuity and disarticulation in accounts of the operation of globalization processes with respect to the real existing circumstances of human actors. Saskia Sassen, for example, has insisted on the need for the methodological deployment of a research strategy of "social thickness" (2000, p. 216). By this, she encourages scholars to especially pay attention to the co-articulation of economic, cultural and political forces in any instantiation of global processes, underscoring the unevenness of the different vectors of globalization: the speed of time-space compression in financial services may not often be matched by the speed of change in culture, education, law and so forth. Sassen shows how late-modern states, under the pressure of new developments, are not in demise but are morphing into new collections of practices marked by the disarticulation of authority, territory and rights. The concrete human experiences derived from this are what Ong (2006, p. 7) calls "graduated sovereignty" and graded forms of citizenship. In her "Power-Geometry" essay, Doreen Massey maintains that space/place is not monochromatic but hosts plural identities, usages and attachments. Aihwa Ong points to the rational calculation of government actors in post-developmental states such as Taiwan, Singapore and Malaysia and their radical combination of neoliberal globalization and powerful drives towards upgrading the social commons.

With this wonderful text, *Reading the World, the Globe, and the Cosmos*, we must now add Suzanne Choo to this venerable list of feminist intellectuals who want us to consider a wider range of subjects concerning globalization than we normally explore. Choo writes from the perspective that all of these logics related to globalization are now fully articulated to schooling and must pass through the pedagogical encounter in the classroom. Ultimately, globalization must be brought into dialogue with pedagogical criticism. Here the task is to construct from the encounter with literature — reaching back into previous centuries and forward into the twenty-first century — models of thoughtfulness and meaningful, empathetic relationships. The techniques and aesthetics of literature study should not be a self-enclosing, self-isolating enterprise but should foster the conditions of production of a deep engagement of the self with the other as Tzvetan Todorov tells us in *The Conquest of America* (1984/1999). We must be, as Todorov suggests, much more open to surprise and the improvisatory — learning from each other as we build ever new forms of collaboration, affiliation and feeling. This idea of shared community and shared responsibility for each other and the fate of the human species is the starting point of a new kind of cosmopolitanism that might help us better transact the devaluing of our intellectual labor in the present age of neoliberal globalization. The project here is ambitious but urgent. The teaching of literature has often insulated the literary text from the world, recuperating and preserving the "literary" for a vain form of aesthetics. On the other hand, teaching about the world in geography, social studies, etc. has often ignored the imaginative domain of literature. Scholars like Edward Said have sought to overcome this gulf in the disciplines in such powerful ripostes as *Orientalism* (1979*), The World, the Text and the Critic* (1994), *and On Late Style: Music and Literature against the Grain* (2007). Homi Bhaba, in his *Locations of Culture* (1994), also points to the critically important work of the text in relation to the vigorous life world of subaltern actors. For Bhabha, texts take on their significance in an encounter with human actors at the extremes of Empire: "a literature of empire . . . played out in the wild and wordless wastes of colonial India, Africa, the Caribbean" (Bhabha, 1994, p. 102). The text then is conditioned by the play of globalization's asymmetries.

Choo builds on these insights by introducing a form of pedagogical criticism that brings the globe into the literature classroom. Her interest here is not to describe the world as it is. Neither is it merely to improve the pedagogy of literature. Choo raises, instead, the issue of teaching new cosmopolitan values through pedagogy by integrating the "hospitable imagination." The hospitable imagination is a space for the gestation of creative and critical reflexivity. The classroom, after all, may be the place of a kind of last stand in an age of the ever-expanding refeudalization of the public sphere. As such, it offers possibilities for elaborating networks to the world — networks for a New-World imaginative geography and the building up of subaltern knowledges. In this manner, the classroom becomes a space for the staging of a new enterprise in literature studies—for thinking about the world as we mediate aesthetics. The radical promise of Choo's intervention here is to bring the entire range of aesthetic critique and "reply" (Paz, 1990, p. 5) to the West into a dialogue with globalization from below. Here the concatenation and plurality of voices might serve to reinvigorate the now deeply invaded space of the modern classroom where one might argue the future of humanity resides.

Cameron McCarthy
Director of Global Studies in Education
University of Illinois at Urbana-Champaign

References

Bhabha, H. (1994). *The location of culture*. New York: Routledge.

Castells, M. (2009). *Communication power*. Oxford, UK: Oxford.

Castells, M. (2012). *Networks of outrage and hope*. Oxford, UK: Oxford.

Fairclough, N. (2006). *Language and globalization*. New York: Routledge.

Friedman, T. (1999). *The lexus and the olive tree: Understanding Globalization*. New York: Farrar, Straus and Giroux.

Friedman, T. (2005). *The world is flat*. New York: Farrar, Straus and Giroux.

Massey, D. (1993). Power-geometry and a progressive sense of place. In J. Bird, B. Curtis, T. Putnam, & L. Tickner (Eds.), *Mapping the futures: Local cultures, global change* (pp. 59–69). London: Routledge.

Massey, D. (2007). *World city*. Cambridge, UK: Polity

Ong, A. (1999). *Flexible citizenship: The cultural logics of transnationality*. Durham, NC: Duke University Press.

Ong, A. (2006). *Neoliberalism as exception: Mutations in citizenship and sovereignty*. Durham, NC: Duke University Press.

Paz, O. (1990). *In search of the present*. New York: Harcourt Brace Jovanovich.

Ritzer, G. (2010). Globalization and McDonaldization: Does it all amount to . . . nothing? In G. Ritzer (Ed.), *McDonaldization: The reader*. Thousand Oaks, CA: Sage.

Said, E. (1979). *Orientalism*. New York: Vintage.

Said, E. (1994). *The World, the Text, and the Critic*. New York: Vintage.

Said, E. (2007). *On Late Style: Music and Literature against the Grain*. New York: Vintage.

Sassen, S. (2000). Spatialities and temporalities of the global: Elements for a theorization. *Public Culture 12*(1), 215–232.

Sassen, S. (2008). *Territory, authority, rights: From medieval to global assemblages*. Princeton, NJ: Princeton University Press.

Todorov, T. (1999). *The conquest of America: The question of the other*. New York: Harper and Collins. (Original work published 1984)

Walters, M. (2010). McDonaldization and the global culture of consumption. In G. Ritzer (Ed.), *McDonaldization: The reader*. Thousand Oaks, CA: Sage.

Acknowledgments

This book developed from my dissertation at Teachers College, Columbia University, USA. I am grateful to Dr. Ruth Vinz for her mentorship and guidance throughout the four years of this research, from its initial sketches to its present form. The many insights I gained from our conversations have been vital to the development of this project. I would also like to thank Dr. Yolanda Sealey-Ruiz for her consistent support in helping me discover my voice and shaping my thinking on this subject; Dr. David Hansen for pushing me to ask philosophical questions essential to this work and for powerfully expanding my thinking on cosmopolitanism and education; Dr. Gauri Viswanathan for her penetrating wisdom, whose work on the ideological institutionalization of the discipline of English literature first inspired me with ideas that have led to this book; and Dr. Sheridan Blau, whose expansive knowledge of the field of English education has provided rich layers to this work.

I am thankful for critical friends without whom this project would have been less enjoyable and less enriching. Nick Sousanis, in particular, has journeyed with me throughout my entire writing process and our regular discussions have contributed to strengthening this work. I have also been fortunate to be able to partner with Deb Sawch and Alison Villanueva on various fieldwork projects that have opened my eyes to twenty-first century education around the world.

I thank my editor, Dr. Cameron McCarthy, for his constructive comments and guidance throughout each stage of this project. I am appreciative of Chris Myers, Sophie Appel, Phyllis Korper, and the editorial staff of Peter Lang for the time and effort invested into the production of this book.

I am grateful to the National Institute of Education, Nanyang Technological University, Singapore, for providing funding to conduct this research.

I owe much of this work to the unwavering support of my family. I am grateful to Wilson Tan, my husband, for his tremendous patience and the unconditional love he has shown me.

I thank my parents, Dr. Richard and Tina Choo, for their love, prayers, and everyday acts of concern. Finally, I thank God for His daily provision of grace and strength and in whom all things are possible.

CHAPTER ONE

Introduction:
Toward a Pedagogical Criticism of
Literature Education

At the front of the classroom, children gather in eager expectation as their teacher, sitting in the middle, begins a story about the little cuckoo and the nightingale. The cuckoo, chancing upon a nightingale, begins to earnestly wish that he could sing as beautifully. But to sing beautifully, the nightingale tells the cuckoo, is something that just cannot be learned; it is simply a gift that one is born with. On hearing this, the cuckoo's wife stubbornly refuses to believe it and decides to test the nightingale's theory by hiding her egg in the nest of a hedge sparrow. When the egg hatches, a young cuckoo emerges and is nourished and cared for exactly like the other hedge sparrows. As it grows up, however, the cuckoo finds that it is unable to fly like the others, nor can it sing like the others. The only sound it makes is just that of a cuckoo. The teacher stops at this point, turns to the children, and asks them to tell her what the moral of the story is.

At first glance, there is nothing unusual about this scene of teaching. This educative use of storytelling in formal settings of modern-day classrooms inherits oral traditions in premodern enchanted worlds where hunters with their children would gather around fires under starlit skies to listen to heroic tales or moral fables. The storyteller could be a teacher employed by the state as in the case of the former or a village shaman or prophet in the case of the latter. Whatever the scenario, stories have been used, since time immemorial, to captivate the imagination and to provide vicarious experiences in order to exemplify moral messages.

Consider another scene of teaching set three thousand years ago in which tribal Mayan communities gathered to listen to an old fable[1] about a sad, lonely man who is offered various gifts by the animals of the world. The vulture gives him sight, the jaguar gives him strength, the serpent gives him wisdom, but in the end, the man's inner emptiness, the hole in his heart, remains. The moral of this Mayan fable is similar to the cuckoo story told in the modern classroom; that is, a leopard cannot change its spots and one's innate nature cannot alter. However, there is one vital difference between the two scenes of teaching. While the Mayan story was told to premodern, porous communities in which the material and the spiritual coexisted[2] in order to caution its members against neglecting the soul in pursuit of the material, the cuckoo story was told in German elementary classrooms during the Second World War. This story was specifically used to promote Nazi racial ideology by insisting on the idea of the German *volk* or "pure blood" (Kamenetsky, 1984; Pine, 2010). Within this context, children would learn to recognize the nightingale as a metaphor of a pure Aryan race and would understand the story's moral principle that since race, blood, and character are inherited rather than acquired, those of Jewish and non-Aryan descent would always be deemed inferior.

This brief comparison demonstrates that two fables can contain a similar moral message but can be used in starkly different ways, one to promote spiritual sensitivity and the other to promote racism. Thus, if we are to examine the power and influence of literature and storytelling across history, our attention cannot be placed solely on the text itself; instead, we need to examine the ways in which literature is utilized, taught, or, to use a better term, mediated. Diagrammatically, the function of mediation can be represented as shown in figure 1.1. As depicted, before the literary text is received, it is already mediated by what Stanley Fish (1980) terms "interpretive communities" that share strategies for making sense of and assigning value to texts. These interpretive communities may be present in many different domains in the public sphere, and some examples are the publisher and editorial committee that decide whether a book is worth publishing by considering economic and other demands; the literary critical community such as reviewers of the *New York Times* or the committee comprising the Nobel Prize and the Booker Prize that decide which literary authors can join the circle of those already honored; academic committees that review university curricula and decide whether new categories of courses and their respective texts such as Korean or Caribbean literatures can be formally introduced into the curriculum; and scholarly communities operating through journals, conferences, or think tanks that evaluate literary works and circulate the discursive language and terminology to discuss these works.

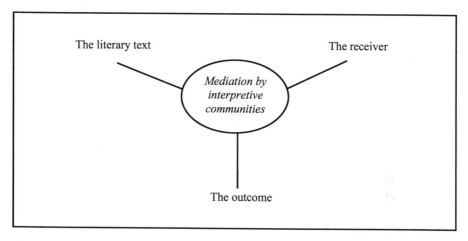

Figure 1.1 Mediation between the literary text and the reader

The main interest, in this book, is the interpretive community comprising literature educators who, from the preschool level to higher education, make important decisions about what kinds of texts to teach, how to organize the literature curriculum, and what instructional strategies are best to employ. If we consider the classical model of communication in which a sender transmits a message to the receiver and the transmission is interrupted by noise (Chandler, 1994; Shannon & Weaver, 1949), then, in this case, the author who sends a message via the literary text to the reader or student is disrupted by a noise source such as the interference of the teacher. While the term "noise" misleadingly contains a negative connotation, it can sometimes be beneficial. For example, if a student suffers from low motivation, the "noise" of the teacher can wake the student from slumber and lethargy; or if a student too hastily reaches a reductive conclusion about the text, the "noise" of the teacher can disrupt this train of thought and push the student to think further and deeper about the text.

What is clear is that, in the context of the classroom, the literary text is never purely received by the student without direct mediation by the teacher or indirect mediation by the school administration that directs educational goals and the state that establishes national curriculum standards. One particularly important aspect of mediation concerns the way the literary text is taught, which then governs how it is received, perceived, and interpreted by students. Yet, as John Guillory (2002a) notes, while there is a wealth of research about literary history, literary genres, and the nature of the literary text, research on approaches to teaching literature is insufficient. Consider, for instance, how, across the history of literary criticism, there have been various scholarly movements contributing influential research to one of these five areas — the author (biographical criticism), the reader (reader-response criticism, psychoanalytic criticism), the text (formalist criticism, new criticism), the language of the text (deconstructive criticism), and the context (Marxist criticism, political criticism). Absent from these movements is what I term pedagogical criticism. This interrogates the ways in which approaches to teaching literature shape the interpretation and reception of the text. In my investigation, I seek to employ pedagogical criticism to analyzing approaches to teaching across the historical evolution of the discipline of English literature.[3]

Reclaiming the Role of Pedagogy in Debates Concerning the Value of Literature Education in the Twenty-First Century

The Decline of Literature Education

The need to consider the influence of pedagogy is particularly pertinent in debates concerning the value of literature education that have garnered increasing attention in recent years. Once described as the "supremely civilizing pursuit" (Eagleton, 1996, p. 27) and the most central subject in British and American schools,[4] literature education has now lost its place of prominence. Even more worrying is its increasingly marginal role in relation to the overall goals of education, particularly in economically advanced nations today. In her book *Not for Profit: Why Democracy Needs the Humanities*, Martha Nussbaum (2010) articulates a disturbing trend that nations, thirsty for profit, are investing their systems of education in applied skills, particularly in science and technology, so as to stay competitive in the global market. The result is that literature and the humanities, perceived by policymakers as useless frills, are being cut away. She cites evidence from various sources including the U.S. Department of Education's *Commission on the Future of Higher Education*, published in 2006, which argues for greater emphasis in highly applied learning designed to contribute to the national economy while leaving little room for the arts and humanities. "If this trend continues," Nussbaum (2010) observes, "nations all over the world will soon be producing generations of useful machines, rather than complete citizens who can think for themselves, criticize tradition, and understand the significance of another person's sufferings and achievements" (p. 2). The trend that Nussbaum is concerned about may be observed in two main forms of decline across different countries.

The first obvious form is a decline in enrollment numbers. In Singapore, English literature remained a compulsory subject in the school curriculum for several decades as part of its British colonial legacy. Shortly after the local government came into power in 1959, students were encouraged to study literature in their mother tongue alongside English literature, which was still deemed conducive to the government's promotion of English language as an official first language in this multiracial island-city. The decline in English literature occurred most dramatically after 1991 when the Ministry of Education publicized the ranking of schools and many schools began dropping the subject since it affected their overall academic standing. The drop was exacerbated in 2001 when the Ministry declared social studies a compulsory elective humanities subject to be studied along with one of three other elective humanities subjects: geography, history, and literature in English. Now that most students had to choose one of the three humanities subjects for study, more than 90 percent chose elective geography or history. Broadly, enrollment rates in literature in English as a full paper at the high-stakes national examination offered to secondary four (grade ten) students fell over two decades from 47.9 percent in 1992 to 21.8 percent in 2001 to 9 percent in 2012 (Heng, 2013).[5]

Like Singapore, the decline in literature education in the United States is most obviously apparent in enrollment figures as observed in the following: the number of students majoring in English literature declined by 57 percent in just ten years from 1970 to 1980 (Bennett, 1984); from 1980 to 1990, those majoring in the humanities dropped a further 30 percent to less than 16 percent while those majoring in business climbed from 14 percent to 22 percent (Chace, 2009); at the high school level, students are turning away from literature in particular and from the humanities in general as observed in the fact that among the millions who take the Preliminary Scholastic Aptitude Test (PSAT) in the tenth grade, only 9 percent indicate interest in the humanities (Delbanco, 1999). Finally, in terms of job listings in English, literature, and foreign languages, the Modern Language Association reports that these declined by 21 percent from 2008 to 2009, the biggest decline in thirty-four years (Cohen, 2009).

Even more surprising is the decline of literature education in the United Kingdom. In recent years, the number of students enrolled in the General Certificate of Secondary Education (GCSE) English Literature Advanced Level examination (a high-stakes nationwide examination taken at the end of secondary education) dropped from 77 percent in 2004 to 72 percent in 2009, which is equivalent to one in four students opting out of taking the subject (Curtis, 2009). While enrollment figures are still considerably higher than other countries, the drop has raised alarm bells among politicians, particularly given the historical primacy of the subject and its connections to British national identity. Michael Gove, the Secretary of State for Education, expressed shock at the current figures and reiterated the importance of English literature in public education (Paton, 2009).

The second form of decline is more subtly observed in the diminution of standards. Despite the drop in enrollment figures in the United Kingdom, a more pressing issue concerns the very rigor of the subject itself. A review of the GCSE English Literature Advanced Level examination papers from 2005 to 2009 by the Office of Qualifications and Examinations Regulation (Ofqual), an independent watchdog, brought to light several problems with current assessment standards. In particular, they found that the questions asked were too formulaic, predictable, and increasingly less demanding. Even the texts assessed had become less challenging. For example, one accreditation board had replaced two texts, *Captain Corelli's Mandolin* and *Catch 22*, with *The Adventures of Huckleberry Finn* and *Northern Lights*, which they argue are more appropriate for earlier grade levels (Ofqual, 2011). The dilution of standards perhaps points to a more deep-seated issue concerning the subject's growing ambivalence and irrelevance in contemporary society. When the National Curriculum for English was first introduced in 1989, it faced tremendous controversy, so much so that the curriculum was revised four times within five years (Raban-Bisby, 1995). However, despite various amendments to the curriculum, scholars charged that the GCSE English Literature Advanced Level examinations had not changed since the 1950s. The assessment contained few new authors and questions typically remained the same. Further, while English departments in universities were already engaging with literary theory, the secondary curriculum continued to focus on the traditional analysis of themes, plot, character, and style. The result was a wide disparity between the study of literature in schools and in universities so that students were often found bewildered and disoriented in their first few undergraduate years (Ballinger,

2002; Eaglestone & McEnvoy, 1999). A more scathing attack occurred in 2005 when the National Association of Teachers of English (NATE) produced a report recommending that English literature be scrapped at the GCSE Advanced Level. The key argument was that the subject failed to give students the skills needed in universities, that it relied too narrowly on a small number of texts, and that the study of literature had little relation to the development of a broader understanding of contemporary culture (Bluett et al., 2006; Garner, 2005).

Doubts about the rigor of English literature and its capacity to be relevant have also been echoed by various policymakers in Australia. While English continues to be the only compulsory subject for students seeking to graduate high school, the emphasis on literature has shifted from the early twentieth century when policy papers such as the 1921 Newbolt Report by the Board of Education in England greatly established its centrality in the national curriculum. By the 1980s, there was increasing pressure to design English courses to cater to the substantial increase in recently arrived students from non-English-speaking backgrounds. This led to the formation of a new "Contemporary English" course that placed more emphasis on language and literacy skills (Manuel & Brock, 2003). The result was a sharp rise in the number of students who opted for this watered-down English curriculum since they considered it to be less demanding and had no intention of pursuing literature in the university anyway. Thus, enrollment in this course increased from 2,000 students in 1989 to 18,000 in 1995 (McGaw, 1996). By the late twentieth century, there were growing concerns about the emphasis on basic English literacy in the secondary curriculum with a corresponding movement away from the teaching of literature (Maslen, 2008). Some politicians described English as a "back to basics" curriculum (Brock, 1984, p. 58), while scholars lamented that the predominance of mechanical English in the curriculum was failing students by underdeveloping skills in critical thinking and aesthetic appreciation (Walshe, 2008).

These trends across different countries have consequently contributed to a global consciousness of literature education's demise that is most obvious in the titles of numerous books and articles published on this topic in the late twentieth century (see table 1.1):

Table 1.1. Titles of books and articles related to the decline of literature education from the 1990s to the present

Country	Titles
Australia	"After English: Toward a Less Critical Literacy" (Hunter, 1997)
	"W(h)ither the Place of Literature?" (Manuel & Brock, 2003)
	"Australia: Humanities Face Global Crisis" (Maslen, 2008)
	"It's Time Australia Reshaped English" (Walshe, 2008)
Singapore	"On Literature's Use(ful/less)ness: Reconceptualizing the Literature Curriculum in the Age of Globalization" (Choo, 2011)
	"On the Nation's Margins: The Social Place of Literature in Singapore" (Holden, 2000)
	"Valuing the Value(s) of Literature" (Liew, 2012)
	"The Politics of Pragmatism: Some Issues in the Teaching of Literature in Singapore" (Poon, 2007)
	"Literature: A Dying Subject in Schools" (*Straits Times*, 2002)
	"Reigniting the Spark of Literature" (*Straits Times*, 2013)
United Kingdom	"Number Taking GCSE in English Literature Falls" (Curtis, 2009)
	"A Critical Time for English" (Eagletsone & McEnvoy, 1999)
	"Scrap English Literature A-level, Teachers Demand" (Garner, 2005)
	"Teenagers 'Shunning English Literature' at School" (Paton, 2009)
	"The State of English in the State of England" (Raban-Bisby, 1995)
United States	"An Elegy for the Canon" (Bloom, 1994)
	"The Decline of the English Department" (Chace, 2009)
	"The Decline and Fall of Literature" (Delbanco, 1999)
	"'The Age of Criticism': Debating the Decline of Literature in the US, 1940-2000" (Ekelund, 2002)
	"Will the Humanities Save us?" (Fish, 2008)
	"Reading Literature: Decline and Fall?" (Iannone, 2005)
	The Death of Literature (Kernan, 1990)
	Not for Profit: Why Democracy Needs the Humanities (Nussbaum, 2010)
	The Rise and Fall of English (Scholes, 1998)

The Marginalization of Pedagogy in Arguments Defending Literature Education

It would not be too far-fetched to say that the discipline of English literature has, toward the late twentieth century, entered a self-reflexive phase. Questions concerning literature education's usefulness, value, relevance, or contribution, stemming from a cross-section of the public including scholars, educators, and policymakers, ultimately undergird debates about the contemporary state of literature education. At the same time, one of the problems with many of the arguments defending literature education is that these reflections often fall into the trap of their being premised on the ontological power of the literary text. Thus, they do not adequately make a clear distinction between the private and public spheres concerning the role of literature education. Put another way, arguments concerning literature education's demise are commonly grounded on the value of literature and not the value of teaching literature in the context of schooling. The focus is therefore on the power of the literary text as a basis for literature education rather than the pedagogical power of teaching literature.

The following are two examples that highlight this fallacy. The first is found in a chapter titled, "An Elegy for the Canon," in which Harold Bloom (1994) passionately seeks to restore the significance of the Western canon. He states, "Originally the Canon meant the choice of books in our teaching institutions, and despite the recent politics of multiculturalism, the Canon's true question remains: What shall the individual who still desires to read attempt to read, this late in history?" (p. 15). Here, Bloom centers the reader's attention on the main problem for discussion: the problematic institution of the canon as an elitist act of text selection in English departments. At the same time, Bloom directs the true question of the canon to the individual and, more specifically, his or her choice of texts for private reading. In other words, the "Canon's true question" should have been: What shall institutions who still desire literary readers attempt to teach, this late in history? This disjointed logic occurs elsewhere in the chapter as well. Shortly after Bloom insists that the study of literature has no effect on improving society or the individual, he proceeds to develop his case that literary engagement is a solitary act between the reader in dialogue with the text after which he claims that "education founded upon the Iliad, the Bible, Plato and Shakespeare remains, in some strained form, our ideal, though the relevance of these cultural monuments to life in our inner critics is inevitably rather remote" (p. 31) and that teaching the canon is necessarily an elitist enterprise since it is grounded on principles of selectivity.[6] Bloom shuttles between literary reading in the private sphere and literary study in the public sphere; the result is that he is unable to get to the bottom of the question concerning the value of literature education or, in the case of his essay, the value of teaching the canon in the public sphere of schools and colleges.

Another example of defenses concerning literature education that tend to be grounded on the ontological nature of the literary text may be found in some of Nussbaum's arguments that address the question of how literature education can play a role in educating citizens of the world and, more specifically, "what sorts of literary works, and what sort of teaching of those works, our academic institutions should promote in order to foster an informed and compassionate vision of the different" (Nussbaum, 1997, p. 89). In contrast to Bloom, Nussbaum proposes a curriculum that is more inclusive of other literary works beyond the Western canon. Her rationale is that reading the "Great Books" as well as literary works from other cultures broadens one's worldview and cultivates what she (1997) terms the "narrative imagination" (p. 10), in which one is able to think and perceive from the standpoint of someone else. This leads to "habits of empathy" (p. 90), "compassion" (p. 92), and "an expansion of sympathies" (p. 111). While Nussbaum begins by considering pedagogical approaches to teaching literature appropriate for preparing students to be world citizens, in various portions of her book, she bases this on the power of literature to foster the empathetic imagination. Here, her focus is on the significance of literary readings performed in the solitude of the private sphere rather than the important role of teaching literature in the public sphere of schools. Even though the reading of literature does have the potential to shape the imagination, it is insufficient to base an argument affirming literature education on the transformative power of a literary work without taking into account the fact that the literary text is mediated by a multiplicity of interpretive actors in the public sphere of education.

First, with specific reference to the context of schooling, students do not simply read literary works in the classroom; more often, they are engaged in the interpretation of literature and the writing of criticism upon which literature assessments are entirely based. It would therefore be too narrow an argument to ground any value of literature education solely on the value of reading literature since one could even argue that the transformative power of a literary work operates best when reading is performed as a private solitary act rather than in the public arena of the classroom where reading becomes affected by the pressures of standardized assessments and the pursuit of good grades.

Second, the effect on the imagination that occurs through one's engagement with the literary work is different in the private versus the public sphere. In the private sphere, texts are chosen by the reader based on personal interests or inclinations; in the public sphere, texts are chosen for the reader based on different agendas by the interpretive communities of the school, the state, or the dominant class. This difference is based on the primary distinction between the private sphere and the public sphere in which the former prioritizes individuality and individual choice whereas the latter prioritizes membership or citizenship in the larger society. In this sense, since literature education is a politicized institution in which its values are fashioned through mediations by the state, the universities, and other public agents, it necessarily belongs to the category of the public sphere rather than the private sphere.

Grounding the Value of Literature Education on Theorizations of Pedagogy

I have shown that arguments defending the value of literature education should give attention to literature education's contribution to the collective society even though such arguments often conflate literary readings in the private sphere with literature education in the public sphere. Since the moment the teaching of literature was not solely confined to the realm of the private but instead became institutionalized through state-managed education systems, this marked a shift in the location of literature education in the public rather than the private sphere. In the light of literature education's increasing decline, it is all the more crucial for scholars and educators to adequately defend literature education based on the pedagogical value of teaching literature in the public sphere.

What accounts for the insufficient attention paid by scholars to the role of pedagogy in contributing to literature education's perceived value to collective society? One reason could be related to the widely held view in education of the distinction between theory and practice that privileges the former and marginalizes the latter (Thomas, 1997). While theory is perceived as intellectual and rigorous, practice is seen as intuitive and involving the mere application of theory. Mary Kennedy (1997, 2002) makes a distinction between "systematic knowledge" and "craft knowledge." While the former stems primarily from research and emphasizes conceptual and analytical methods of processing knowledge, the latter stems from experience and its method of processing knowledge is idiosyncratic relying on intuition. Implicit in this distinction is already a bias that links craft knowledge to models of learning associated with apprenticeship, artisanship, and the vocational as opposed to academic learning. This bias is transmitted in top-down theory-into-practice models commonly employed in teacher education courses in which university-based researchers position themselves as knowledge generators while teachers are merely technicians who transmit and apply theory to their teaching (Gravani, 2008).

In this sense, theorizations regarding the function of narrative to provoke empathetic sensibilities or the power of literary texts to cultivate the aesthetic imagination contribute to seemingly more convincing arguments about the need for literary study in schools. Conversely, pedagogy involving practices of teaching in the public sphere of schools is marginalized and perceived as stemming from mere application of theory. The logic is as follows: If one can prove that reading literature can expand one's perspective of other cultures and worldviews and foster an imagination more hospitable toward marginalized others, the commonsense assumption is that teaching literature in the classroom can similarly encourage such dispositions. However, as I have argued, such logic fallaciously conflates literary engagements in the private versus public spheres and does not account for the fact that pedagogical approaches to teaching literature interrupts and disrupts any "pure" experience of reading the literary text.

From the twentieth century, various scholars have attempted to challenge the hegemony of theory and have called for a closer integration of theory and practice. For example, in theorizing independent artisanship (Huberman, 1993), collaborative artisanship (Talbert & McLaughlin, 2002), and apprenticeship learning (Lave & Wenger, 1991), these scholars are essentially theorizing pedagogy by arguing that practice is already informed by tacit theorizing whether by the teacher in the form of personal critical reflection or the teacher as situated within a collaborative professional learning community. In relation to literature education, Sheridan Blau (2003) has conceptualized a pedagogical approach centered on the workshop model in which he argues for an "antitheoretical theory of practice" (p. 14). This is a bottom-up approach that can be applied to literature education courses. It begins with practice and then encourages teachers to reflect on the tacit theories informing their teaching within communities of practice.

Toward a Method of Pedagogical Criticism

Pedagogy has conventionally denoted the art and science of teaching as observed in various movements that have given stress to methods and strategies of teaching. One example is constructivist pedagogy inspired by the influential theories of John Dewey, Jerome Bruner, and others. Dewey (1915) advocated situating learning within the "immediate instincts and activities of the child himself" (p. 34) and emphasized developing the child's innate and experiential knowledge through stages (Dewey, 1902), relating knowledge to the real-world (Dewey, 1915), transforming the child's experiences with his physical and social world into an educative exercise (Dewey, 1938), and using knowledge of the past as a means to understanding the present (Dewey, 1938). Similarly, Bruner (1961, 2006) argues that teachers need to encourage students to discover on their own, to engage with play and experiential learning. While scholars in the field of constructivist pedagogy focus on the learner, other scholars draw attention to the substance of teaching, such as the New London group's (1996) pedagogy of multiliteracies that offers a framework for teachers to incorporate multimodal texts and tasks in instruction. Yet others emphasize the need for culturally responsive pedagogy. Gloria Ladson-Billings (1994) argues that teachers who apply such a pedagogy can sensitize students to invisible power structures that sustain and justify inequity and exploitation; this eventually contributes to a more inclusive education. Culturally responsive pedagogy's emphasis on social justice is closely interconnected with the critical pedagogy movement that gained momentum in the late twentieth century. Critical pedagogy encourages reflection about the ways in which race, gender, and class identities are constructed and how certain forms of knowledge are legitimated and for whose benefit (Giroux, 1988, 1989; McLaren, 1989). Extensions of critical pedagogy include feminist pedagogy, focusing on issues of sexism and gender oppression (Weiler, 1991), and ecopedagogy, focusing on the ways in which teaching can draw attention to the destructive effects of globalization on the environment and on marginalized communities (Bowers, 2003; Kahn, 2009).

A key contribution of critical pedagogy is that it has served to dislodge the conventional idea of pedagogy as narrowly bounded and reductively tied to methods, strategies, or "best practices" of classroom teaching. Conversely, critical pedagogy scholars draw attention to the ways in which curriculum and pedagogy are shaped by broader institutional, national, and transnational forces and advocate the role of teachers as public intellectuals empowered to critically read and respond to the social and political factors constructing knowledge, texts, and subjectivities (Apple, 1999, 2004; Giroux, 1998; Kincheloe, 2008). This then points to the need for a specific methodology of reading pedagogy or pedagogical criticism. While connected in principle to critical pedagogy, it does not aim so much at valorizing political postures of Freirean resistance or Deweyan ideals of democracy; rather, pedagogical criticism prioritizes an analytical methodology that proposes historicized and critical readings of interventions occurring in the enactment of disciplinary knowledge.

The overarching aim of the book is to characterize and critique four pedagogical approaches to teaching literature in English — nationalistic, world, global, and cosmopolitan — from the late eighteenth century to the present. To do so, I apply the method of pedagogical criticism to reading the history of literature pedagogy by focusing specifically on three significant areas: conceptual values, the public sphere of the nation-state, and the global public sphere.

Conceptual Values

What drives pedagogy and its corresponding tacit theories are underlying impulses, desires, and beliefs. In fact, one of the most powerful drivers underlying any action, whether this involves the formulation of new ideas or the application of new teaching strategies, is values. As Dewey (1939) notes, "All conduct that is not simply either blindly impulsive or mechanically routine seems to involve valuations" (p. 3). Values, valuing, valuations, and value systems can all essentially be characterized by two main features. First, values involve a set of beliefs and second, these beliefs are "about desirable end states or behaviors" (Schwartz & Bilsky, 1987, p. 551). Another way of saying this is that values are beliefs about "the good" where "the good" refers to that which is desirable. This attachment of values to "the good" is found in *valere*, the Latin root of the term *value*, which denotes the good or worth of something, and it is also evidenced in a range of philosophical writings. For instance, at the beginning of *Nicomachean Ethics,* Aristotle (trans. 1985) argues, "Every craft and every investigation, and likewise every action and decision, seems to aim at some good; hence the good has been well described as that at which everything aims" (Book 1.1, 1). "The good," therefore, underlies every value and action. Similarly, Dewey (1939) discusses valuation in relation to the verb sense of the term "to value," involving the act of assigning significance to something, and the noun sense of the term "values" or value systems, involving beliefs about the good or significance of something. Thus, values are essentially ideals or aspirations that primarily center on the notion of the good. However, this leads us to a conundrum, for how can "the good" be defined? Even G. E. Moore (1903) acknowledges the elusiveness of this term in *Principia Ethica*:

> If I am asked, "What is good?" my answer is that good is good, and that is the end of the matter. Or if I am asked "How is good to be defined?" my answer is that it cannot be defined, and that is all I have to say about it. (p. 6)

The problem is that beliefs about what is good are never fixed and escape definition. Indeed, it is the very ambiguity of the term that has provided space for a range of interpretations. On one hand, there are values that emphasize a belief in the good of self-improvement and self-fulfillment. To Aristotle (trans. 1985), for example, the highest good is *eudaimonia*, which, translated from the Greek, means living fully (Kraut, 2010). One who subscribes to such a value may act and make decisions in ways that lead one to live fully, and he or she might agree with Aristotle that all other goals such as wealth, health, and education are subordinate to this sense of fulfillment. On the other hand, there are values that emphasize a belief in the good of treating others justly. For example, right after his trial in which he is sentenced to be executed, Socrates argues that the most important human aspiration should center not on what it means to live but on what it means to live well. Here, living well is interchangeably translated in the Socratic dialogues as living the "good life,"[7] which does not refer to a kind of self-centered, comfortable living; rather, it refers to a life in which one conducts oneself appropriately in the world, as observed when Socrates states that "the good life, the beautiful life, and the just life are the same" (Plato, trans. 2002, Crito, 48b). One who subscribes to such a value may act and make decisions for the good of another person.

Across the history of literature pedagogy, one may observe different values containing beliefs about the good of teaching literature that subsequently inform the decisions teachers make in the classroom concerning what texts to select or what instructional strategies to employ. Some of these involve values of socialization based on a belief in the good of teaching literature for ensuring cultural continuity; some of these are instrumental values based on a belief in the good of teaching literature for equipping students with linguistic skills and cultural creativity necessary to contribute to the national or global economy; some of these are cosmopolitan values based on a belief in the good of teaching literature for developing open-mindedness and the critical, reflective capacities to engage with other human beings in a complex world. In this sense, one may say that the teaching of literature is a form of values education. Often, literature teachers do not see themselves as constructing values or educating for values. Yet, in their daily routine of teaching, literature teachers unconsciously enact, reflect, and reconstruct their beliefs about the good of teaching literature for their students, their community, their country, and for the global world. It is thus the task of my research to trace the ways in which various values involving beliefs about the good of teaching literature have been defined and redefined from the moment English literature was formally instituted in schools from the late eighteenth century to the present.

Given that values are intangible and abstract, one way in which changing values in literature education may be traced is by highlighting concepts that have become dominant at particular moments in history and that are subsequently articulated via pedagogical discourse. These concepts reflect an ethos about the value of teaching literature, and analyzing conceptual turns provides an insight into understanding the emergence of new pedagogical paradigms to teaching literature and the changing values they embody.

The Public Sphere of the Nation-State

What determines changes in values or beliefs about the good of teaching literature? I have argued that the moment the reading and study of literature was not solely confined to the realm of private reading but instead became institutionalized and hence entered the realm of public schooling, arguments defending the value of literature education needed to center more specifically on its location in the public sphere. The distinction between the private and public spheres is primarily a feature of modernity. Prior to the sixteenth century, premodern societies comprised disparate and small communities that lacked complex institutional structures. In *A Secular Age*, Charles Taylor

(2007) describes such societies as characteristically "enchanted, porous" in nature (p. 42). On one level, the enchantment was due to the unchallenged belief that God was implicated and present in every part of society and was, in fact, the very existence of society. Here, the spiritual existed independently outside of human agency and had the power to possess and control human beings. For example, if one fell sick, this illness was naturally attributed to a sinful condition.

On another level, premodern societies were porous in the sense that there was no clear boundary between the spiritual and the physical. Within this context, the notion of the unreality of God could not possibly be conceived, since accepted reality was one in which living man interacted with spiritual forces that were present in all natural and material things. Since God figured as the dominant spirit, the individual and the collective society were a microcosm subordinate to God's larger macrocosmic universe. Within such a context, it could be argued that literature education was valued for both enhancing the spiritual and emotional well-being of the individual and his or her family or community. Sitting at the feet of the old sages and prophets, one acquired values of loyalty, hard work, and courage as well as respect for nature and God through stories and myths vital to maintaining order and unity in the tribe. Beliefs about the good of literature education changed with the emergence of a secular age that occurred as a consequence of scientific discoveries, increasing cynicism toward the dominance of the church and, more importantly, a growing awareness of active human agency so that God was no longer unquestionably the determinant of the course of human history but became an option among others so that one now had the choice of subscribing to faith in God or not. Hence, the prophetic interpretation of God's laws and its application to human life no longer formed the central basis for everyday existence; instead, man's agency now entailed the power to choose between affirming or denying the reality of God and His involvement in human lives. Taylor (2007) notes that the coming of modern secularity correlates with the rise of a "self-sufficing humanism" (p. 20) concerned with humanity's own flourishing. Consequently, a secular age is characterized as "one in which the eclipse of all goals beyond human flourishing becomes conceivable" (p. 19). Instead of a porous world, this self-sufficing humanism manifested itself in a distinction between the private sphere and public sphere, which became increasingly evident in Europe during the seventeenth and eighteenth centuries.

While the private sphere refers to the domain that constitutes the individual and the family to the exclusion of the state, the public sphere refers to the domain where private individuals identify themselves as members of a larger community and engage in the social and political affairs of society (Habermas, 1991). While the private sphere is the space where the private experience of reading the literary text is valued for its effect on the individual, the public sphere is the space where the study of the literary text is valued for its effect on both the individual as well as society. What is clear here is that with the advent of secularism and modernization, along with the development of state-controlled public education, the interpretive function mediating the literary text and the reader has shifted from the village storyteller operating at the personal level of family and community to the teacher who is typically an employee of the state operating at the level of the public sphere of schools. Within the context of contemporary modern societies, it is clear then that understanding various values containing beliefs about the good of literature education must stem from the domain of the public rather than private sphere.

More specifically, the public sphere is itself located within the territorial borders of the nation-state. Since the eighteenth century, with the exception of a minority of wealthy families, the education of individuals has been largely determined and managed by the modern nation-state with the spread of mass public education in Europe, which then provided models of secular education to other parts of the world. The state was not only integral to the construction of schools and the development of administrative infrastructures, it also managed all aspects of the curriculum conceived under the broad goals of education for citizenship. Education for citizenship initially involved the public construction of national identity through the apparatus of a state-directed education system.[8] At its broadest level, citizenship denotes membership to a community that recognizes that man is a social being and, thus, there is a distinction between public and private spheres of living. It is at the public level where the citizen participates in the governance of the community and shares particular rights of membership as well as obligations to maintain the freedom and security of that community.

Since the establishment of public education in the form of schools is inherently bound to the objectives of education for citizenship, these objectives play a key role in shaping literature pedagogy involving ways of organizing the curriculum, choices of texts to include for study, and instructional strategies to employ. This is primarily because any discrete subject (including English literature) is situated within the broader context of education in the public sphere. The curriculum is therefore a public rather than private document that considers the aspirations of members of the nation-state and those who hold political power; these actors then heavily influence the intentions and values of the curriculum (Apple, 2004; McLaren, 1999; Ross, 2002). The implication, therefore, is that the goals of literature education are determined by and therefore subordinate to the goals of education for citizenship in the public sphere of schooling in the nation-state.

The Global Public Sphere

While the public sphere that arose in Europe in the seventeenth and eighteenth centuries was specifically tied to the nation-state, this model has become problematic. From the late eighteenth century and more evidently from the end of the Second World War, the sovereignty of the nation-state has been increasingly challenged by various factors attributed to the phenomenon of globalization. This includes the rising influence of transnational institutions and corporations that have eroded the authority of the state as the sole decision maker in matters concerning the nation. Subsequently, globalization has served to dislodge the traditional notion of the public sphere as connected to the nation-state so that new possibilities for the public sphere may be imagined, such as the inclusion of multiple public spheres within the nation-state as well as the global sphere.

What this means is that if beliefs about the good of teaching literature are located in the domain of the public sphere of the nation-state, then these beliefs must be necessarily redefined as the forces of globalization impact it. Correspondingly, arguments that defend literature education must therefore account not only for its role in the public sphere of the nation-state but also how this role is shaped by transnational forces in the global sphere.

One example of a study that limits itself by not addressing the forces of globalization is an influential report by William J. Bennett (1984) that was the outcome of a research group sponsored by the National Endowment for the Humanities, a U.S. government agency comprising prominent teachers, scholars, and administrators. The main aim of the Bennett report is to evaluate the state of learning in the humanities in American colleges and universities and its recommendations are based on an analysis of empirical data collected within the country. For example, the report begins by detailing the declining enrollment in literature and humanities and, right at the beginning, it becomes clear that the report lays the blame largely on faculty and administrators who have "given up the great task of transmitting culture to its rightful heirs" (p. 1). It gives the example of how a collective loss of nerve on the part of faculty and academic administrators in the late 1960s and 1970s led them to give in to students who were demanding more autonomy in setting their own educational agendas. As a result, administrators relinquished course requirements and, along with this, the intellectual authority to establish important learning outcomes. This reluctance toward anything seemingly prescriptive also resulted in intellectual relativism so that no one subject or discipline was deemed more important than another. Presumably, the report is suggesting that this is a main reason why literature and the humanities have lost their central place in the curriculum in higher education.

At the same time, there is little attempt to understand the factors involved in the democratization of colleges and universities, particularly in relation to broader forces stemming from the increasing marketization of higher education globally. Instead, the Bennett report accuses colleges and universities of having lost a sense of their educational mission and, in doing so, reverts to a romanticized idea of the university as the bastion of a nation's heritage. Thus, it references Matthew Arnold's (1861/1993) claim that the business of culture and criticism is "to know the best that is known and thought in the world" (p. 37). Along the lines of this argument, the value of teaching literature and the humanities is in their perceived benefit to the development of an informed sense of community in which participants share a common culture rooted in Western civilization's highest ideals and aspirations. Despite its well-intentioned and lofty aims, the report assumes that ideals and aspirations are fixed and unchangeable. Additionally, in calling for a return to a "common culture," it further appeals to the myth of authenticity and neglects to examine how such a culture was imagined and constructed in the course of history and how global forces in the present age have served to challenge and reconstruct it so that it is no longer the common culture of nation but of humanity as a whole that has taken center stage.

In short, arguments defending literature education need to provide more holistic examinations of national and broader transnational forces that shape it. For example, while the teacher may mediate the text and the student, there are multiple factors mediating the teacher and his or her students, including the various actors operating at both the level of the public sphere of the nation-state (e.g., the minister of education, officials from the education ministry, superintendents of schools, school leaders, parents, and other stakeholders involved directly or indirectly in education) and at the level of the global sphere (e.g., international accreditation and assessment boards such as the International Baccalaureate, and transnational organizations such as the Organization for Economic Cooperation and Development, or OECD, that internationally benchmarks schools all over the world using tests such as the Programme for International Student Assessment).

Hence, a more nuanced and historicized analysis of the value of literature education should be inclusive of the forms of intersection between the nation-state and the global and the tensions that arise as the nation-state grapples with the forces of globalization. Such an analysis recognizes that the effects of globalization are not uniformly experienced across time and space. Various scholars, notably Samuel Huntington (1991) and Immanuel Wallerstein (2004), have traced how globalization accelerates and intensifies at specific historical periods and have described these phenomena in the form of global waves. This intensification is brought about by innovations in communication and transportation such as occurred during the Industrial Revolution, large-scale political events such as the spread of colonization from the late eighteenth century, the effect of two global wars in the twentieth century, and the rise of terrorism and the influence of transnational actors such as the United Nations and the World Bank in the late twentieth century. The intensification of globalization directly impacts the nation-state primarily because the global sphere and the nation-state are intimately connected.

On one hand, globalization is dependent on the pervasiveness of the nation-state system as evidenced historically when the rapid extension of the nation-state system to other parts of the world during the age of the British and European empires of the nineteenth century facilitated cultural globalization involving the global spread of Western culture and Western habits of thought. This also corresponded with economic globalization as observed in the increase in international trade and the development of a world economy. Before the nineteenth century, the world economy was fragmented and countries largely depended on domestic markets (O'Rourke & Williamson, 2002). The acceleration of economic globalization therefore correlates with the spread of the nation-state system throughout the world. At the same time, this spread encouraged technological globalization as the prospect of expanding markets internationally led to various innovations such as steam engines and railroads that made the transportation of goods more efficient, hence facilitating international trade among nation-states.

On the other hand, the nation-state too is dependent on globalization, specifically in relation to a stable transnational governing system that can grant recognition of its sovereignty. This argument is grounded on what Jürgen Habermas (1998) describes as the coexistence of internal sovereignty and external sovereignty that defines the nation-state. In order to call itself into existence, the nation-state must first demonstrate its capacity to maintain law and order internally while protecting its borders from foreign interference. Here, it appeals to internal sovereignty. However, it attains a status of sovereignty only when this is recognized by other sovereign nation-states in the international community so that its internal sovereignty is dependent on external sovereignty or recognition of its autonomy in the global sphere. This then implies that the nation-state is dependent on the stability of transnational organizations that can grant recognition of its sovereignty. Historically, the most influential organizations have been the delegation involved in signing the Treaty of Westphalia, enacted at the end of the Thirty Years War in 1648 when a system of nation-states in Europe became clearly demarcated along with an articulation of principles of sovereignty, a recognition of the formal equality of nation-states, and an agreement of non-intervention into the domestic affairs of nation-states (Held, McGrew, Goldblatt, & Perraton, 1999); the League of Nations, spearheaded by American president Woodrow Wilson after the First World War to promote international cooperation that included a covenant guaranteeing political independence and territorial integrity of all member nations against foreign aggression and a proposal to establish a Court of International Justice; and the United Nations, formed after the Second World War to strengthen harmonious relations among nations and aimed also at providing an important platform for nations to dialogue on key global issues. The degree to which the security, stability, and sovereignty of the nation-state can be guaranteed is dependent on the strength and power accorded to such global actors who can put in force transnational governing treaties that, in varying degrees, grant recognition to nation-states. Paradoxically, while these treatises may give validity to the sovereignty of nation-states, they also serve to erode the authority of governments to gain complete control of their own nation.

Given the close and complex relationship between the nation-state and the global sphere, the objectives of education for citizenship in the public sphere of schools must therefore shift according to their changing relations. In his seminal work, *Imagined Communities*, Benedict Anderson (2006) explores how a "nation came to be imagined and, once imagined, modeled, adapted, and transformed" (p. 141) so that even the notion of national identity is not immune to significant conceptual transformations. This has been precipitated by various forces of globalization, specifically cultural, economic, and technological globalization resulting in the notion of national citizenship becoming harder to define. The acceleration of globalization from the early twentieth century has led to new conceptions of citizenship, such as the world citizen, global citizen, and the cosmopolitan citizen. These concepts work to broaden the goals of education for citizenship and, subsequently, the goals of literature education. Thus, from the early twentieth century, one may note a shift away from nationalistic to world, global, and cosmopolitan pedagogical approaches to teaching literature.

A Framework for Pedagogical Criticism

In this book, I utilize a method of pedagogical criticism that encompasses the three aspects I have outlined above, namely, I examine how pedagogical approaches to teaching literature have been informed by values emerging as salient at particular periods of time and I then analyze how these values arise as a result of forces in the public sphere of the nation-state and the global public sphere. Figure 1.2 provides an illustration of this methodology.

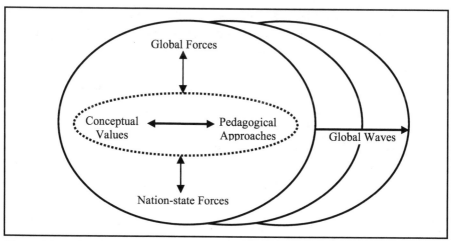

Figure 1.2. A framework for employing pedagogical criticism to an analysis of literature education

First, the center circle examines the emergence of pedagogical approaches informed by conceptual values containing beliefs about the good of teaching literature. These values are shaped by dynamic and intersecting forces operating at the nation-state and global spheres. To identify these values, I focus on concepts that have emerged via disciplinary movements or philosophical contributions by key scholars. My method of identifying these concepts follows a similar logic adopted by Margaret Masterman (1970) in her application of Thomas Kuhn's paradigm theory into a research framework comprising three domains which she terms the "construct," "sociological," and "metaphysical." In the construct domain, a new paradigm is located by investigating concrete changes in a field or discipline. Here, my interest is in locating the emergence of new pedagogical paradigms to teaching literature. In the sociological domain, social and political institutions acting as catalysts for change are examined. Here, I look at how various movements in the discipline of literature education lead to the dominance of particular concepts and how values underlying these concepts inform pedagogical practices. Finally, the metaphysical domain investigates not so much the nature of being but the kinds of metaphysical ideas and philosophical questions that gain salience at particular historical moments. Similarly, I am interested in exploring how the predominance of philosophical ideas of key scholars at various moments in time contribute to particular concepts and how the values underlying these concepts inform pedagogical approaches to teaching literature.

Second, I examine how pedagogical approaches change across time via conceptual turns as a result of various global waves in history. The idea of a conceptual turn follows the notion of a paradigm that was thoroughly developed by Kuhn in his non-linear approach to studying the history of science. Although Kuhn had as many as twenty-one different definitions of a paradigm (Masterman, 1970), a central thread that runs through these definitions is that it is "an organizing principle which can govern perception itself" (Kuhn, 1962, p. 112). This "organizing principle" arises through several stages in which theories or concepts rise to prominence, become reiterated in sociopolitical and academic discourse, and become extended into a school of thought. Take the example of world literature or *weltliteratur*, first employed by the German writer Christopher Martin Wineland in 1813. This concept was later developed by Johann Wolfgang von Goethe when he used the term to push German intellectuals toward greater exposure to literature from other European cultures. As the term became popularized, it was eventually used to designate a discipline that developed in the United States (Pizer, 2006) and was introduced to schools in the early twentieth century.

Historical paradigms may be analyzed in a number of ways. One way is by focusing on dominant organizing structures such as genres or canons. For example, Mad Thomsen (2008) applies a historical-paradigmatic approach in his study of the history of world literature. He focuses on identifying shifting focal points in the history of world literature that lead to new literary genres and new canons. He gives the example of Tolstoy's and Dostoyevsky's contributions to the rise of the epic novel in the 1860s. By locating moments in which these writers transcended already existing genres of the novel, he then explores their impact on the emergence of a new canon in world literature. Another way is by focusing on dominant ways of interpretation. To some extent, Fredric Jameson's (1982) influential work titled, *The Political Unconscious: Narrative as a Socially Symbolic Act* utilizes a paradigmatic analysis of literary history:

> In the area of culture . . . we are thus confronted with a choice between study of the nature of "objective" structures of a given cultural text (the historicity of its forms and of its content, the historical moment of emergence of its linguistic possibilities, the situation-specific function of its aesthetic) and something rather different which would instead foreground the interpretive categories or codes through which we read and receive the text in question. (p. 1937)

Jameson is essentially arguing that texts come to us "always-already-read" (p. 1937) by prior interpretations and interpretive traditions that underlie objective structures of texts. By reminding the reader to "always historicize!" (p. 1937), he then proceeds to examine various literary movements and the interpretive codes that gain salience in these movements. Whether one chooses to analyze historical paradigms through genres, canons, or interpretive codes, one always has to give name to them. This act of naming relies on abstract, generalized ideas or, in other words, concepts. A concept is similar to a paradigm since it is articulated as a term that embodies a set of ideas, values, beliefs, and precepts and can provide a glimpse of the way reality is perceived. Just as history is marked by paradigm shifts, it is also marked by conceptual turns referring to moments when particular concepts attain dominance. The advantage of studying history through conceptual paradigms is that it avoids examining history in terms of events so that more attention is paid to the history of ideas, and further, paradigms disrupt the notion of a linear history that then allows for historical overlaps. For example, world approaches to teaching literature, conceptualized by Goethe in 1827, continue to be incorporated in schools today along with more contemporary global approaches.

In this research, I focus on key concepts that characterize various pedagogical paradigms to teaching literature via four waves of globalization. Part of the challenge with identifying these global waves is that scholars have not come to an agreement on when globalization first occurred and when it accelerated. For example, Wallerstein (1974) attributes globalization to the establishment of the modern world in the sixteenth century. With the crisis of feudalism in the century before, Europe transited to a new capitalist world economy that propelled an age of exploration and conquest in order to expand trade. More recently, Kevin O'Rourke and Jeffrey Williamson (2002) debunk this theory and argue that the modern world economy only developed after the nineteenth century. Before this period, international trade was limited to products catered for the elite classes. They argue that it was only after the 1820s that trade expanded to include basic goods for the masses, which meant that globalization had become sufficiently widespread as to affect overall living standards. Admittedly, these waves remain contestable but at the same time, the identification of waves of globalization is useful in providing parameters that would allow a more focused analysis of the impact of globalization on literature education. One way to resolve this complexity is to provide broad historical periods rather than specific historical dates. Further, my main interest is not in the historical period but on how the processes of globalization correlate with particular turns leading to changing beliefs about the good of teaching literature. In summary, the four waves and their relation to four pedagogical paradigms are as follows:

1. The first wave of globalization (late eighteenth century to the nineteenth century): Nationalistic approaches to teaching literature
2. The second early wave of globalization (early to mid-twentieth century): World approaches to teaching literature
3. The second later wave of globalization (mid- to late twentieth century): Global approaches to teaching literature

4. The third wave of globalization (late twentieth century to the present): Cosmopolitan approaches to teaching literature

In summary, I employ pedagogical criticism to provide a holistic and historicized examination of four key paradigms that have emerged and their underlying values containing beliefs about the good of teaching literature. Part of the aim is to characterize rather than define each of these pedagogical paradigms. The difference is that definitions seek to impose a limitation on an idea and thus aim at closure. Conversely, the act of characterizing suggests a posture of openness, an acknowledgment that one cannot fully comprehend or objectify an idea but can only provide glimpses of this idea through description. It is thus the aim of this book to characterize, through these multiple dimensions, various paradigms to teaching literature particularly those that have become pertinent to the value of literature education in the twenty-first century.

More importantly, this book addresses literature teachers in the hopes that it would encourage a greater consciousness of themselves as ethical actors. Literature teachers are not mere pawns enacting a curriculum scripted by the state, nor do they passively function to prepare students for high-stakes standardized tests. In the everyday reality of the classroom, literature teachers consciously or unconsciously enact values concerning beliefs about the good of teaching literature that are then conveyed through the choices of texts they select and the teaching approaches they employ. By introducing teachers to the different approaches to teaching literature, it is hoped that this will broaden their consciousness and repertoire of pedagogical approaches as well as equip them to be more purposeful in their applications of these to the classroom.

In order to strengthen the sense of ethical agency, teachers need to be equipped to critically reflect on their craft. The depth of critical reflection depends on the extent to which teachers can engage with two important capacities. The first concerns the capacity to engage in a historical reflection of the discipline. As teachers become more aware of how literature in English emerged and evolved as well as how different beliefs about the value of literature education came into vogue across history, they become more sensitized to the global, sociopolitical, and institutional factors underlying these belief systems. The second concerns the capacity to engage in philosophical reflection particularly of concepts that appear naturalized in literature curriculum, assessment, and pedagogical objectives. My research hopes to facilitate such philosophical reflection by contextualizing concepts in history, thereby denaturalizing them, and by engaging teachers with the ideas of key philosophers and thinkers who have significantly contributed to theorizing these concepts. In short, the book provides an exhortation to literature teachers to think critically, historically, and philosophically about their discipline.

Author's Situatedness

Part of my interest in this research evolves from the paradox of "East" and "West" that remains embedded in my psyche. My grandfather emigrated from Foochow in China to Singapore in the 1930s because of the looming threat of war at the time. While in Singapore, he sent two of his children, including my mother, to English-medium schools and the other two to Chinese-medium schools. Thus arose the strange conundrum that my mother would speak in a Chinese dialect to her parents while conversing with the rest of her family in English. During my childhood, I too found it strange that I would speak to my mother in English, since she knew no Mandarin, and to my grandparents in Mandarin, since they knew no English. This linguistic contradiction was also evident in my high school education. Since I had more exposure to the English language from my parents at home, they decided to enroll me in a conservative Chinese school that had been established by Chinese merchants in 1917 and was historically infamous as a center for pro-communist activities in the 1940s and 1950s. The year I entered secondary school in the late 1980s was a tumultuous moment for Chinese-medium schools such as the one I was enrolled in. Under a new directive from the government, schools in Singapore were in the midst of transiting to teaching all subjects in English, which was also to be taught as a first language given its emergence as a dominant global language. In short, I was immersed in a dizzying bilingual experience in which teachers who previously taught subjects such as mathematics and physics in Mandarin now had to struggle to teach these subjects in English. Perhaps what was most puzzling to me concerned literature education. Why was it that in this conservative school with its strong emphasis on Chinese tradition and culture, English literature was a compulsory subject, whereas Chinese literature was an elective subject? Why did the school emphasize Chinese values and culture in its assembly speeches and its celebration of traditional Chinese festivals while in the everyday learning that occurred in classrooms, English remained the language of dominance and privilege?

It is this confusing cultural mix of "East" and "West" that forms a significant aspect of my history and identity even at this moment as I, a Chinese-Singaporean, attempt to write about historical developments concerning the teaching of English literature. Those who claim that only the Westerner can write about any history related to the discipline of English literature are appealing to a myth of authenticity, the myth of a pure Anglophone race that can speak on behalf of English culture and cultural texts. The historicity of literature education in English is incomplete without the participation of voices belonging to countries in which the subject was introduced, appropriated, and rewritten. Thus, I approach this subject marked by a strong sense of justification that English literature belongs as much to the shaping of my identity and the identity of second- and third-generation Singaporeans as it does to a "native" English person. Yet, mingled with this sense of justification is also a sense of ambivalence, for it must be remembered that English literature as a subject was imported from the British curriculum, the English language was considered the language of foreigners, and its rise as a dominant language was deemed threatening to native languages and culture particularly in the mid-twentieth century. Thus, part of the ambivalence is whether such a study undertaken by a non-Westerner is complicit in the colonizer's project of infiltrating and fashioning the imagination of other worlds.

I have come to terms with this ambivalence by shifting my attention not on a historical examination of English literature as a subject but on literature in English. While the former centers on literature as a subject pioneered during the British Empire, privileging Western canonical texts, the latter centers on a broader view of literature as a subject involving the study of a range of texts from around the world. In Singapore, this shift in terms was most evident when the Ministry of Education implemented a nationwide initiative in 1998 to rename the subject literature in English instead of English literature as an indication of the emancipation of the subject from its colonial roots. Thus, the scope of this research is twofold. First, it will begin with an analysis of English literature from the late eighteenth century. I have chosen this period because, though literature education had occurred since the dawn of mankind when families and communities in earlier civilizations utilized myths and stories to transfer moral and religious values to their children, the formal institutionalization of English literature in schools within the public sphere only occurred with the spread of state-controlled mass education during this time. This also means that the research will largely focus on literature education occurring at the precollege stage, where exposure to and education in literature is at its maximum reach. Second, the main interest of the investigation is how, following this period, the processes of democratization, decolonization, and globalization have led to the emergence of education centered on literature in English instead of English literature.

It should also be noted that historical developments underlying the disciplines of English literature and literature in English are not wholly discrete and may even overlap with the historical development of non-English literature education. For example, in my analysis of world literature education, I discuss how the study of German literature expanded to include other European literatures and how this influenced the incorporation of world literature in English as a subject in schools in the United States during the early twentieth century. In order to make clearer distinctions among the different terms, in the rest of this book, I use the term "literature education" to refer specifically to the subject English literature in the second chapter and literature in English in subsequent chapters. In cases where I refer to other non-English literature subjects, I use specific terms such as "German literature," "Chinese literature" and so on. When referring to terms such as English literature or world literature as school subjects rather than specific genres of literary texts, I make the distinction clearer by describing them in relation to "the study of," or "the teaching of," as well as by explicitly connecting them to terms such as "course," "discipline," "education," or "subject."

Organization of the Book

This book is divided into six chapters. With the exception of the introduction and conclusion chapters, each chapter begins with an initial glimpse of one of the four pedagogical paradigms in the historical period concerned. The first section then provides a historical context of the period, specifically how the relation between the global sphere and the nation-state led to shifting goals of education for citizenship in the public sphere. The second section examines how particular concepts, as a result of disciplinary movements or key philosophical contributions, become connected to the pedagogical paradigm concerned. The third section seeks to characterize this pedagogical paradigm and offers practical approaches regarding how they may be applicable in the context of the twenty-first century literature classroom.

Following the first chapter, in which I contextualize and introduce the methodology of this research, in the second chapter, my aim is to characterize a nationalistic paradigm to teaching literature in the context of the first wave of globalization from the late eighteenth to the early nineteenth century. I begin with the late eighteenth century because, though literature education had occurred since the dawn of mankind when families in earlier civilizations utilized myths and stories to transfer moral and religious values to their children, the formal institutionalization of English Literature in schools only occurred with the spread of state-controlled mass education during this time. This period, occurring during the first global wave, is significant given the development of the world economy, the entrenchment of state power and bureaucratic control, the dominance of liberalism as a form of political organization conducive to globalization, and the development of interstate government organizations and communication services. More importantly, this period witnessed the rapid expansion of the British Empire and the consolidation of the modern state system. Focusing on linguistic developments and the influence of print capitalism, Benedict Anderson (2006) argues that this period was catalytic in developing and spreading nationalistic consciousness worldwide through the proliferation of nation-states throughout the world. In this chapter, I explore how the first wave of globalization contributed to an emphasis on education for nationalistic citizenship that was foundational to the goals of English literature when it was institutionalized in public schools. I show how the concept of taste became tied to this pedagogical paradigm as a result of various disciplinary movements. Through an analysis of the philosophical contributions of key thinkers on aesthetics and aesthetic education, including Alexander Baumgarten, Immanuel Kant, Friedrich Schiller, Friedrich Schelling, and Georg Hegel, I examine how the concept of taste becomes associated with concepts of the beautiful and morality, which culminates in the concept of the Absolute. I conclude the chapter by discussing how these interrelated concepts inform a nationalistic approach to teaching literature particularly via the pedagogy of reproduction and didactic pedagogy.

Following this first global wave, the processes of democratization, decolonization, and the intensification of globalization have led to the emergence of education centered on literature in English instead of English literature. In the third chapter, my aim is to characterize a world paradigm to teaching literature in the context of the second early wave of globalization from the late nineteenth to early twentieth century. This wave saw the spread of the nation-state system throughout the world coupled with an increasing concern with the goal of education for world citizenship that subsequently influenced the goals of literature education. I discuss the emergence of a world paradigm with the institutionalization of world literature in schools as well as the introduction of comparative criticism as a typical pedagogical approach. I then critique this paradigm by examining how the concept of collective taste was prioritized and, through an analysis of Goethe's contribution to a philosophy of world literature, I argue that this was problematically tied to the concept of universal humanity. I conclude the chapter by providing examples to show how world approaches to teaching can foster critical open-mindedness in the contemporary literature classroom.

In the fourth chapter, my aim is to characterize a global paradigm to teaching literature in the context of the second later wave of globalization from the mid- to late twentieth century. This period saw the spread of liberal democracy and a renewed emphasis on human over citizenship rights. I explore how this period contributed to a rising global consciousness that shaped the ethos of education for global citizenship. I look at the emergence of a global paradigm through two movements, namely, new criticism and British cultural studies. I then critique the concept of empowerment valorized in this paradigm by examining its underlying impetus toward depolarizing universal and particular values of humanity. I conclude the chapter by providing examples to show how global approaches can promote critical empowerment and activism in the contemporary literature classroom.

In the fifth chapter, my aim is to characterize a cosmopolitan paradigm to teaching literature in the context of the third wave of globalization from the late twentieth century to the present. The phenomenon of globalization intensified during this period and issues related to global mobility increasingly challenged the sovereign authority of nation-states. I discuss how the phenomenon of extraterritoriality as a consequence of global mobility influenced the goal of education for cosmopolitan citizenship. I examine the emergence of a cosmopolitan paradigm through reader-response and critical literacy movements. I then critique this paradigm by arguing that the concept of responsible engagement valorized in this paradigm was tied to a particular valuation of alterity. I conclude the chapter by providing examples to show how cosmopolitan approaches can promote ethical-philosophical criticism in the contemporary literature classroom.

In the concluding chapter, I return to my initial premise of literature education as a form of values education. I argue that in a nation-state model of values education, engagements with values and explorations of identity are conveyed in superficial, didactic ways. What is needed then is a transnational model of values education that promotes critical engagements with values in an interconnected, globalized world. In relation to such a model, the teaching of literature is especially powerful in educating beyond the ideological values of the nation-state by promoting world, global, and cosmopolitan orientations and dispositions. Not only do these orientations serve to develop a greater sense of ethical agency in both teachers and students, more importantly, they also foster the cultivation of a hospitable imagination.

CHAPTER TWO

Nationalistic Approaches to Teaching Literature

After the student is handed a selected passage, such as a poem by Blake, he or she is asked to first learn it by heart and then to rewrite it from memory. The copy is then compared to the original and corrections are made. This process is repeated until the student is able to replicate the complete text accurately. It is recommended that such a method of studying literature be implemented for two mornings in a week for four to five years (Michael, 1987). Though such a method may appear draconian today, it was the common strategy of teaching in the eighteenth century when the formation of a national system of education in Britain had just begun (Richardson, 1994). Even up until the first decade of the twentieth century, this strategy of reproduction was expanded to include teaching students to learn lists of useful words from the text by heart (Board of Education, 1905), getting students to copy phrases wholesale from original texts, and getting them to imitate the style and content of the texts they memorized (Myers, 1996; Welton 1906). It was hailed by the Board of Education (1910) as the most effective approach to the teaching of English language and literature. David Shayer (1972) notes the underlying belief behind this strategy of reproduction was that "if the pupil were to start doing things for himself, he would make mistakes and this could not be tolerated because 'successful' learning [was] seen as the complete avoidance of errors" (p. 13). Perhaps one might argue that the strategy of reproduction was probably the most effective approach, given the immense challenge the state faced in tackling illiteracy when the national system of education was instituted. But the emphasis on accuracy coexists with the emphasis on imitation, and it is this latter concept that contains a deeper significance that this chapter aims to uncover.

The First Wave of Globalization and Education for Nationalistic Citizenship

The Consolidation of the Nation-State

The entry of literature education into the public sphere was propelled by what scholars have termed the first wave of globalization. The exact period when this occurred is contentious, with some scholars pointing to its origins in sixteenth century Europe. Wallerstein (2011) notes that the world system came into being during this time as Europe transited to a new capitalist world economy and Europeans started building trade connections with other territories. However, it is more likely that the first wave of globalization occurred later, from the late eighteenth to nineteenth centuries. There are several reasons for this. First, scholars have rebutted Wallerstein's claims and argued that it was, instead, the early nineteenth century that a world economy came into being. Prior to this period, trade was limited to non-competing luxury goods meant for the elite classes, which meant that international trade had little impact on the masses. It was only from the 1820s that trade involved basic goods such as wheat and textiles, indicating that globalization now had a more pervasive influence on society as a whole (O'Rourke & Williamson, 2002). Even Wallerstein himself admits that it was only toward the latter part of the eighteenth century that the world economy expanded geographically to more territories and that it had become better established with the growing influence of the merchant capitalist class, the entrenchment of state power and bureaucratic control, and the development of stronger interstate relations (Shannon, 1996). Second, liberalism, the political organization conducive to globalization only became dominant from the nineteenth century onward. Huntington (1991) describes the period from 1828 to 1926 as the first wave of democratization that saw the emergence of national democratic institutions with roots in the American and French Revolutions. The nineteenth century also saw the rapid expansion of the British Empire and the consolidation of the modern state system. The need to manage these vast overseas territories led to innovations in communication and transportation to facilitate transnational exchanges. Further, the devolution of control to colonized territories led to the development of government organizations and the establishment of international banking services (Held, McGrew, Goldblatt, & Perraton, 1999). Third, focusing on linguistic developments and the influence of print capitalism, Anderson

(2006) notes that the latter part of the eighteenth century was significant in developing and spreading nationalistic consciousness worldwide. The decline of Latin and the power of the clergy in its influence on political affairs coupled with the proliferation of secular books and vernacular languages meant that a larger community of people within a shared language field could now connect with each other. This, he states, was the embryo of a nationally imagined community that proliferated in the consolidation of nation-states throughout the world.

Synthesizing these different perspectives concerning the world economy, liberal democracy, and print capitalism, one can surmise that the phenomenon of globalization first emerged from the period of the late eighteenth to the nineteenth century. This was the period when globalizing forces of the British and European Empires led to the modern state system involving the centralization of political power, expansion of state administration to colonized territories, and the development of an organized military force, while the nation-state also fueled economic and technological globalization.

The Formation of a Literary Public Sphere

Of the different perspectives, Anderson's argument regarding the spread of print capitalism during this period is particularly interesting in pointing to the fashioning of a literary public sphere. It must be noted that the concept of literature first appeared in Europe in the fourteenth century and its root is the Latin *littera*, denoting a letter of the alphabet. At this time, it referred specifically to what we today understand as being literate or possessing the ability to read (Williams, 1977). But reading predominantly occurred in the private space of the home. How did reading literature transit from a private experience to the public sphere? Habermas (1991) provides an account of the emergence of the public sphere by first tracing the etymological history of the terms "public" and "publicity." He notes that these terms first appeared in German during the eighteenth century and even until the close of the century, they were not commonly used. What this suggests is that the public sphere first emerged in Germany and acquired its function during this period, which was limited to the realm of commodity exchange and social labor. Such a space, distinctly separated from the private sphere, could not have existed in feudal societies of the High Middle Ages. Thus, it was the gradual emergence of capitalism that became a globalizing catalyst to the introduction of a public sphere. The traffic of commodities resulted in a demand for traffic of news gradually leading to the publication of commercially distributed newsletters and newspapers. With the expansion of trade to more distant locations, it became imperative to ensure a regular supply of news to the public. Habermas (1991) makes a further argument that the establishment of public information and news, coupled with the rise of a bourgeoisie class comprising public officials, doctors, pastors, and scholars that formed the core of the public sphere, suggests that this was primarily a "reading public" (p. 23). There are two connotations to this term. On one level, the public sphere comprised an educated and literate group that had the ability to access news and information, formulate opinions, and engage with social and political affairs of the time. In this sense, Habermas (1991) defines the public sphere as the space where private people could come together as a public to collectively exercise their reason even to the extent of confronting the authority of the state. On another level, this public sphere did not simply remain within the political realm but evolved to include the "public sphere in the world of letters" (p. 30) in which literary discussions occupied a vital place. In seventeenth century France, this public gathered together with aristocrats in theaters, court houses, and later salons to discuss political and economic issues along with works of art and literature. In various parts of Europe, the emerging public sphere gathered in coffeehouses of which as many as three thousand were in existence in London by the eighteenth century.

The vehicle through which discussions on art and literature occurred was in the form of the periodical, and its articles became the center of conversations at coffeehouses. In Britain, the most popular periodicals were the *Tatler* (1709–1711), the *Spectator* (1711–1714), and the *Guardian* (1713), published by Joseph Addison and Richard Steele, and it became almost routine for gentlemen both in the cities as well as the countryside to gather in coffeehouses to collectively interpret and discuss articles in the periodicals. Essentially, these articles were concerned with the shaping of public opinion and the development of public taste through reflections on morals, literature, art, and manners (Cowan, 2004). The *Spectator* itself acquired a literary nature, since its opinions on society were articulated through a fictional cast of characters known as the Spectator Club, who engaged in imaginary conversations. In summary, the emergence of a critical public via the vehicles of coffeehouses and periodicals had two very significant effects on the important place of literature in the public sphere.

First, it was in these coffeehouses that engagements with literary works transited from the private sphere of the individual and family to the public sphere of civil society. Second, it was in these coffeehouses that literature acquired a legitimate status as a serious platform for public discourse. In both these instances, what is clear is that literature became tied to an educative function in the public sphere in that it was the avenue through which public opinion could be shaped and through which serious discourse could occur. This then made it conducive for the study of literature to be institutionalized in the public sphere of schools later on.

Education for Nationalistic Citizenship

The formation of a critical, literary public typically involved a minority bourgeoisie class, which meant that the larger public sphere as a whole was highly fragmented, and thus, it became imperative for the state to intervene. This was the period of the Industrial Revolution, which had contributed to a highly discontented working class. On one level, the British Empire was expanding and enormous profits from the slave trade and from colonialism meant that Britain was becoming the world's first industrialized capitalist nation. On another level, secularism and materialism, which were becoming increasingly characteristic of the period, resulted in an impersonal political and economic system apathetic to the conditions of the working class. Along with material prosperity, therefore, was the looming threat of political instability from an increasingly dissatisfied working class (Eagleton, 1996). The fault lines in the public sphere were becoming increasingly clear and it was necessary for the state to address its apparent fragmentation. In the 1780s, the state found an avenue to tackle this fragmentation; this was through the provision of mass education via key initiatives such as the Sunday schools movement and the first attempts to legislate schooling for working class children (Richardson, 1994). At the same time, the mass education system was burdened by the colossal task of addressing social problems such as illiteracy. Interestingly, large scale illiteracy in the country served to provide an opportunity for literature education to establish itself as a core subject in the national curriculum, since encouraging the reading of literature could be an effective conduit to improving students' competence in mechanical reading. Another major problem was the moral gap left by the failure of religious studies. Previously, religion had been an effective tool to enact a "pacifying influence, fostering meekness, self-sacrifice and the contemplative inner life" throughout all sectors of society (Eagleton, 1996, p. 20). However, cynicism toward the church and clergy in the nineteenth century meant that there was now a need to look for an alternative tool for the moral education of the masses. Here, literature education was found to be an appropriate secularized alternative to religion. Thus, in the early curriculum, didactic popular fiction was the most common genre adopted for its capacity to civilize the masses (Michael, 1987; Richardson, 1994). In summary, the problem of illiteracy and the failure of religion provided the impetus for the introduction of literature education in the national curriculum. Literature was now accorded the quasi-religious function of civilizing the masses and the functional task of raising literacy standards. Additionally, literature as a genre had already acquired a respectable status in the public sphere as a platform for individuals to engage in social and political discourse. This therefore gave the state some assurance that the study of literature would eventually occupy a significant role in fulfilling the aims of mass education.

By the latter part of the nineteenth century, English literature had become the most important subject in Britain and her colonies and was the "spiritual essence of the social formation" (Eagleton, 1996, p. 27). However, it should be noted that the respect given to English literature was only gradually realized. During the early nineteenth century when mass education was evolving into a nationally organized system of education, it was still considered a new subject occupying a lesser position compared to the study of classical Greek and Latin literature and languages that dominated the core curriculum in higher education.[1] It was only toward the latter half of the nineteenth century that English literature was introduced to colleges. Even then, English literature courses appeared first in provincial universities such as Leeds in 1874, Birmingham in 1880, and Liverpool and Nottingham in 1881 (Shayer, 1972) before they were offered in prestigious colleges such as Oxford and Cambridge in the 1890s. Despite this, classical methodological approaches continued to be transferred and applied to teaching English literature (Collins, 1891; Doyle, 1989).

The entry of English literature into prestigious universities in Britain secured its influential and dominant position. Aside from its quasi-religious status and its functional capacity to improve literacy, English literature acquired an ideological function. This is particularly evident at the level of mass education in the public sphere. The institution of a state-controlled organized system of mass education essentially meant the intrusion of state ideology and state goals that served to politicize the goals of education. Thus, in the context of schooling, it was not the education of the public but the education of the nationalistic citizen that became the central goal of education. While both the terms "public" and "citizen" refer to the individual's membership to the larger society, the latter term has the added category of obligation to that society. The goal of education for nationalistic citizenship therefore involves educating individuals about their roles and rights as citizens in society (membership) as well as the responsibility they have in contributing to it (obligation). This latter concept of obligation was particularly important to the state, as it sought, through public education, to inculcate values of civility to promote a more passive, ordered citizenry and, more importantly, to promote a conscious sense of nation in order to cultivate a greater degree of loyalty and subjugation among its citizens. In the eyes of the state, English literature was the vital weapon that could be used to appease a highly fractured public sphere and so secure its own hegemonic position.

The Conceptual Formation of a Nationalistic Pedagogical Paradigm

The Institutionalization of English Literature

The discipline of English literature emerged in Britain when a nationally organized system of education was established from the late eighteenth century onward. Whether taught at schools or colleges, English literature from its very beginning was constructed as a subject to complement the goals of nationalism. This occurred through the state's implicit projection of the ideal citizen via the vehicle of English literature. Such an ideal citizen was one who demonstrated two essential qualities. The first quality was bourgeoisie English values or "Englishness" and literature education was to provide the essential training ground (Doyle, 1989). The civilizing mission of literature education was most vocally expressed through the contributions of Matthew Arnold (1861/1993) who, in *Culture and Anarchy*, regards culture as "a study of perfection" (p. 59) involving a sentiment for beauty that opposes "animality" (p. 73) and the materialism of the modern age. Similarly, literature education participated in the project of culture by cultivating the moral and intellectual capacities of a working class increasingly drawn into a mass education system. In the essay, "Common Schools Abroad," Arnold (1888/1960) makes a comparison between the system of education in Britain and those of schools in Europe (France, Germany, and Switzerland). He criticizes the present goals of mass education for focusing on skills or what he calls "useful knowledge" (p. 292). This over-emphasis on the pragmatic, he argues, is what has caused English schools to fall short of European schools. He (1888/1960) then proposes that education should move beyond mere transference of knowledge to focus on what he terms training students in being "human":

> I found in the common schools abroad entire classes familiar with the biography of the great authors of their countrymen; capable of comparing and discussing their productions and of indicating the sources whence these productions draw their power to move and delight us. I found classes trained to that which is human. (p. 300)

Training in the human is evidently linked to cultural knowledge, and here, Arnold sees literature education as serving an important civilizing function. His argument provides an example of how, by the nineteenth century, literature's role in cultivating ideals in humanity had become associated specifically with cultivating the ideals of bourgeois civility.

The ideal citizen not only demonstrated civilized values of Englishness, he or she was also characterized by a second quality which was a strong sense of affinity and loyalty to Britain. Literature, by this time, had shifted away from its broad notion of printed works to a specialization in fictive and imaginative writing. Yet, inherent in the notion of imaginative writing is the sense of projection or vision. It is precisely literature education's capacity to project a vision of the ideal citizen that made it such a powerful and subtle tool for the state. In his proposal to grant English literature greater significance and autonomy in universities, John Churton Collins (1891) writes:

> [The people] need political culture, instruction, that is to say, in what pertains to their relation to the State, to their duties as citizens; and they need also to be impressed sentimentally by having the presentation in legend and history of heroic and patriotic example brought vividly and attractively before them. (p. 148)

Here, Collins relates an education for citizenship with literature education that involves affecting a sense of nationalism by evoking images of a national ideal. This is the myth of the nation or Empire that literature education was called upon to sustain through romanticizing English history. Subsumed under the broader goal of education for nationalistic citizenship, literature education was centered on the mission of fashioning the ideal citizen as one who would exhibit civilized values of Englishness and one who was nationalistic in spirit. Such a mission was essentially an ideological one, grounded on visions about the value of teaching literature in cultivating Englishness and nationalism. Yet, how could these visions be accomplished in practice? The answer was through literature education's emphasis on the concept of taste.

The Concept of Taste in Disciplinary Movements

In order to understand how the concept of taste became emphasized in the discipline of literature, it is necessary to examine how taste rose to prominence in the literary public sphere. While the concept of literature originally referred to the capacity to read, which distinguished an educated person from an uneducated one, its meaning began to shift with the emergence of the public sphere in the eighteenth century. Raymond Williams (1977) notes that the ability to read now meant the ability to read particular kinds of texts. In other words, the concept of literature now became associated with the idea of taste. This marked a change from learning to taste or sensibility as a criterion for defining literary quality. The emergence of the periodicals in the literary public sphere is a clear demonstration that taste had become associated with the reading public. For example, Brian Cowan (2004) counters Habermas' claim that the periodicals served to provide a democratic space for public debate; instead, he argues that the periodicals, undergirded by anxieties about lack of restraint in English society, served to police the public through surveillance of its social foibles in order to promote taste and decorum.

The manner in which this concept of taste was translated into practice was via the activity of criticism. More specifically, in the literary public sphere, taste became conjoined with the activity of criticism and whereas the original meaning of the function of the critic was used interchangeably with the function of the grammarian and philologist in the Middle Ages, it later emancipated itself from these two disciplines and became connected to taste and the judgment of the beautiful (Wellek, 1963). This latter idea of criticism as connected to taste was launched in the seventeenth century with John

Dryden's "The Grounds of Criticism in Tragedy" (Wellek, 1963). Written as a preface to Shakespeare's *Troilus and Cressida*, Dryden (1679) does not explicitly discuss what criticism is nor its function. In fact, the term is hardly used in the essay. What Dryden does instead is to model the act of criticism through his application of Aristotelian notions of tragedy to the English plays of Shakespeare and Fletcher. Here, Dryden states that good drama should contain a single action so as not to distract the attention of the audience. Another such rule that criticism should focus on is with regard to the manners or inclinations of the characters that must be exhibited in such a way as to make clear the moral of the work that directs the whole action of the play. In other words, to Dryden, a critic must exhibit taste in classical works and have a sound knowledge of its rules in order to apply these to a contemporary critique of literary works.

By the eighteenth century, taste and criticism began to gain a greater degree of emancipation from the Ancients as observed in the publications of John Dennis' (1704) "The Grounds of Criticism in Poetry" and Alexander Pope's (1711) "An Essay on Criticism." Criticism at this time became a social act or part of polite conversation (Patey, 2005), which essentially means that the focus had shifted from criticism as a method or as application of set classical rules to the critic as a person who engages in public discourse. For example, Pope's essay begins by arguing for the importance of learning the rules established by the Ancients. At the same time, he suggests that modern authors may divert from the classical rules as long as this rationale can be defended. This then implies that the modern critic should have a certain degree of flexibility and need not be completely subservient to classical rules of writing:

> Moderns beware! Or if you must offend
> Against the Precept, ne'er transgress its End,
> Let it be seldom, and compell'd by Need,
> And have, at least, Their Precedent to plead.
> The Critick else proceeds without Remorse,
> Seizes your Fame, and puts his Laws in force. (Pope, 1711, para. 12)

Here, Pope paints a negative description of the critic who, wholly loyal to the ancient code, becomes overly harsh and is unable to appreciate a modern literary work for its own merits. Though Pope continues to venerate ancient authors like Homer and Horace, upholding them as benchmarks to critique modern works, his essay shows some initial, albeit restricted attempts to remind critics to be more open-minded in judging a work for its intentions and its own worth; hence, a "perfect Judge will read each Work of Wit / With the same Spirit that its Author writ / Survey the Whole, nor seek slight Faults to find" (para. 16). The push toward even greater autonomy can be observed in Dennis' review of Pope's essay in which he criticizes Pope for still remaining servile to the authority of the Ancients.[2] These tensions only demonstrate the emergence of a new paradigm of literary engagements in the public sphere in which to engage in literature involved engaging in literature as a critic occupying the space between tradition and autonomy.

As the occupation of the critic grew in influence in the eighteenth century, periodical writers saw it important to establish standards for criticism. Addison (1711a) therefore describes periodical articles as "papers of criticism," the objective of which is encapsulated in this statement: "As the great and only end of these my speculations is to banish vice and ignorance out of the territories of Great Britain, I shall endeavour as much as possible to establish among us a taste of polite writings" (para. 2). One method commonly applied by Addison and Steele, in order to establish standards of criticism, is to promote greater discernment in the public by specifically identifying critics whom they regard as shallow and vulgar. Such a critic is described as an "importunate, empty, and conceited animal," since they mechanically assess the works of writers based on whether or not they adhere to those various rules and principles (Addison, 1710, para. 2). Addison (1711b) even provides a hyperbolic caricature of an actual person who often sits in the upper gallery of the playhouse and, when pleased with something witnessed on stage, would express this with a loud knock on the benches that can be heard over the whole theater. The shallow critic is then directly set at odds against what Addison (1714) describes as the true critic who is knowledgeable about classical rules of writing and is able to intelligently formulate his or her own opinions about the work; however, this is an opinion that is grounded in taste and not tied to such prior knowledge. Addison and Steele themselves typify early cultural critics, a phenomenon unprecedented at the time, who would provide critical commentaries on all forms of social life ranging from fashion, propriety and manners at public places, parental treatment of children, and dueling to artworks such as literature, drama, opera, dance, and music in order to cultivate taste among the public.

Thus, when literature entered the public sphere in eighteenth century Europe, it comprised the concept of taste carried through the activity of criticism, which was a mark of refinement and civility appropriate to the bourgeoisie intellectual public. Guillory (2002b) observes that the practice of criticism from the beginning was closely tied to moral philosophy; that is, criticism of literature provided the platform for public intellectuals to engage in moral philosophizing particularly that pertaining to right manners and conduct. Similarly, he notes that the introduction of belles lettres in the university, which is a precursor to modern literary criticism, also emerged out of the discipline of moral philosophy. In practice, belles lettres combined the act of judgment with the concept of taste that became foundational to literature education as it developed more fully in the nineteenth century, for if literature education in the public sphere had comprised only the function of taste, then there was no reason why the tasteful reading of literary masterpieces would not result in tasteful writing (or our modern day equivalent of creative writing). Instead, the centrality of taste required the necessity to educate for a greater degree of discernment in the public. Hence, criticism, particularly in the form of writing, was deemed more valuable than creative practices. As Williams (1977) astutely notes, literature was not a category of production but a category of consumption, since public discourse on literature encompassed the development of discerning capabilities in the consumption of cultural products.

The Connection among Concepts of Taste, the Beautiful, Morality and the Absolute in Philosophical Contributions

Though it is easy to dismiss the cultivation of taste through the vehicles of the literary public sphere and literature education in the public schools as elitist snobbery, underlying this was a powerful belief in the moralizing potential of taste that, until today, remains foundational to literature education. To understand this more fully, I suggest it is necessary to step away from the history of English literature education as we have been discussing to consider a parallel discipline that developed at the same time. This was the discipline of philosophical aesthetics. The question is, what can an examination of philosophical aesthetics offer us in our investigation of the conceptual history of English literature education? Here, I argue that philosophical aesthetics, which developed in Germany also during the late eighteenth century, represents the first systematic discussion about the value of aesthetic education, including literature education. While the value of literature and the arts have been debated since the time of Plato and Aristotle, discussions about the value of aesthetic and literature education only emerged formally through the institutionalization of an autonomous and systematic philosophical discipline known as aesthetics during this period. An understanding of the beliefs underlying literature education must therefore be located here rather than in the historical development of the discipline. In what follows, I will examine how the concept of taste becomes associated with concepts of the beautiful, morality and ultimately, the concept of the Absolute through five core philosophical works central to the development of the discipline of aesthetics: Alexander Baumgarten's *Aesthetica* (1750–1758), Immanuel Kant's *Critique of Judgment* (1790), Friedrich Schiller's *On the Aesthetic Education of Man* (1795), Friedrich Schelling's *The Philosophy of Art* (1790), and Georg Hegel's *Lectures on Aesthetics* (1818–1829).

The first person to provide a comprehensive philosophy on aesthetics and aesthetic education is Alexander Baumgarten who is commonly regarded as the father of aesthetics. He published his lectures in the 1740s in a work titled *Aesthetica* and some of his crucial ideas were developed later by Immanuel Kant. Baumgarten was aware that the senses were regarded as a lower faculty inferior to cognition, which may be traced to the philosophy of Cartesian dualism in the seventeenth century that privileged mind over body. However, his lectures and published works on aesthetics marks the beginning of attempts to establish rigor in a study of aesthetics by associating this with reason: "Experience will demonstrate that our art can be subjected to proof; it is clear a priori because psychology etc. provide a sure foundation; and the uses mentioned among others show that aesthetics deserves to be elevated to the rank of a science" (Baumgarten, 1750/2000, p. 491). Thus, Baumgarten defines aesthetics as the "science of perception" (p. 489). While Kant later developed the relation Baumgarten had established between aesthetic judgment and reason, the main point of departure is that whereas Baumgarten attempts to connect aesthetics to perception and sense, with Kant, there is a shift toward that which is transcendental, beyond the empirical, and that concerns aesthetics as a science of the beautiful (Pluhar, 1987).

Kant further defines the concept of the beautiful by distinguishing it from the good and the agreeable. According to Kant (1790/1987), "Good is what, by means of reason, we like through its mere concept" so that "we call something (viz. if it is something useful) good for [this or that] if we like it only as a means" (p. 48). The good is always purposive and is connected to a practical use. The agreeable is "what the senses like in sensation" (p. 47) or what provides feelings of subjective pleasure (p. 48), enjoyment (p. 50), gratification (p. 52), and it is determined by the empirical and conditioned by stimuli (p. 51). Unlike the good and the agreeable, the beautiful is "liking devoid of all interest" (p. 53); it is a disinterested liking based on the mere contemplation or reflection of the artwork and not based on any instrumental or utilitarian purposes. What is particularly important is that the concept of taste then becomes associated with the concept of the beautiful and, correspondingly, criticism becomes associated with aesthetic judgments of the beautiful. The logic of Kant's argument is as follows.

First, free beauty or a liking of the beautiful is disinterested and does not involve a predeterminate concept. Kant gives the example of flowers, which are free natural beauties because there is no predeterminate concept of what an ideal flower is meant to be. Therefore, any judgment of the flower will be based on what it is, not what it can do (the good) or how it can satisfy the senses (the agreeable).

Second, this disinterested nature of the beautiful implies that aesthetic judgments of the beautiful forms the basis for universal liking or what he (1790/1987) terms "subjective universality": "For if someone likes something and is conscious that he himself does so without any interest then he cannot help judging that it must contain a basis for being liked [that holds] for everyone" (pp. 53–54). Kant is not suggesting that when we claim an artwork as beautiful, everyone must necessarily agree with us; instead, he is proposing that such a claim is a public rather than a private one so that it contains a basis for being liked that is communicated to everyone. Elsewhere, Kant (1790/1987) states that there is no pleasure in the beautiful in solitude so that a man abandoned on a desolate island would find little reason to engage in beautiful artworks (p. 163). Since humans are social beings, there is a natural propensity to share with others that implies that part of the pleasure in our engagements with aesthetic works is that they provide an opportunity for communication. This point is suggested in the only section in *Critique* where Kant explicitly discusses aesthetic education. Here, he (1790/1987) states that the highest aim of aesthetic education is in "cultivating our mental powers by exposing ourselves beforehand to what we call *humaniora*; they are called that presumably because humanity [Humanität] means both the universal feeling of sympathy, and the ability to engage universally in very intimate communication" (p. 231). Embedded within Kant's mission of aesthetic education is an ethics of communicability or a belief that aesthetic education opens public spaces for discussions about artworks.

Third, the beautiful is connected to taste as observed in Kant's (1790/1987) claim that "When we judge free beauty (according to mere form) then our judgment of taste is pure" (pp. 76–77). Here, Kant equates aesthetic judgments of the beautiful with pure judgments of taste. It follows then that if aesthetic judgments of the beautiful facilitates "universal communicability," then it contributes to the "taste of everyone" (p. 79). Another way of saying this is that an aesthetic judgment of the beautiful publicly expressed contributes to the cultivation of taste in the public sphere. In relation to literature education, the connection between the beautiful and taste promotes disinterested reflection on "beautiful" literary works. This means that the practice of criticism, which centers on an aesthetic judgment of the beautiful, is also centered on passive appreciation aligned with a posture of reflection and awe in the presence of "beautiful" literary works. This opposes our modern day notion of critical reading and criticism as involving the active evaluation of a literary work.

As previously discussed, Kant had made the radical proposal that any claim that an object is beautiful must have a basis for universal assent. The only way that Kant's proposal can be logically conceivable is by connecting an aesthetic judgment of the beautiful and, correspondingly a pure judgment of taste, to morality. Indeed, various scholars (Crawford, 1974; Elliott, 1968) have argued that it is this connection that validates Kant's principle of subjective universality for pure judgments of taste as encapsulated in the following:

> Now I maintain that the beautiful is the symbol of the morally good; and only because we refer the beautiful to the morally good (we all do so naturally and require all others also to do so, as a duty) does our liking for it include a claim to everyone else's assent, while the mind is also conscious of being ennobled, by this, above a mere receptivity for pleasure derived from sense impressions, and it assesses the value of other people too on the basis of [their having] a similar maxim in their power of judgment. (Kant, 1790/1987, p. 228)

Based on the above formulation, the beautiful is not equivalent to morality; instead, the key phrase is that the beautiful is a "symbol of" morality.

According to Kant, symbols operate indirectly and by analogy when a concept is applied to another object and then reflected upon. For example, Kant gives the example of a despotic state and a hand mill. While these are two different things, our reflection on how one operates (e.g., the hand mill) helps us to understand how the other operates (e.g., a despotic state). Thus, there is an analogous relationship between a hand mill and a despotic state so that the former serves as a symbol for the latter. Since Kant does not specify how the analogous relationship between the beautiful and morality operates, this has led to a range of speculations by various scholars. Henry Allison (2001) argues that although judgments of the beautiful are independent from moral judgments, the former prepares one for the latter. This is because judgments of the beautiful involve a transition from the contemplation of sensible to supersensible concepts (such as God or freedom) thereby mirroring the way moral judgments operate. By performing aesthetic judgments, the individual learns to distance him- or herself from sensuous inclinations so that the "the transition effected through reflection on the beautiful is not itself a transition to morality, it does facilitate that transition" (p. 264). Kant (1790/1987) provides several examples of this transition in different parts of *Critique*: "The beautiful prepares us for loving something, even nature, without interest" (p. 127); "a lily's white color seems to attune the mind to ideas of innocence" (p. 169). Donald Crawford (1974) provides a different perspective by connecting the beautiful with Kant's theory of the sublime. The beautiful in nature, art, and the sublime symbolizes the basis of morality by leading us not only to reflect on the supersensible but to contemplate its immense and limitless potential. The sublime is what Kant (1790/1987) defines as "what is absolutely large" (p. 103) and may be found in threatening rocks, thunderclouds, volcanoes, and hurricanes with all their destructive power. While the sight of them makes us fearful, they also allow us to discover our capacity to perceive and apprehend the infinite which then makes us aware of our own superiority over the sublime. Crawford argues that the beautiful in artworks represents a microcosmic presentation of the way we apprehend the sublime by exposing our supersensible faculty of imagination and reason that allows us to transcend the sensible and the material. This therefore accounts for the symbolic relationship between the beautiful and morality because aesthetic judgments of the beautiful parallel moral judgments, since the basis of moral judgments is a capacity to apprehend the sublime in the supersensible.

In summary, Allison argues that the symbolic relationship between the beautiful and morality is based on the capacity of aesthetic judgments of the beautiful to attune the mind to the supersensible which parallels the operation of moral judgments, while Crawford argues that it is the capacity of aesthetic judgments of the beautiful to allow the mind to apprehend the sublime which parallels the operation of moral judgments. Unlike Allison and Crawford, Paul Guyer (1997) emphasizes pleasure as the main symbolic connection. Aesthetic judgments of the beautiful and moral judgments may be different but they share a structural similarity — both forms of judgments are pleasing in themselves. They are not a means to some further end and are grounded in disinterestedness. In relation to aesthetic judgments of the beautiful, the condition of disinterestedness does not mean the absence of all interest. Instead, Kant is referring to the absence of empirical interest such as an interest based on a thing's usefulness (the good) or an interest based on the pleasure given to the senses (the agreeable). The pleasure that aesthetic judgments of the beautiful provide is an intellectual interest or pleasure arising solely from the contemplation or reflection of the object based on a free and autonomous will not influenced by any external causes. Similarly, the pleasure from moral judgments is derived from a reflection on moral laws and based on a free and autonomous will adhering to the categorical imperative — to "act only according to that maxim by which you can at the same time will that it should become a universal law" (Kant, 1785/1995, p. 38).

These different interpretations concerning the way the beautiful is a symbol of morality then addresses Kant's proposal of subjective universality. Following Allison's attunement thesis, there is a universal duty to attend to the beautiful, since reflection on the beautiful prepares one for moral reflection, and following Crawford's apprehension thesis, the implication is that pleasure in the beautiful rightfully demands universal assent, since it is an expression of humanity's capacity to cognize the supersensible or more specifically, the sublime.[3]

Kant's important contribution to aesthetics was his extension of Baumgarten's theories into a comprehensive philosophy concerning the correlation between aesthetic judgments of the beautiful and pure judgments of taste as well as the connection between both these judgments with an ethics of communicability or a condition of universal assent, thereby giving significance to their place in the public sphere. More importantly, by showing how both these judgments parallel and facilitate moral judgments,

Kant had implicitly attached a transcendental value to the discipline of aesthetics. This involves the belief that the good of aesthetic education, including literature education, is that it allows man to transcend the sensible, empirical world in order to contemplate the supersensible. This transcendental value was to become even more strongly tied to aesthetic and literature education following other key German aesthetic philosophers of this period who provide varying descriptions of the supersensible.

The publication of Kant's *Critique of Judgment* had a profound influence on Schiller who, in the early 1790s, not only devoted time to an intensive study of Kant's works, he also began employing the new critical vocabulary in his own work (Kooy, 2002). Five years after the publication of Kant's *Critique*, Schiller published *On the Aesthetic Education of Man*. While Kant had argued that the beautiful is the symbol of the morally good, Schiller's (1795/2004) main argument is that engaging in the beautiful facilitates the transition from man's engagements in the sensual or physical to the moral. At the same time, the moral impulse is directed at the divine and it is divinity that man carries within him- or herself. Schiller argues that this results in the inherent tension within humans between their sense faculties that insist on reality and what Schiller terms their personality (or spirit) that is aware of the infinite divine potential within them. This tension is necessary in order to keep humans grounded in the case of the sense faculty and to motivate humans to strive for higher, more transcendental goals in the case of their consciousness of spirit. The beautiful in the form of artworks then mediates the domain of the empirical in relation to their sense faculties and the domain of the moral in relation to their spiritual consciousness. Schiller (1795/2004) strongly insists that the most important goal of aesthetic education is to "make him [man] aesthetic as far as ever the realm of Beauty can extend, since the moral condition can be developed only from the aesthetic, not from the physical condition" (p. 110). While Kant had suggested that aesthetic judgments of the beautiful are conditioned by universal assent, Schiller goes even further by stating that aesthetic education cultivates man's social character because it develops an affinity with other members of society; this affinity recognizes the divine spirit within man that is also present in others. In this light, aesthetic education enables us to become aware of ourselves as individuals but also as representatives of the human race and the human spirit. The process of reading and analyzing a "beautiful" literary work in the public context of school, for example, is then an act of reading and recognizing this human spirit that expresses itself through the text. To

Schiller then, aesthetic education facilitates man's transition to a contemplation of the supersensible that he describes as divinity inherent in the human spirit and correspondingly in artworks.

A few years later, from 1801 to 1804, Schelling gave a series of lectures on the philosophy of art where he identifies the supersensible more specifically as God. At the beginning of the text, Schelling (1801/1989) describes the complete autonomy and independence of God. Since God is absolute in identity and totality, He is therefore not dependent on anything, particularly time and space. In other words, God is both eternal and infinite. From here, it is clear that Schelling takes a broader notion of God beyond a specific entity. A more accurate term is the Absolute, referring to that which is completely independent of all things and cannot be contained in any title since titles can never capture the totality of the divine (Beiser, 1993). The Absolute is expressed in the universe as a whole which is fully self-contained and this expression of the Absolute in the universe implies that the universe itself is a work of art. This also implies that the Absolute can be known internally through the universe and its components such as nature and artworks. In other words, since the Absolute is the source of beauty and all artistic creativity, artworks reflect the nature of the Absolute. However, artworks mediate the ideal and the real in that, while they express the divine Absolute, they are also part of created reality. This mediating vehicle in artworks is found in poetic language that allows for more insight into the nature of the Absolute compared with philosophical language (Hammermeister, 2002). Schelling then shows how this poetic language provides the gradual revelation of the Absolute across history, first through the depiction of the gods in Greek mythology followed by the depiction of God in Christian allegory. His point is that poetic language, whether in mythology or allegory, only conveys a partial revelation and not the totality of the Absolute. In this sense, only poetic language is capable of representing the infinite and this is expressed in the form of artworks. Therefore, it is not the form of the artworks but the idea of the Absolute it represents that renders it significant and allows artworks to share a close affinity with religion. Without the idea of the Absolute, the content of artworks would be shallow and impotent, never able to transcend sensual and material experiences; without artworks, the Absolute would not adequately manifest its manifold attributes.

Like Schelling, Hegel shares the view that the Absolute can be conceived in naturalistic terms and all forms of nature manifest aspects of the

Absolute's infinite qualities. In his lectures on aesthetics, which he gave between 1818 and 1829, Hegel argues that this divine nature of the Absolute is knowable through an examination of the development of the history of the world. He then shows how, with each passing civilization, artworks display a greater degree of humanity's self-consciousness of the Absolute. For example, he divides art history into three distinct periods: the beginning of art where the symbolic form dominates, the period of ancient Greece where the classical form dominates, and the period of Christianity where the romantic form dominates. To Hegel, it is the last category that represents the highest ideal and most genuinely beautiful form of art (Houlgate, 2009; Wicks, 1993). This is the example of art "transcending itself, while remaining within the artistic sphere and in artistic forms" (Hegel, 1820/1993, p. 87). Romantic art distinguishes itself from all other forms by its transcendental capacity to bring to consciousness the divine nature of the Absolute. By delineating three different stages of art according to the symbolic, classical, and romantic forms, Hegel is also providing a model for aesthetic education in which the study of artworks should be based on a prioritization of the transcendental value so that the artwork in the form that best expresses the Absolute is considered more profound and more valuable. At the same time, by suggesting that history progressively reveals the Absolute through art forms, Hegel is suggesting that one historical period may contain a belief system expressed through artworks that provides a more accurate understanding of the Absolute. This leads to his claim that oriental artworks cannot be compared to Greek or Christian artworks because they lack any clarity with regard to the nature of the Absolute. He argues that such works are externally defective because they are internally flawed. By saying this, Hegel is also suggesting that the Christian and Greek belief systems are superior to other belief systems such as those stemming from primitive animistic cultures or oriental beliefs such as Buddhism, Hinduism, or Taoism.

Thus far, one may observe that from Kant to Hegel, there is an attempt toward a greater comprehension of the supersensible through aesthetics. Kant had established the connection between the beautiful and the supersensible. He describes this supersensible realm as the sublime, which is the realm of chaos, of the infinite, and the divine that is beyond cognition. The sublime exists in an external realm and our rational contemplation of it can be facilitated by aesthetic judgments of the beautiful. It was Schiller who then turned the sublime into an internal divine quality man intuits within him- or herself and is found in beautiful works of art. But Schiller does not clarify exactly what this divine essence is. Instead, it is Schelling who describes the divine essence as the Absolute being that is beyond time and space, infinite and eternal. The world and its created beings exist within time and space or, in another word, historicity. Schelling argues that only poetic language can mediate between an ahistorical Absolute and a historical world. Hegel then shows how this poetic language manifests in forms of art that progressively provide a revelation of the divine nature of the Absolute across history.

What may be clearly discerned is the prioritization of a transcendental value in aesthetics and, correspondingly, aesthetic education. By the late eighteenth century, Aesthetics had become established as a significant discipline concerned with the philosophical study of artworks largely through the key German philosophers discussed. Though the discussions occurred in the domain of the philosophical, they provide a deeper understanding of how the goal of education for nationalistic citizenship, as prioritized in literature education, was connected to the concept of taste that was itself grounded on concepts of the beautiful, morality, and ultimately, the Absolute.

Applications of Nationalistic Approaches to Teaching Literature

The interconnected conceptual relation of taste-beautiful-morality-the Absolute informing a nationalistic paradigm to teaching literature is premised on a perspective that the value of teaching literature is in its capacity to promote a consciousness of the divine, allowing one to transcend the material and sensual world. In considering what this implies in practice, two key teaching approaches involving the pedagogy of reproduction and didactic pedagogy appear significant.

First, the emphasis on the concepts of nationalistic citizenship and taste in literature education points to approaches to teaching literature that center on the promotion of elitism. From the late eighteenth to the early nineteenth century, the teaching of literature contained the functional aim of increasing literacy, since a more literate population would contribute to greater political stability. More importantly, the teaching of literature centered on the mission of fashioning the ideal citizen as one who exhibited civilized values of Englishness and who was nationalistic in spirit. This meant that approaches to teaching literature had to be necessarily elitist and the basis for this may be observed even up to the early twentieth century, as evidenced in the influential Board of Education (1921) report concerning the teaching of English in Britain:

> If we explore the course of English Literature, if we consider from what sources its stream has sprung, by what tributaries it has been fed, and with how rich and full a current it has come down to us, we shall see that it has other advantages not to be found elsewhere. There are mingled in it, as only in the greatest rivers there could be mingled, the fertilizing influences flowing down from many countries and from many ages of history. Yet all these have been subdued to form a stream native to our own soil. (pp. 16–17)

Here, elitism is observed in the promotion of English culture as the greatest of all rivers originating from ancient traditions deemed authentic to this myth of nation. One of the most effective strategies for supporting elitism was to center approaches to teaching literature on texts deemed worthy of being read. At universities and colleges, approaches to teaching literature focused on the study of classical English literary texts such as the following from an Oxford University examination text list in the 1890s:

> Old English texts (Beowulf and Sweet's Anglo-Saxon Reader)
> Middle English Texts (King Horn, Laurence Minot, Sir Gawain)
> Chaucer (selections) and Piers Plowman
> Shakespeare (about six plays)
> History of the English Language
> History of English Literature to 1800
> Gothic (Gospel of St. Mark) and unseen translations from Old and Middle English (Palmer, 1965, p. 113)

The emphasis on older, more classical English texts served to dichotomize classical works from popular vernacular fiction. Only the study of "valuable works" was legitimized in the early national literature curriculum and this was similarly observed in schools. A report from the Board of Education in 1900 describes typical approaches to teaching literature from year one, when students are seven years old, to year seven, when students are thirteen years old. From years one to four, students are simply required to read a short passage from a book. At year five, they are required to read a passage from a standard author, though names of authors are not mentioned at this point. At years six and seven, they are required to read a passage from Shakespeare or Milton (Shayer, 1972). Typical textbook anthologies such as F. C. Cook's *Poetry for Schools*, published in 1849, were specifically written as an introduction to the "great classical poets of England" so that "children of peasantry and artisans would come to understand and sympathise with the sentiments and principles by which well-educated persons are influenced" (Michael, 1987, p. 221). Among the list of authors selected in textbook anthologies, the most popular comprise Byron, Shakespeare, and Wordsworth followed by Cowper, Longfellow, Pope, and Scott (Michael, 1987).

In order to cultivate an appreciation of canonical texts, the pedagogy of reproduction was commonly employed to initiate students into a habit of tasteful reading. An example of such a strategy, stressing rote memorization and regurgitation, has been provided at the beginning of the chapter. At lower levels, teaching strategies emphasized recalling of information, identifying or locating information from a text, explaining meanings of words and phrases, and paraphrasing the text (Michael, 1987). At higher levels, the teaching of literature involved hunting for allusions and figures of speech, which was a method of teaching and assessing literature derived from the classical curriculum (Shayer, 1972). If students were taught to critique or evaluate a text, this was at a rudimentary level. A typical exercise involved the following steps: the teacher would read a selected poem aloud to the class; he or she would then provide biographical details about the poem, explain interesting allusions and figurative expressions, and explain the general meaning of the poem. The teacher would then tell the class about what the writer intended to achieve and would then describe the author's life and what critics have said about him or her (Michael, 1987). Presumably, students were expected to model these steps of criticism later on in their evaluation of the poem. This form of modeling could perhaps be tied to the low levels of literacy during the period. However, it emphasized a particular posture that students were to adopt — passivity with regards to the text in question. Passivity meant that students were not expected or encouraged to question the text. Instead, their task was to demonstrate an appreciation of the text by complimenting its poetic language and by displaying an understanding of the moral of the story. What we observe then is that approaches to teaching literature, centered on an elitist selection of texts, require teaching strategies that encourage students not to think for themselves but to think in the shoes of the author. In so doing, students learn to emulate model authors and acquire an education in taste in the process.

Second, the relation between the concept of taste and the concept of the Absolute suggests the connection between teaching literature and the teaching of moral and religious values. For example, another common approach adopted during this period involved didactic pedagogy. Here, poems and stories that promote desired moral virtues were read aloud by the teacher to young students who passively listened. Following this, the teacher would go on to explain the story to the students (Shayer, 1972). The prevailing view during this time was that literature, and poetry in particular, needed to be explained to students and therefore explanation should comprise a large part of teaching (Michael, 1987). Once again, this suggests a pervasive distrust that students could read and formulate opinions on their own. Teachers primarily directed students to particular virtues and moral messages, such as courage, that students were to appreciate from texts, and students would then passively regurgitate their teacher's explanations in their written responses.

In the British colonies, didactic pedagogy, as it was applied in schools, masked a more insidious aim of conversion. This is particularly evident in Thomas Macaulay's infamous "Minute on Indian Education" presented to the British government in 1835. Macaulay was a British politician who served on the Supreme Council for India and his aim was to create a specific class of native Indians who would be Indian "in blood and colour, but English in tastes, in opinions, in morals and in intellect" (1835, para. 34). One vehicle to facilitate this was through the teaching of English literature. Though Macaulay admits to not knowing Sanskrit or Arabic and confesses to having read only a few translated works from the East, he unashamedly states that among all his acquaintances, he has "never found one among them who could deny that a single shelf of a good European library was worth the whole native literature of India and Arabia" (para. 10). Macaulay goes on to argue that the teaching of local literature in India should be stopped and replaced with the teaching of English literature. The reason he gives is as follows:

It is said that the Sanskrit and the Arabic are the languages in which the sacred books of a hundred millions of people are written, and that they are on that account entitled to peculiar encouragement. Assuredly it is the duty of the British Government in India to be not only tolerant but neutral on all religious questions. But to encourage the study of a literature, admitted to be of small intrinsic value, only because that literature inculcated the most serious errors on the most important subjects, is a course hardly reconcilable with reason, with morality, or even with that very neutrality which ought, as we all agree, to be sacredly preserved. It is confessed that a language is barren of useful knowledge. We are to teach it because it is fruitful of monstrous superstitions. We are to teach false history, false astronomy, false medicine, because we find them in company with a false religion. (para. 31)

What Macaulay suggests here is that oriental literature is inferior because Eastern beliefs, fraught with superstition and lacking in attention to scientific rationality, are essentially "false religion." Therefore, there is a need to replace oriental literature with English literature which is aesthetically superior and can function to expose colonized natives to a better and more rational belief system. Gauri Viswanathan (1989) provides an account of how the colonial government in India used English literature as a vehicle to convert students from Hinduism to Christianity. In the eyes of the British government, Hindu beliefs were strongly embedded in Indian culture and identity but they were also obstructing the introduction of modern sciences and the more empirical subjects into the curriculum. Direct conversion of the colonized subjects was sure to result in violent reactions, since they were already suspicious of their colonial ruler's involvement in educational reform in the country. The only way was through the indirect medium of English literature instruction. Hence, the British government, acting on the advice of Thomas Macaulay, made English the medium of instruction in local schools in India and, more importantly, endorsed a new function for English instruction in the dissemination of moral and religious values (Viswanathan, 1989). The reading of selected secular texts served as a good replacement for the reading of scripture by evoking the imagination through graphic imagery (e.g., of heaven and hell).

Though literature continued to be taught "classically," with the emphasis on the history and structure of the language, its potential usefulness in leading Indian youth to a knowledge and acceptance of Christianity quickly became apparent. For example, without once referring to the Bible, government institutions officially committed to secularism realized they were in effect teaching Christianity through Milton, a "standard" in the literary curriculum whose scriptural allusions regularly sent students scurrying to the Bible for their elucidation. (Viswanathan, 1989, p. 85)

Literary texts such as Milton's *Paradise Lost* were selected specifically because they were aligned with Christian values. Other selected texts include the poetry of the Romantics as these conveyed the deeper connection between nature and the human soul as well as highly imagistic poems by Wordsworth as these provided a bridge to understanding the imagery in religious texts. The plays of Shakespeare were chosen not just for aesthetic reasons but also for their capacity to promote subordination to religious values such as in *Macbeth* where the murder of the king, who is a representative of God, disrupts the chain of being and leads to disharmony in the world.

To conclude, a nationalistic paradigm informing the teaching of literature was fundamental to establishing the discipline of English literature and ensuring its key contribution to strengthening the British Empire. English literature's rise to prominence toward the late nineteenth century must be partly attributed to the goal of education for nationalistic citizenship demonstrated through the propagation of concepts such as taste and the Absolute that were then translated into pedagogical approaches centered on reproduction and didacticism. Both these strategies served to fortify nationalistic sentiments through the transmission of a common heritage via canonical literary texts glorifying English history and culture; they also served to civilize the masses, increasingly incorporated into public education, through promoting taste and the refinement of sensibilities. More importantly, given that public education was now overseen by a secular state rather than the clergy, literature education inherited a quasi-religious function of transmitting moral and religious values. Underlying this function was a belief that the good of teaching literature enabled one to transcend material interests in order to be more conscious of the divine. Particularly in colonized countries, literature education was a powerful conduit facilitating conversion and colonial subordination through encouraging native subjects to passively appreciate literary texts that extolled Christian values.

With the gradual decline of the British Empire in the twentieth century, particularly following the end of the Second World War, coupled with the acceleration of globalization and the expansion of conceptions of citizenship beyond the nation, the concepts associated with nationalistic approaches to teaching literature were increasingly challenged. As Viswanathan (2002) argues, it became more difficult for literature education to sustain any vision of a singular, universal moral-religious value system as the reality of religious and cultural pluralism grew even more pervasive. Consequently, literature education underwent a process of transformation as new roles geared toward developing a stronger sense of agency in students to cope with the diversity of values and beliefs could now be imagined. In short, the goals of literature education have shifted in two main ways. First, literature education's goals have shifted away from its oppressive ties to nationalism toward a focus on developing students' understanding of their membership and participation in the wider global community. Second, its goals have also shifted from a transcendental concern with the Absolute to an emphasis on responding and engaging with otherness. In subsequent chapters, I explore these shifts in greater depth through three paradigms, namely, world, global, and cosmopolitan approaches to teaching literature.

CHAPTER THREE

World Approaches to Teaching Literature

A large outline of the map of the world is placed on the front wall of the room. Next to it are two huge charts. One chart is organized according to lists of nations — America, France, Greece, Persia, and so forth. Another chart is organized according to distinct periods — eighteenth century, nineteenth century, twentieth century, and so on. Surrounding the chart are a set of pictures that vividly display the setting and background of key places and events within some of these geographical regions. Throughout the entire school year, students engage in reading world literature and the front wall is transformed into a giant notepad as they categorize the books according to place and time and note brief descriptions about the texts. The difficulty of mapping the world is evident in this disorganized space of huge charts, handwritten notes, pictures, and connecting lines. In the middle of the program, the teacher observes that national prejudices surface as students begin to make stereotypical associations such as that between Jew and moneylender, Chinese and laundrymen, Italian and bootblack. As they articulate these in their discussions, the teacher encourages them to refer to the map and consider from where these biased impressions are derived, why the text conveys a particular association, and what are the social and political forces conditioning events in the story. If the Chinese in story A is depicted in a particular way in the nineteenth century, how is this similar or different from the way the Americans are depicted during this period in story B? What historical circumstances inform these differences? The teacher is careful to maintain neutrality; his aim is to trouble his students' thinking, to lead them to recognize their own assumptions, and to raise further questions for deeper understandings of foreign cultures. In this year-long world literature class, historical knowledge intersects and disrupts literary readings. This is coupled with comparative approaches that draw students in and out of their familiar social world. At the end, they learn that cultural differences are historically contextualized and their visual, geographical, and temporal mappings of literary texts give them a broad idea of the aesthetic expression of human beings across history. In spite of the differences they find, a common theme begins to emerge at the end of the year — that of the human being or, more specifically, the human being's quest to survive and flourish.

There is an immense sense of pride as the teacher of this American high school in 1935 reflects on the key objective of this program: to convey the importance of historical perspective in understanding cultures of the world through literature (Stolper, 1935). His lesson is comprehensively described in a published article in the *English Journal* which perhaps is an indication of the novelty of world literature courses in schools at the time. In fact, it was only nine years prior in 1926 that the first formal world literature course was introduced in American high schools (Stolper, 1935). At the tertiary level, world literature courses only began to emerge in American colleges in the late 1920s (Pizer, 2006). The early twentieth century therefore marks a focal period in the recognition of the importance of a world paradigm in the teaching of literature, and it was primarily through the subject of world literature that such a paradigm may be discerned. Several observations may already be made with regard to a world paradigm in this short scene of teaching. The most obvious observation is that it seeks to be inclusive even as it remains exclusive. Its inclusivity is evident in the fact that such a program centers on literature in English rather than English literature. On one hand, the flatness of the map on the wall emphasizes the neutrality with which its components are to be approached. Britain stands out no more than China, India, or Russia. The map conveys visually the idea of the larger world; everything falls within the space of the map which is a cohesive and inclusive space in which all nations, large or small, are connected and bound together by land and sea. On the other hand, the map also has lines and markers distinguishing the territory of the United States from Canada, Britain from Ireland, India from Pakistan, and China from Mongolia. If a map is organized according to the boundaries of nation-states, then a mapping of world literature must correspondingly be organized by these same boundaries. Hence, when world literature later evolved into the Great Books and comparative literature courses in universities, the syllabus was also categorized by geographical territories. For example, the first semester of a course titled "Books That Made Civilization" offered to comparative literature students at the University of Wisconsin in 1960, includes texts representing five regions: Greece, Rome, India, China, and the Near East (now more commonly referred to as the Middle East) (Alberson, 1960). Here then we arrive at the troubling crux of an approach to teaching literature informed by a world paradigm that is precisely this very activity of mapping the world. In order to include the other, one must name and define the other; hence, inclusivity involves exclusivity when the articulation of lines, borders, and divisions serve to highlight differences and the separation of one nation-state from another. Further, a world paradigm informed by such an ethos may misguidedly assume that the boundaries of nation-states are fixed and determinable and while the pedagogy of mapping paradoxically promotes reflection on the historical constructedness of literary texts in nations of the world, it fails to question the historicity of the very boundaries that compartmentalize and construct the world in the first place.

In what follows, I seek to provide a deeper understanding of a world paradigm informing the teaching of literature particularly through the introduction of world literature in schools during the early twentieth century. Despite some of the challenges of this pedagogical paradigm as suggested above, I want to consider how it can also offer possibilities in expanding literary engagement in the classroom.

The Second Early Wave of Globalization and Education for World Citizenship

The Formation of a Geoculture Based on a Recognition of Territorial Sovereignty

The period from the late nineteenth to the early twentieth century was marked by a growing recognition of the nation-state as the best model of political organization. I term this the second early wave of globalization in order to establish continuity with the second later wave of globalization following the Second World War in which the nation-state became the dominant form of political organization in the world. This is in contrast to Huntington (1991) who describes this period or, more specifically between 1922 and 1942, as the first reverse wave of democracy when quite a number of previously democratic nations, such as Italy and Germany, turned to authoritarian rule and totalitarianism. At the same time, Huntington's mapping of waves is quantitative in nature. He (1991) defines a wave of democratization as "a group of transitions from non-democratic to democratic regions that occur within a specified period of time and that significantly outnumber transitions in the opposite direction during that period of time" (p. 15). If, however, rather than limit the definition of a wave to a quantifiable figure (in this case, the number of nations who turn to or away from democracy), such a definition includes the idea of influence, then the period of the early twentieth century can no longer be described as a reverse wave. If one turns instead to Wallerstein, a different picture concerning this period emerges.

In the fourth volume of his comprehensive historical analysis of the modern system, Wallerstein (2011) identifies the period between 1789 and 1914 as involving the development of a geoculture of the modern world-system. He defines a geoculture as "the values that are widely shared throughout the world-system, both explicitly and latently" (p. 277). Prior to this period, there had been a gap between the operations of an expanding capitalist world economy and an acceptable ideological value-system. This gap was overcome by the doctrine of what he terms "centrist liberalism" which is a form of liberalism adopting a center position in-between the left (the radicals, democrats, socialists, or revolutionaries who advocate equality, freedom, and change) and the right (the conservatives who resist change and seek to preserve some measure of order and authoritarian rule). Centrist liberalism negotiates between the two impulses by, on one hand, supporting the free market and the maximization of the rights of the individual while, on the other hand, strengthening the nation-state and its interstate relations in the global sphere. Centrist liberalism was introduced in the nineteenth century as it aligned for the capitalists an ideal economic and political system, since the maintenance of a free market required the establishment of strong nation-states to facilitate open trade and to guarantee social stability against the discontent or revolt of the working class. Centrist liberalism not only depends on strong nation-states, it also depends on the spread of the nation-state as a political model in the global sphere and the recognition of the sovereignty of nation-states in the interstate system. Already, we see that what the ideology of centrist liberalism does is to contribute to a world paradigm. Such a paradigm envisions the world as organized by a collective system of sovereign nation-states. This perspective of the world had been developed by the mid-nineteenth century as centrist liberalism became the principal political system in Europe led by the British Empire. By the early twentieth century, it became the dominant way of envisioning the political organization of the world. As the British Empire receded, it was the entry of the United States as a global superpower during the early twentieth century that was particularly catalytic in securing a world-oriented vision of a collective system of sovereign nation-states operating within the ideology of centrist liberalism.

The United States was also to play a significant role in another crucial area that strengthened the pervasiveness of this world paradigm. This concerns its leadership in the establishment of an intergovernmental organization comprising nation-states. What was distinctive then about this organization was that it was dedicated not to protect the interests of specific nations but to provide collective security in the global sphere. In his "Fourteen Points" speech, the American president at the time, Woodrow Wilson (1918), states in the fourteenth article, "A general association of nations must be formed under specific covenants for the purpose of affording mutual guarantees of political independence and territorial integrity to great and small states alike" (para. 16). Wilson terms this general association the League of Nations and one may note that it is grounded on the mutual recognition of sovereignty of nation-states and that it encompasses a vision of economic liberalism promoting free trade among nations as far as possible. Though the League of Nations never materialized in reality and was pronounced defunct in 1946, it was the precursor to the formation of the United Nations and it also represented an important change in the geopolitical sphere involving the recognition that old ways of diplomacy consisting of secret alliances and wars were no longer sufficient (MacMillan, 2003). The modern world-system required an effective intergovernmental organization that could secure peace and security globally by more importantly securing the sovereignty of nation-states. Once again, this contributed to a world-oriented vision of a world divided into disparate and autonomous nation-states. The League of Nations, in guaranteeing sovereignty of nation-states at an international level, was particularly important in turning such a vision into reality.

At the same time, the tension between inclusion and exclusion was apparent in this world paradigm that informed the League of Nations. While such a perspective sought to be inclusive of all nation-states, it operated through exclusion in its attempts to define and legitimize territorial borders. Further, another level of exclusion had to do with the fact that even if a nation-state's sovereignty was recognized, this did not mean that it was accorded equal recognition. For example, one of the main points of contention was why the League was led by representatives of only five nations — Britain, France, Italy, Japan, and the United States. This caused some resentment among smaller, less powerful nations that grew when the Council later excluded Japan from its deliberations so that once again, European nations were left in charge of deciding about matters concerning the rest of the world (MacMillan, 2003). The most controversial matter, however, involved the clause regarding racial equality that the Japanese delegation proposed. Representatives of Japan wanted to expand the religious liberty clause in the League's covenant to include racial equality. Their draft proposal read: "The equality of nations being a basic principle of the League of Nations, the High Contracting Parties agree to accord, as soon as possible, to all alien nationals of States members of the League equal and just treatment in every respect, making no distinction, either in law or in fact, on account of their race or nationality" (cited in MacMillan, 2003, pp. 317–318). The British delegation strongly opposed the new clause and various members were afraid that the inclusion of such a clause would stir up racial issues all over the world; even Wilson knew that he would lose votes from key politicians back in the United States (MacMillan, 2003). As a result, the clause was never included in the covenant which was a crucial factor that deterred Japan from cooperating with the West leading to its eventual withdrawal from the League. It must be added that the whole irony of the episode was that the Japanese who fought so hard to end discrimination within the League through the inclusion of this racial equality clause were themselves guilty of the worst racist acts of violence when they massacred thousands of Chinese in Nanking, China, a few years later during the event known as The Rape of Nanking or the Asian Holocaust. As Iris Chang (1997) has documented, Japanese soldiers were taught that they "must not consider the Chinese as a human being but only as something of rather less value than a dog or cat" (p. 56). The point is that in the international order of things, there was no law, no principle that the League of Nations could have referred to deter Japan from their maltreatment of the Chinese. In fact, without the racial equality clause, the League's covenant was simply an empty statement, for how could there be equality among nation-states if equality among races and people groups was not recognized in the first place? If, for example, those of African origins and Asians were deemed inferior to whites, then how was it possible to recognize the equal standing of countries like Africa or China in the League of Nations?

In summary, the first wave of globalization in the late eighteenth and nineteenth century primarily brought about the formal organization of the nation-state via the concrete establishment of infrastructures such as government bureaucracies, organized military, and innovative applications of technology and communication to facilitate trade and exchanges with colonies and other nations. This second early wave of globalization from the late nineteenth and early twentieth century saw the spread of a powerful ideology in the form of centrist liberalism that both supported the free market and economic and technological globalization while strengthening the power of the nation-state. The difference between the first wave and the second early wave is that while the former is characterized by the consolidation of the nation-state, the latter is characterized by both the spread of the nation-state as well as controversies about its definition within the global sphere concerning which nation-states comprised and were accorded equal recognition in the world. This second early wave also led to the promotion of a world paradigm that essentially operated through bounded recognition, which means recognition of membership in the global sphere based on bounded autonomous nation-states. In short, bounded recognition is the primary basis of territorial sovereignty that was highly coveted by nation-states.

Education for World Citizenship

A world paradigm in the geopolitical sphere carried over to the public sphere of education and this was largely articulated through the goal of education for world citizenship. The goal of education for world citizenship must be understood in the light of its opposite — education for nationalistic citizenship. In fact, these two impulses were increasingly obvious in the early twentieth century leading to the Second World War. At one extreme, education for the hyper-nationalistic citizen may be found in totalitarian countries such as Germany and in militaristic states such as Japan. In Germany, Hitler sought to reform the entire education system to promote German national identity. German teachers were introduced to concepts such as "blood" or "soil"; they were taught about the supremacy of the Aryan race, how its purity could be polluted by racial mixing, and they were extolled to transmit these values to their students as encapsulated in the following Nazi directive to elementary school teachers in 1940: "It is not the task of the elementary school to impart a multiplicity of knowledge for the personal use of the individual. It has to develop and harness all physical and mental powers of youth for the service of the people and the state" (Pine, 2010, p. 41). Literature was an important part of the curriculum, particularly the inclusion of stories involving German mythology and folklore, since these texts contributed to the development of the German spirit or *volk*. Just as English literature was utilized to cultivate Englishness, as discussed in the previous chapter, German literature was used to develop a consciousness of Germanness. Similarly, in Japan, subjects such as history and literature were used to strengthen the sense of nationalism by portraying the Japanese as a super race. Students from a young age were taught that obedience and submission to the nation was a virtue and that next to the emperor, all individual life including their own was worth nothing (Chang, 1997).

At the other extreme — and perhaps in reaction to these hyper-nationalistic impulses — was the growing awareness of the importance of education for world citizenship. Though the necessity of education for world citizenship, as opposed to hyper-nationalistic citizenship, would only be fully recognized at the end of the Second World War following the Jewish and Asian Holocausts, its seeds were already sown in the early twentieth century. Derek Heater (1990) provides an account of various movements during this period that sought to free education from state control. Some examples include the revision of textbooks in the Netherlands to ensure the absence of national bias (a move that was pursued later by the League of Nations and the United Nations) as well as the promotion of Peace Education as a discipline in Europe in 1907. These movements helped create awareness of the importance of having a broader vision for education beyond the nation-state and it was given further impetus through the work of two key reformers. The first is Maria Montessori in Italy who, during a lecture she (1947) later gave in Sri Lanka, outlined her vision for a new education: "Moral education, which is so necessary today, must insist upon the appreciation of civilization rather than upon the appreciation of the character of one's country or of one's race, as has been the case in the past. . . . The new education must foster a new understanding of the real values of humanity and gratitude must be felt for those workers upon whom human life depends" (p. 3). Education that gears one toward a deeper understanding and engagement with the world was also a vision by another reformer, Rabindranath Tagore, in India. When Tagore later established the Visva-Bharati University, he encouraged the study of foreign cultures and introduced a curriculum that aimed to deconstruct binaries such as East and West, modern and traditional, elite and masses (Williams, 2007). His aim was to build the institution "upon the ideal of the spiritual unity of all races" (Tagore, 1961, p. 217). In this light, compassion was a fundamental disposition to be cultivated in all students, since one first needed compassion before moving out of one's own worldview. The ultimate objective was to educate in students "a sympathy with all humanity, free from all racial and national prejudices" (Tagore, 1961, p. 216).

In short, a comparison of education for nationalistic citizenship that occurred in Germany and Japan and education for world citizenship that was emphasized by Montessori and Tagore shows how each is framed by the other in a dichotomous binary. Education for nationalistic citizenship insists on sole loyalty to the state or emperor while education for world citizenship emphasizes loyalty to the broader humanity; the former operates by instilling fear and demanding submission while the latter operates by promoting love and compassion and by encouraging cooperation and understanding; finally, the former defines citizenship according to exclusion in which specific races or communities are not accorded the economic or political privileges of membership while the latter defines citizenship according to inclusion in which all human beings are part of a world brotherhood or family.

The Conceptual Formation of a World Pedagogical Paradigm

The Introduction of World Literature in Schools

Given that the goals of literature education were subsumed under broader educational goals in Western nations, the vision of a world brotherhood grounded on democratic ideals of citizenship influenced the development of a world paradigm to teaching literature. This was largely demonstrated in the shift from the teaching of literature with a nationalistic focus via English literature to an international focus via literature in English. Though a world paradigm may inform approaches to teaching literature in English in multiple ways, one of the primary avenues was through the subject of world literature that was introduced to schools during this second early wave of globalization.

From the early twentieth century, world literature was slowly introduced to schools in the United States while in Britain and her colonies, the teaching of English literature remained dominant. A survey of high schools across the United States in 1922 found that America, Britain, Canada, and France were well represented in the literary texts studied although there were calls for broader representation from other parts of the world (Bryan, 1922; Koch, 1922). Broadly, world literature began to be taught in American schools only after two important institutional movements.

The first was the elimination of the college entrance uniform reading lists. Arthur Applebee (1974) provides a comprehensive account of how, by the beginning of the twentieth century, English literature was universally offered in all schools. A key catalyst was the college entrance requirements that tested graduating high school students on a list of literary texts. At first, there was no uniform list of texts so that colleges such as Harvard and Yale were setting different requirements; but as a result of pressure from schools for some form of standardization, various committees and conferences were established that eventually led to a high school literary canon. This canon was centered on classical works of English literature such as *David Copperfield, Ivanhoe, Julius Caesar, Silas Marner, The Lady of the Lake,* and *The Merchant of Venice*. By this time, literature education was a core aspect of the national curriculum and the formalization of the college entrance requirements dictated the kinds of texts studied in the literature classroom. However, the appropriation of English literature education in a non-British context foreshadowed future resistance, and thus, it was only a matter of time when American schools began to question the dominance of these texts in the syllabus. Perhaps the first movement leading to the introduction of world literature in schools then began with abolishing the standardized canonical list. Applebee (1974) provides several reasons for how this happened: the growing confidence of English teachers about their profession and their ability to shape a curriculum independent of the dictates of colleges; the formation of the National Council of Teachers of English to develop an English program for schools so that they would not need to depend on the uniform lists; and the broader progressive movement led by John Dewey that stressed the need for students to engage in contemporary concerns that then challenged the relevance of studying classical texts. By 1916, college entrance requirements no longer made it mandatory for students to study the lists of literary texts that the colleges recommended. Thus, the hegemony of the college lists ended and schools now had the freedom to construct the literature curriculum. This democratization of the curriculum was significant in providing space for the entry of other literatures in English.

The second significant event was the introduction of American literature in the curriculum, especially since schools no longer had to center their literature curriculum on the study of English literature. Following the First World War, there was increasing pressure to include the teaching of American literature in order to instill a sense of national history and heritage. The subject became firmly established in the curriculum by the late 1920s and its goal was encapsulated in this statement given by a teacher: "The first great aim in the literature course is a training for citizenship by a study of our national ideals embodied in the writings of American authors, our race ideals as set forth by the great writers of Anglo-Saxon origin, our universal ideals as we find them in any great work of literary art" (cited in Applebee, 1974, p. 68). This statement is particularly enlightening because, here, the teacher is envisioning a literature course as encompassing three parts: the study of literary texts from America followed by Britain and other parts of the world. In this curriculum, the first part emphasizes the nation; the second, race; and the third, humanity. Such a goal must have been significantly radical given that the United States has a much shorter history and literary tradition compared to Britain. However, this example shows how the provision of space in the curriculum for American literary texts at the same time allowed the possible insertion of other world literatures for study irrespective of the length of their historical literary tradition. As calls for the inclusion of American literature received greater prominence toward the middle of the century, English literature became subsumed under the category of world literature as observed in the recommendations of a proposed world literature curriculum:

> Time devoted to literature in the four-year high school would be proportioned on a 2-2 basis. The first half of the course would be devoted to American literature. The last half section would treat world literature, with Britain's contributions rated along with outstanding works of other nations. (Carter, 1948, p. 419)

Thus, as American literature began to be introduced into more schools, it correlated with the introduction of world literature as well. It was literature from America rather than other formerly colonized countries that provided this space given the increasing sense of confidence of the United States as a leader and global superpower in the world.

The Concept of Collective Taste in Disciplinary Movements

Underlying the teaching of world literature in American schools was a world paradigm that had earlier been conceptualized by Johann Wolfgang von Goethe in 1827 but that was now revitalized. In a comprehensive history of the discipline of world literature, John Pizer (2006) notes that while world literature as a pedagogical practice and program of study is almost exclusively a development in the United States, world literature as a philosophy is closely related to Germany and the ideas of German thinkers, particularly Goethe. Though Goethe's philosophical contributions to a world paradigm in literature education will be developed at greater length in the following section, my focus here is on Goethe's contribution to the comparative movement within the discipline and, more importantly, how this movement was grounded on the concept of collective taste.

The first author to have employed the concept of *weltliteratur*, or "world literature," was the German scholar Christopher Martin Wineland who, in 1813, mentioned this in a series of handwritten notes. However, many scholars consider Goethe as the first scholar to have fully articulated the broad parameters of *weltliteratur* (Auerbach, 1969; Damrosch, 2003; Lawall, 1994; Moretti, 2000, Pizer, 2006). When Goethe outlined world literature, the Napoleonic Wars had ended a few years earlier in 1815 and Germany was politically disintegrated. At the same time, improvements in publishing and communication technologies provided the conditions for greater dialogue and exchange of ideas with Germany's neighbors. Goethe was particularly concerned that German intellectuals remained caught up in their own world despite these new opportunities for broader communication following the war. Thus, he turned to literature in the public sphere (involving both the public discourse about literature as well as literature education in the public sphere of schools) as the vehicle for an international exchange of ideas (Goethe, 1921a). His proposal was foundational to literature education, especially since he was directing his argument at scholars and teachers in the universities as observed in his recorded conversations with his friend and disciple, Johann Peter Eckermann:

> But, really, we Germans are very likely to fall too easily into this pedantic conceit, when we do not look beyond the narrow circle that surrounds us. I therefore like to look about me in foreign nations, and advise everyone to do the same. National literature is now rather an

unmeaning term; the epoch of world literature is at hand, and everyone must strive to hasten its approach. (Eckermann, 1836/1998a, pp. 165–166)

The ideal citizen for Goethe is not the nationalistic citizen whom he would have categorized as one displaying "pedantic conceit"; instead, his focus is on a world citizen who, though rooted in his or her own culture, shares an affinity with the larger humanity at the same time. In some ways, Goethe's implicit notion of a world citizen parallels the term "citizen of the world" originally coined by Diogenes the Cynic 404–323 BC, who set up his home in the marketplace out of disdain for material comfort and out of a desire to develop a philosophical detachment from home (Nussbaum, 1997). In a similar spirit, Goethe describes a condition of mental exile for the world citizen: "The poet, as a man and citizen, will love his native land; but the native land of his poetic powers and poetic action is the good, noble, and beautiful, which is confined to no particular province or country, and which he seizes upon and forms wherever he finds it" (Eckermann, 1836/1998b, p. 425). Thus, the world citizen is one who privileges the world over the provincial, the universal over the particular, and common humanity over one's own countrymen.

Goethe himself modeled what it meant to have a world orientation. Not only did he travel frequently, he exchanged letters with writers from all over the world even opening his home to meet them (Boerner, 2005). Goethe was also a wide reader of "great" literature from around the world but more so from Europe and he wrote many critical essays on the authors he admired. Among the English were Lord Byron, William Shakespeare, and Sir Walter Scott; among the French was Victor Hugo; among the Greeks were Aristotle, Homer, Plato, and Sophocles; and among the Italians was Dante. More importantly, Goethe provided the foundations of a method of comparative criticism for studying world literature. In his writings, he suggests how comparative criticism may be performed using two methods. In the first method, Goethe suggests that contemporary European works may be studied by comparing them to classical Greek and Latin literary works which, to him, represent the epitome of world literature:

But, while we thus value what is foreign, we must not bind ourselves to some particular thing, and regard it as a model. We must not give this value to the Chinese, or the Serbian, or Calderon, or the

Nibelungen; but if we really want a pattern, we must always return to the ancient Greeks, in whose works the beauty of mankind is constantly represented. (Eckermann, 1836/1998a, pp. 165–166)

Throughout his writings, Goethe makes constant references to both Greek and Latin literary works that he advocates must be studied in close detail and that form the benchmark for assessing contemporary literature. Using the example of *The Odyssey*, comparative criticism modeled after this approach is as follows. It begins by appreciating the aesthetics of this Greek literary classic and extolling its philosophical wisdom. This is then followed by a comparative analysis in which this text is connected to a contemporary literary text by a national or regional writer such as *Ulysses* by Irish novelist James Joyce or the *Cantos* by American poet Ezra Pound involving the section that recounts Odysseus' journey to the underworld. Goethe's methodology was highly influential in providing a method for studying modern literary texts when these were first introduced to universities in the mid-nineteenth century. Thus, in early comparative literature courses, students were required to read the classics alongside contemporary European works and Goethe's method of comparative criticism was employed so that the classics formed the standard to which modern works were evaluated (Milner, 1996). On one hand, Goethe's comparative methodology seeks to be inclusive in that it provides space for the entry of more contemporary works by reaffirming their value through their ties to the classics. On the other hand, such an approach is exclusive, since only selected modern works qualify and the anchor for comparison remains the classical Western canon.

In his second method, Goethe shows how comparative criticism may be applied to studying non-European literature. Though Goethe demonstrates a curiosity about literature primarily from Europe, he also read literature from China and India. In his discussions, he suggests how such literature may be approached as observed in his reflections after reading a Chinese novel:

The Chinamen think, act, and feel almost exactly like us; and we soon find that we are perfectly like them, except that all they do is more clear, pure, and decorous, than with us. With them all is orderly, citizen-like, without great passion or poetic flight; and there is a strong resemblance to my Hermann and Dorothea, as well as to the English novels of Richardson. They likewise differ from us in that with them external nature is always associated with human figures. (Eckermann, 1836/1998a, p. 164)

Here, Goethe is performing a comparative criticism of non-European literature. First, this involves using the literary text as a platform for understanding foreign culture. For example, having read the Chinese novel, he extracts from it an understanding about Chinese ways of thinking, social living, as well as Chinese styles of writing. To some extent, the generalizations Goethe makes about the orderliness of Chinese society based on one novel borders on the stereotypical. Second, literary masterpieces are at the center of these comparisons so that he compares a presumably well-known contemporary Chinese novel to the works of the English novelist Richardson as well as his own works. Third, in this comparative approach, established Western texts remain the central frame of reference. This is observed when Goethe states that the Chinese are "almost exactly like us"; here, the foreign is critiqued on familiar grounds (Lawall, 1994). The construction of foreign culture is also used to inform Goethe's own European culture which is an instance of what Gayatri Spivak (1988) has described as the production of the other to support the constitution of the subject as Europe. Furthermore, throughout the rest of the letter, "Chinese novel," "Chinese Romance," and "Chinese poet" are used but no specific names are mentioned, whereas he specifically lists the titles of German and English texts. Hence, the form of cross-cultural exchange enables the dominant culture to critique the foreign culture, and the voice of the other is noticeably absent in such an exchange.

Inherent in the two methods comprising Goethe's model of comparative criticism is a tension between inclusivity and exclusivity that, as discussed in the previous section, was also evidenced in the global sphere as observed in the formation of the League of Nations. Goethe's comparative methodology, on one hand, is premised on a vision of inclusivity through promoting world communication via world literature. This vision entails a belief that the good of literature is in its educative potential in fostering world communication, which not only broadens a nation's perspective, dialogues, and exchanges at an interstate level, it also leads to the collective improvement of society and humanity. Although this belief in world communication seems noble in its desire to promote an inclusive space for international dialogue and exchange, on the other hand, such a perspective also promotes exclusivity. This is primarily observed in the way comparative criticism becomes connected to the concept of collective taste. For example, the two methods of comparative criticism described above involve engagements with literary masterpieces whether this concerns classical works, European, or non-European literatures. Thus, when Goethe proposes that the platform through which nations can connect with other nations is world literature, he is not referring to all literatures written around the world. Instead, he argues that world communication should focus on the best ideas and the best literary masterpieces that each nation can offer, thus foreshadowing the Arnoldian (1861/1993) call "to know the best that is known and thought in the world" (p. 37). Underlying this focus on the best literary works is a fear that with the push for world literature, the literary market would be open to other forms of low-culture literary texts from other countries that would eventually threaten high-culture literary works, including his own published works. The best way to guard against this dilution of standards is then to emphasize inclusivity and exclusivity at the same time. That is, one needs to be open to literature from around the world but to only engage with world literature of the best kind.

This twin function of promoting world literary exchanges on one hand and cultivating collective taste by focusing on the best literary masterpieces on the other hand was to become one of Goethe's key projects as described by George Lewes (1908) who wrote one of the earliest biographies on Goethe. Goethe had attacked the German public calling them philistines and had accused them of having such widespread taste in cultural works that they could watch a performance of Hamlet on one night followed by a crass comedic act the following night (Eckermann, 1836/1998c, p. 281). In other words, the German public lacked a consistent cultivated taste in contrast to the French and Italians.[1] Goethe then became invested in broadening a network of elite literary intellectuals who could be distinguished from the masses in terms of their preference for fine writing from different parts of the world as opposed to popular texts. Essentially, this elite literary citizenry would demonstrate the capacity for taste in beautiful world literary masterpieces and the capacity to provide an informed appreciation of these works through public discourse. This elite network was to then take on the burden of educating the rest of the public and would look into establishing standards of taste, thereby improving society and the world's collective taste in world literature.

Essentially, Goethe's key contribution to a world paradigm informing the teaching of literature is his bridging of a belief about literature's power to promote world communication and, correspondingly, a consciousness of world citizenship, with a belief in literature's power to improve collective taste in the world via the sharing of world literary benchmarks. This then distinguishes the concept of taste as associated with a world paradigm informing approaches to teaching literature from that associated with a nationalistic paradigm. Whereas in the latter, taste is aimed at cultivating nationalistic values and sentiments through a literary canon that elevates English history and culture, the former is aimed at progressing humanity's collective taste and discernment through a world literary canon.

The Concept of Universal Humanity in Philosophical Contributions

A world paradigm subscribes to a belief in the good of the collective. It is the human rather than the divine that is privileged, and this implies the prioritization of the concept of universal humanity. In this section, I focus on Goethe's philosophy of *weltliteratur* with particular attention to unpacking this concept.

One reason why Goethe emphasizes world literary masterpieces is because what they all have in common is their capacity to depict a "universal" human condition. Engagements with world literary masterpieces then facilitate moral reflection about this common humanity. When Goethe states, "but if we really want a pattern, we must always return to the ancient Greeks, in whose works the beauty of mankind is constantly represented" (Eckermann, 1836/1998a, p. 166), his interest is in works representing the "beauty of mankind" or, in other words, works that contain a "universal aesthetic," works that beautifully philosophize about humanity. Georg Brandes (1899), who elaborated on Goethe's universal aesthetics, argues that in reality, only a handful of writers belong to the category of world literature. One example is Shakespeare, by virtue of the fact that his works delve into universal themes and issues. On the other hand, despite the literary quality of their works, authors such as Christopher Marlowe and Samuel Taylor Coleridge possess the status of "English" authors and do not belong to the category of world literature. What Goethe and Brandes assume is that one can dichotomize aesthetics at the local level versus aesthetics at the world level. Ironically, they discount the fact that much of the literature of ancient Greece was influenced by other civilizations. For example, David Damrosch (2009) cites a study about how illiterate bards in Yugoslavia were composing and singing epic poems containing many of the oral techniques used in the Homeric epics later on. In addition, Goethe does not adequately provide convincing reasons why classical Greek literature belongs to the category of universal aesthetics and not other classical works such as Tang Dynasty or Sanskrit poetry that contain deep spiritual and philosophical reflections about the meaning of human existence. Despite these discrepancies, the point is that Goethe's interest in the beautiful is based on a view that it is only through such works that one can transcend the superficial and material world in order to contemplate the universal human condition.

At the same time, Goethe is far from being consistent about this notion of universal humanity. Two evidences point to this. First, Goethe's definition of the "universal" in world literature once again seems to suggest a tension between inclusivity and exclusivity. A survey of secondary readings highlights this contradiction. On one hand, Goethe is portrayed as one who advocates the "universal man" (Goethe Bicentennial Foundation, 1950, p. x), who has faith in humanity that is inclusive of all nations (Hutchins, 1950), and who celebrates diversity regarding it as an innate part of human nature (Wilder, 1950). On the other hand, a distinctly nationalistic impulse underlies Goethe's call for world literature. According to Goethe, a cohesive national literature and a corresponding cohesive spirit of nationalism must precede world literature and the ideal of world citizenship. Goethe had complained that the German writers were isolated, disorganized, and self-absorbed. This was in contrast to France which had a vibrant literary public sphere consisting of journals and book clubs as well as the sense that French writers had a common spirit in that they grappled with issues of the nation and of Europe (Strich, 1949). The problem was that, unlike their European rivals, German writers tended to focus on trivial issues about their own personal lives or that of their own town or province. This overall lack of a consciousness of Germany in their writing resulted in German literature receiving little recognition from other European nations. Thus, Goethe (1827/1921b) argues that as "the military and physical strength of a nation develops from its internal unity and cohesion, so must its aesthetic and ethical strength grow gradually from a similar unanimity of feeling and ideas" (p. 89). The paradox here is that while world literature seeks to be inclusive in promoting intellectual conversations among nations, it is internally exclusive and remains trapped and defined within a nationalistic mode of thinking. As Fritz Strich (1949) observes, the primary function of world literature is to promote universal harmony by making the national characteristics of peoples intelligible to each other. Universal harmony therefore depends on a consolidated and cohesive sense of national unity.

Such a view essentially grounded early conceptualizations of the discipline in the academy. For example, in 1911, when University of Chicago professor Richard Moulton first proposed a syllabus for a world literature course, he began by distinguishing universal literature from world literature. Universal literature refers to the sum total of all literatures while world literature is universal literature "seen in perspective from a given point of view, presumably the national standpoint of the observer" (Moulton, 1911, p. 6). The paradox therefore is that while the universal seeks to oppose and transcend the national, the strength of its meaning is dependent on the national.

Second, Goethe's definition of "universal" in world literature seems to contain a Eurocentric bias. When Goethe speaks of a universal or common humanity, this term often connotes a singular idea since his emphasis is on European culture. Various scholars maintain that although Goethe showed some interest in non-European literature, this attention was only cursory and limited. His main focus was primarily on developing closer relations among European literatures (Finney, 1997; Lawall, 1994). Goethe was aware that unlike France, Germany lacked a core literary tradition. He states that the reason is because "Germany, so long inundated by foreign people, pervaded by other nations, employing foreign languages in learned and diplomatic transactions, could not possibly cultivate her own [common culture]" (Goethe, 1811/1921c, p. 226). Having become culturally fragmented as a result of these foreign invasions, Goethe argues that the Germans had looked to other European traditions, namely French and Latin languages and literatures. This constant centering of national identity through the traditions of other European nations inevitably results in an innate need to develop a German literary tradition and raise the status of German literature. Indeed, this is what Goethe (1827/1921b) seems to suggest when he writes, "I shall merely acquaint my friends with my conviction that there is being formed a universal world literature, in which an honourable role is reserved for us Germans" (p. 89). One way in which this honorable role may be achieved is by situating German literature within the larger context of Western literature, thus creating stronger connections between German literature and a much revered classical literary heritage. Sarah Lawall (1994) notes that Goethe seemed intent on forging continuity between Greek and Roman literatures and contemporary European literature. In so doing, the status of German literature as well as Goethe's own status as a significant figure in the German literary scene is raised as a result of this ancestral linkage. In his conversation with Eckermann on July 15, 1827, Goethe praises a German historian for what he describes as an aristocratic versus a democratic view. In youth, Goethe tells Eckermann (1836/1998b), one knows nothing, possesses nothing, and therefore knows little about how to value anything. One therefore possesses a democratic openness to all things, whereas in old age, one values what one owns and wishes his or her children to inherit them. This aristocratic posture is inevitable in old age, Goethe states, and he then moves on to praise the review of a German historian who claims:

> We are weakest in the aesthetic department, and may wait long before we meet such a man as Carlyle. It is pleasant to see that intercourse is now so close among the French, English, and Germans, that we shall be able to correct one another. This is the greatest use of a world literature, which will show itself more and more. (Eckermann, 1836/1998b, p. 216)

What Goethe means when he distinguishes aristocratic and democratic postures and later states, "Therefore in old age we are always aristocrats" (Eckermann, 1836/1998b, p. 216) is made clearer when he links it to this citation about the aims of world literature as a means to strengthen the connection among French, English, and German literary traditions. In this sense, the aristocratic posture is akin to a posture of partiality, and Goethe makes the justification that one cannot help but be partial as one grows in age, in knowledge, and learning. At the same time, the borderline between partiality and exclusivity seems blurred in this instance. Even though Goethe displays a curiosity about the world via world literature, his partiality toward Europe as a basis for forging continuity among various European literary traditions suggests a danger that partiality can lead to exclusivity. What we are observing is Goethe's construction of a Western canonical tradition that can only strengthen the cohesiveness of a German literary tradition. Ironically, then, though Goethe saw the study of literature as a conduit for human progress and advocated the reading of foreign literature for the promotion of harmony, communication, and understanding among nations, the Eurocentric bias inherent in his conceptions of world literature seems to represent an extension of German nationalism.

The fact that Goethe wavered between a genuinely global transcendental outlook and what seems a nationalistic, Eurocentric perspective concerning engagements with world literature indicates that perhaps he himself was attempting to define the concept *weltliteratur*, or world literature, that he had popularized and was struggling to do so in the process. The tensions result from an attempt to break away from traditional nationalistic modes of thinking while remaining trapped within this framework. As a result, we see tendencies toward inclusivity and exclusivity, the universal and the selective, in this early world paradigm grounded in Goethe's philosophy. At the same time, perhaps such tensions betray a more deep-seated bias, one that is spiritual in nature.

What is the basis of Goethe's nationalistic and Eurocentric bent underlying the concept of universal humanity? In a perceptive analysis of the ideology underlying Goethe's theorization of world literature, Strich (1949) argues that the source of Goethe's idea stems from the Christian notion of brotherhood. Strich demonstrates, through an analysis of Goethe's letters, that the biblical command to "love one another" was Goethe's lifelong creed upon which he based his idea of world literature. This was a vision that involved calling and drawing people together to work toward the development of humanity through mutual exchanges and collaboration. While grounded on the values of Christianity and Christian brotherhood, on the surface it was humanity that was glorified so that "the early fundamental ideas of world literature were formed and developed out of the religion of humanity" (Strich, 1949, p. 39). Here, the concept of universal humanity takes over the religious function of the Absolute or God: It is to be glorified and is to be the cause that would unite the peoples of the world. Underlying this ideology is the assumption that the true religion of Christianity would privilege the idea of universal humanity above the individual, the family, or the nation.

One may argue that Goethe's own beliefs had nothing to do with the development of a world paradigm informing the teaching of literature. However, Goethe's ideas have been influential in spiritualizing the concept of universal humanity and it is particularly evident in the discipline of world literature. This can be observed in the work of two very influential scholars who inaugurated the discipline of world literature in the academy. The first is Hutcheson Posnett who is regarded as a "pioneering scholar of comparative literature" (Damrosch, Melas, & Buthelezi, 2009, p. 50). His privileging of the idea of Christian brotherhood is seen in the use of the religious terminology of a common creed to describe the ethos underlying the study of world literature:

A common creed, whether it be that of Christianity or any other system, rests, and must rest, on the belief of men in their fellow-men, on the sympathy of man with man, on the extension of man's pains and pleasures beyond the narrow circle of his personal being, within which he may be a god or a "glorious devil," but never the possessor of a creed. Moreover, since any literature deserving of the name must address itself to a community of human hopes and fears however narrow, the disbelief of man in his neighbour, which cuts away all sympathies, also paralyses the workings of imagination in its efforts to pass from the individual to a wider and greater world. (Posnett, 1886, p. 243)

According to Posnett, what gains literary texts membership in the discipline of world literature is an aesthetic extolling universal humanity; such an aesthetic entails a spiritual belief in a common fellowship of individuals above the self. Though this common creed may be found in many other cultures and religions, Posnett upholds the Christian religion as a model when he answers in the affirmative to his own rhetorical question, "Are we justified in regarding the social as the dominant aspect of Christian world literature, are we justified in treating the teaching of Christ and his disciples as the most splendid example of the social spirit in world literature?" (p. 286). He then proceeds to show that what he categorizes as Christian world literature, such as the Bible and works by Dante, are marked by an ethos of social brotherhood, since they convey the fall of humanity and the inheritance of sin by all mankind leading to man's need for salvation; these lead the reader toward a transcendental consciousness of the common destiny and fate of humanity.

The second influential scholar is Richard Moulton who proposed a world literature syllabus at the University of Chicago in 1911. His course is organized according to what he terms "literary bibles" beginning with the Bible, followed by classical Greek and Roman literature, and the literature of Dante, Goethe, Milton, and Shakespeare. These are termed bibles to indicate the sacred nature of the text, its ability to transcend the provincial and thereby its significance in contributing to the "autobiography of civilization" (Moulton, 1911, p. 437).

In short, the prioritization of the concept of universal humanity in world literature that is reflective of a world paradigm informing the teaching of literature is a complex term marked by contradictions concerning inclusivity and exclusivity as well as a world embracing aspiration coupled with nationalism and Eurocentrism. A further contradiction is that such a paradigm promotes international exchanges concerning secular literary texts while maintaining ties to a Christian worldview.

Applications of World Approaches to Teaching Literature

I have argued that a world paradigm subscribes to a belief about the good of teaching literature that is tied to the goal of education for world citizenship as articulated via concepts of collective taste and universal humanity. However, as I have shown, inherent in these concepts is the tension of inclusion and exclusion that lies at the heart of a world pedagogical paradigm. What counts as representative masterpieces? Who decides what counts as universal? In earlier sections of this chapter, I have provided various examples of how this tension was manifest at different levels during the early twentieth century. At the geopolitical sphere, the League of Nations sought to promote a collective and inclusive interstate system even as it was led by an exclusive club of Western powers who made decisions for the rest of the world. Further, despite their pursuit of world harmony, they failed to accord equal recognition to all nation-states. In the context of world literature education, underlying the concepts of collective taste and universal humanity is an inclusive ethos that pushes for dialogue and intercultural understandings through engagements with literatures around the world even as these concepts have also been associated with elitism. This suggests that world literature has not completely relinquished its ties to nationalism, Eurocentrism, and a Christian worldview.

Another example of the tension between inclusion and exclusion within a world pedagogical paradigm is evidenced in world literature's emphasis on representative masterpieces. While aiming to be inclusive of a wide range of world literary texts in its emphasis on breadth, it is depth that becomes compromised. Further, students engage in a representative sampling of texts from different regions and countries in the world that can result in superficial or stereotyped understandings of other cultures and communities. It also excludes overlaps and subtle differences among ethnic groups within a region as would occur when subgenres such as Japanese literature, Korean literature and Singapore literature are all classified broadly as Asian literature.

At the same time, this tension between inclusion and exclusion is a necessary reality behind the impossible task of reading the world. Rather than reject a world pedagogical paradigm, I want to suggest that teachers can make powerful use of such a tension to promote more democratically inclusive spaces in the classroom. This can occur through teaching students to read the world by emphasizing boundary recognition. In the rest of this section, I want to suggest four approaches to teaching literature that are related to boundary recognition. I make use of historical examples to show how teachers in American middle and high schools, during this second early wave of globalization, were already experimenting with varied ways of equipping students to read and critique different forms of boundaries observed in literary texts.[2]

World approaches to teaching literature can center on the idea of boundary recognition, and the first approach involves facilitating students to read within the boundaries in which literary texts have been categorized. In his book *How to Read World Literature*, Damrosch (2009) proposes reading across time by tracing characters, themes, motifs, and images across centuries as well as by tracing an image or scene back to its source to observe how texts borrow from other texts. Indeed, teaching students to read across historical time and geographical space seems to be the most common way in which the world literature curriculum was organized in schools between 1900 and the 1930s. For example, it was common practice to teach the great masterpieces according to historical periods such as the classics of the eighteenth century followed by the nineteenth century, and so forth. Within each period, texts from a range of literary genres such as the novel, the epic, the lyric, and drama were then explored (Meader, 1899). This was also a common way of organizing world literature anthologies that were used as textbooks in schools. For example, one text provides a broad survey of great literatures from America, Asia, Europe, and Russia arranged chronologically from the fifteenth century BC to the twentieth century (Shepherd, 1937). The point of these boundaries is to move students from part to whole so that through the study of clusters of world literary texts, students would appreciate a particular historical period, geographical region, or generic convention. Another aim is that through the comparative study of particular texts, students would obtain "a sympathetic acquaintance with scenes in various geographical sections and with historical periods of the world" (Koch, 1922, p. 193) and so would come to an understanding of the universal human condition.

Boundary recognition also involves the second approach of facilitating students' reading of the constructedness of boundaries. Pizer (2006) proposes a metatheoretical approach to teaching literature in which students, as they immerse themselves in world literature, are asked to think about how concepts and categories become attached to texts. For example, he challenges his students to think about what national or regional elements foreground Kafka's story as Czech or Austrian. This would presumably involve getting students to interrogate even the constructedness of national, regional, and ethnic identities. A version of this idea was experimented in a high school in the early twentieth century as the teacher sought to teach the history of literature in English through reading world literature. He had his students trace the development of literary forms (genres and styles) in both English and American as well as foreign literatures in English and explore how these changing forms reflect global, political, and philosophical ideas of the time (Axson, 1906). Such an approach enables students to become aware of how global forces across history contribute to developing literary categories and forms that themselves reflect a kind of progress in the world history of ideas.

The third approach of boundary recognition is to read around boundaries. Reading around the text involves getting students to think beyond the constructedness of the text. This can include pursuing the complex networks of signification suggested by the boundaries presented in the text (Lawall, 1994). In practice, this would mean locating literature within the broader context of other disciplines or fields that would provide a deeper understanding of the world and humanity. During the early twentieth century, some schools subsumed the study of world literature within a broader integrated curriculum so that the emphasis is not the teaching of world literature but the teaching of literature in the world. This is typically organized in two ways. One way is the integration of the subjects, literature and history. For example, a unit on ancient history would be supplemented by texts such as the *Iliad* and the *Odyssey* (Hobson, 1917); the point is so that the study of history would not be reduced to mere facts but would come alive for students. In a tenth grade course at one school, the modern literature curriculum is centered on the theme of the growth of democracy and is divided into six units: the growth of democracy, awakening of national consciousness, escape from the commonplace, revolt against conventions, changing attitude toward war, and science changing the world. In the first unit examining the growth of democracy, selected texts include poems by Walt Whitman, Robert Frost, and the works of Leo Tolstoy (Lyman, 1936). Another way is the integration of literature with other subjects through thematic units. In a survey of 8,799 teachers across schools in the United

States, almost 84 percent agreed that the most urgent need for improving the teaching of English is a cooperative plan to connect English with all other subjects (Hill, 1925). Underlying this is a push to make English more relevant to the contemporary world and, subsequently, more interesting for students. In an evaluation of secondary school English in New York State, the reviewers note that integration of English with other subjects is not common and praised the one school that experimented with such an approach by examining the history of opera. Here, stories of operas are read in English class, opera as a genre is taught and analyzed in music class, and students are trained to act and direct in an opera production in their speech class (Smith, 1941). One example of a successful statewide integration of subjects is the Core Curriculum of Virginia Secondary Schools, which was regarded as a model curriculum in the 1930s (Lyman, 1935, 1936; Meade, 1937). The Virginia curriculum is grounded on the idea that "the school must guide pupils in the development of types of behavior compatible with democratic ideals" (State Board of Education, 1934, p. 1). The curriculum centers on twelve common themes concerning various aspects of social life that a student is expected to participate in as a citizen (such as communication and transportation, expression of religious impulses, and extension of freedom), and every subject in each grade works to expound on these themes. Under the theme of communication, for instance, a grade eight language class would have students involved in "interpreting ballads, folk songs, legends and epics to show their use as a means of communicating common ideas of earlier civilizations" (p. 119) and under the theme of exploration, students are encouraged to "read poems which express the urge to explore on land and sea to understand better the naturalness of this urge" (p. 130). Some of the problems with an integrated literature in the world curriculum, in which literature is integrated with history or other subjects under a common theme, is that literature becomes marginalized and either used to supplement the teaching of history or used to elucidate a theme. The aesthetic quality of the literary work is therefore immaterial, and so, for example, Jane Austen's *Pride and Prejudice* may be less popular compared to Charles Dickens' *Hard Times* since it would be regarded as less relevant in providing insights into the effects of the Industrial Revolution.

The fourth approach of boundary recognition involves reading against boundaries. Having identified the boundaries that constitute the text, teachers can encourage students to think about the issues presented in the text from multiple or counter perspectives. Teachers can also have students examine instances where the text transcends the borders (historical, geographical, or generic) in which it has been categorized. By doing so, students become aware that literary texts refract rather than reflect cultures and nations (Damrosch, 2009). Reading against boundaries also entails recognition of the fluidity of boundaries. This is why Lawall (1994) insists that teachers must emphasize to students that world literature provides only a starting or entry point to understanding the world so that students become aware of the limitations and restrictions of the boundaries categorizing literary texts in the curriculum. Reading against boundaries imposed on literary texts facilitates a universal understanding through the removal of imaginary boundaries in which individuals and communities are classified.

Boundary recognition involving approaches of reading with, of, around, and against the world offers a way that teachers can make educative use of the tensions of inclusion and exclusion inherent in a world paradigm to teaching literature. Since the imposition of boundaries is an inevitable process of attempting to know and name the world, such approaches are all the more significant in enabling the valorization and reconstruction of forms of power underlying the construction of boundaries.

Global Approaches to Teaching Literature

Eternal minstrel of liberty!
Thy shrill voice rends the wintry air
Dost thou sing for want of sympathy?
Or art thou tired of strife and care? (B. C. K., 1935, para. 1)

These lines comprise the first stanza of a poem titled "The Rook." The remaining three stanzas of the poem speculate on the bird's wanderings and its dismal cry. Perhaps it is oppressed by the dreariness of the world, perhaps it knows something of the fate of human existence that the rest of the world does not. In the final stanza, the narrator reflects on his envy of the bird which, in its freedom, appears to express deep wisdom about the condition of humanity. The poem was published in 1935 in the school magazine of Raffles Institution, a premiere all-boys high school. Since the magazine was only published three times a year, it was most likely the case that the poem was selected above others by the teacher or headmaster for its exemplary literary qualities. For example, the poem almost consistently employs the iambic tetrameter throughout; its first stanza ends with two rhetorical questions establishing the yearning, sympathetic tone of the poem which reaches its climax in the final stanza as the protagonist contrasts the rook's freedom and courage to his own helpless resignation toward life.

What is most remarkable about the poem, however, is that the school concerned is situated in Singapore and was established to educate the sons of native elites in the country. At the time this poem was published, the school was essentially an English-medium school attended by predominantly Chinese students though there were also Eurasians, Indians, and Malays. A closer examination of the poem, however, reveals five glaring discrepancies. First, the second line of the poem mentions "wintry air," and yet, winter does not exist in Singapore, since its location near the equator ensures that the weather is consistently hot and humid throughout the year. Second, the term "minstrel" references medieval entertainers or Elizabethan bards, which is again a concept foreign to this island-city made up of a majority of immigrants from China and parts of Malaya. Third, the poem is written in the linguistic style of early modern English from the sixteenth and seventeenth centuries and it seems starkly inauthentic for a native subject to write in this fashion in the 1930s. Fourth, while crows may have been common in Singapore, a rook would have been extremely rare, since it is a species most commonly found in Europe and not in Southeast Asia. Finally, the poem celebrates the rook as an "eternal minstrel of liberty"; yet, Singapore was colonized by the British from the time of its founding in 1819 until 1959, and in the early years of the twentieth century, the country was far from stable. For example, native subjects were segregated according to racial lines, and most Chinese, for example, felt a greater sense of loyalty to their homeland in China than to their British colonial rulers. Furthermore, there were threats in varied forms, from secret societies and gangs, opium addiction, the influence of the Communist Party from China, whose members were rallying the Chinese working class, and strikes instigated by labor unions as a result of dismal working conditions. Amid this political instability, schools were slowly being established, but still, large numbers of children, particularly girls, did not have access to schooling (Turnbull, 2009). It would have been more accurate to say then that security rather than liberty was uppermost in the minds of colonized subjects at this time. Kishore Mahbubani (2008) makes an insightful point that the notion of freedom or liberty is a Western ideological concept that ignores other freedoms such as freedom from want and freedom of security. At particular points in history, these other freedoms would have been more urgently required before freedom of choice, thought, speech, or movement, as associated with liberty, can be conceived. Hence, it is hard to imagine why a native student would foreground liberty as a key theme of the poem given the context of the time.

Though it is no longer possible to find out who the poet is or the circumstances that led him to write this poem, one can safely presume that the poem was written as an imitation of canonical poems studied in his English class. Two clues point to this. First, in the previous issue of the magazine published in April 1935, one article, titled "Books to Read," provides a recommended list of "serious" writers. The list of names mentioned are all British writers most of whom belong to the canon —

Charles Dickens, Arthur Conan Doyle, Thomas Hardy, Ben Johnson, Christopher Marlowe, Sir Walter Scott, William Shakespeare, and Edgar Wallace. One can imagine that these writers also formed part of the list of books required for study in the English class. Second, the syllabus of instruction written by the principal of Raffles Institution, D. W. McLeod, in 1937 provides a description of the literature curriculum. The main objective of the curriculum is stated in this line: "When students have mastered the mere mechanics of reading they must be initiated into the subtleties of language and thought and imagination, which make for true appreciation" (McLeod, 1937, p. 30). Though McLeod makes little mention of the texts used to "initiate" students, he references a few authors such as John Keats, Alexander Pope, and Shakespeare. One can already speculate the dominance of the canonical tradition in such a curriculum. In the light of these two clues, it is therefore reasonable to speculate that the poem "The Rook" may have been chosen from among a list of entries from a class exercise in which students were tasked to craft their own poems modeled after texts they had read in literature class. More disturbingly, this poem, consisting of images and concepts of a foreign culture, is representative of a colonization of the imagination. Perhaps unconsciously, McLeod's initiation progresses along the three stages he lists: the student is first taught to appreciate the subtleties of language, which shapes his thinking about what qualifies as a great work of literature; this then molds an imagination that is sympathetic toward and in awe of British colonial culture. In short, such an "initiation" is merely a guise for indoctrination.

If indoctrination was a key pedagogical instrument utilized in teaching literature in Singapore and, presumably, in other colonized countries, it paradoxically foreshadowed resistance toward its implementation following the end of colonization. In other words, indoctrination provided the platform through which alternative ways of teaching could be imagined once previously colonized countries now had the freedom to design their own curriculum. One such alternative was the development of new literature courses customized to the needs of newly independent countries that then contributed to new categories of literature. For example, "Singapore literature" was constructed and became incorporated into the curriculum eventually becoming a core component of high school assessments in Singapore. Another alternative was the inclusion of translated works into the literature in English curriculum. For example, in India, classical literary texts written in Bengali, Punjabi, and Tamil were translated into English and included for study in literature classrooms. Yet other alternatives involved the expansion of the concept of the "literary" so that, for example, media texts such as advertisements and films could be studied alongside literary texts, as was the case in Australia and Canada. All these alternatives have culminated in the emergence of a category called "global literature" in the late twentieth century.

The teaching of global literature is used to describe approaches aimed at promoting a global mindset in students so that they will perceive themselves and others as members of an interconnected global village. For example, various sessions at the National Council of Teachers of English (NCTE) Annual Convention in 2011 featured the teaching of global literature even though a sign of the embryonic nature of this category can be observed in that these topics tended to be confused with multicultural and culturally responsive approaches to teaching literature.[1] Although global literature remains an ambiguous term and was only popularized in the latter part of the twentieth century, we can trace the emergence of a global paradigm informing approaches to teaching literature much earlier from the mid-twentieth century. While world literature, as it was institutionalized in schools and colleges in the United States, may have opened the way for third world, postcolonial, and other literatures in English to be studied in schools, political circumstances following the end of the Second World War and particularly the end of British colonialism were catalysts for the democratization of literature in English grounded on "reading the global."

The Second Later Wave of Globalization and Education for Global Citizenship

The Significance of Human Rights

The period following the end of the Second World War is generally taken as the period when globalization gained a new impetus in which the modern-state operating under liberal democracy emerged as the principal form of political rule (Held, McGrew, Goldblatt, & Perraton, 1999). This period witnessed the most massive expansion of the world economy. It also marked the hegemonic position of the United States as the most powerful military and economic nation. The rise of transnational corporations in the United States coupled with the development of various international agreements, such as the General Agreement on Tariffs and Trade (GATT), contributed to the removal of trade barriers that facilitated global flows of goods. Other countries in Europe and Asia began to recover from the war and acquired dominance of their domestic markets so that by the 1960s, they were able to compete with the United States. Thus, production in the world-system and the world economy grew as a whole and standards of living rose for many people previously living in poverty (Ikeda, 1996; Wallerstein, 1996). During this period too, allied occupied territories such as Austria, Italy, Japan, Korea, and West Germany became democracies as well as Greece, Turkey, and several countries in Latin America. The end of British colonialism also inaugurated several new nation-states such as India, the Philippines, and Singapore, which, to different degrees, instituted some form of democracy (Huntington, 1991). Thus, Huntington describes this period, specifically from 1943 to 1962, as the second wave of democratization. However, as discussed in the previous chapter, this wave could not have occurred without an earlier wave in the late nineteenth and early twentieth centuries when a geoculture operating on liberal democracy was developed particularly under the leadership of the United States. To establish continuity with this early wave, I term the period following the Second World War from 1945 to 1970 as the second later wave of globalization.

One of the most significant changes that occurred during this later wave was the emphasis on human over citizenship rights. The articulation of human rights contributed to strengthening global consciousness in two main ways. The first was the recognition in the international arena that individuals belong to the larger global community rather than to the nation alone. This recognition led to the securing of fundamental rights basic to all human beings especially concerning equality. The United Nations (UN) was to become the primary apparatus through which a consciousness of human rights could occur. Lessons learned from the failure of the League of Nations (LoN) led to a concerted effort to strengthen international governance through the formation of the UN in 1945. While both the covenant of the LoN and the charter of the UN are directed toward the same goal of maintaining security in the global sphere through international constitutional guarantees, the difference is a clearer commitment toward ensuring collective security in the case of the latter, especially with regard to issues concerning interstate aggression.[2] Collective security not only entails the allocation of real coercive power (economic and military) to the UN, it also necessitates recognition of equality. This marks a key difference between the covenant and the charter. The LoN covenant included a clause requiring member-states to refrain from religious discrimination. However, when the Japanese delegation sought to extend this to include a provision for member-states to refrain from racial discrimination, it was rejected, particularly by Britain and the United States.[3] The eventual rejection of the clause strengthened Japan's belief that the LoN was merely an international system that was unfair and biased in favor of these Western powers. Japan also took this event as a symbolic representation of its rejection by the West which created the impetus to pursue its own independent foreign policy grounded on racial thinking. What is evident is that in 1919, racial equality was still a relatively undeveloped concept that, in the eyes of Western powers particularly the United States, could be compromised for the sake of the formation of an intergovernmental organization. Following the Second World War, such a view was overturned, for the international community now acknowledged that no stable or effective intergovernmental organization could be formed if it were not grounded on principles of equality in the first place. The concept of equality was extended into a document, the Universal Declaration of Human Rights, detailing essential human rights based on the first principle that "all human beings are born free and equal in dignity and rights" (United Nations, 1948, art. 1). The Declaration marked a significant attempt at envisioning rights governing membership to the global community.

The second way in which the articulation of human rights contributed to a global consciousness was that the Declaration indicated a formal international consensus that the rights of individuals no longer belong solely within the jurisdiction of the nation-state. This is in contrast to the Treaty of Westphalia in 1648 following the end of religious wars in Europe. In the Westphalian order, the language of rights, including freedom of religion, was to be determined by the state, and other states had no right to interfere. In other words, rights were solely a national issue and within the sovereignty of the nation-state; rights were framed as citizenship rights rather than human rights. Such a perspective shifted, especially following the atrocities of the Second World War that were crucial to cementing recognition of the importance of universal human rights as opposed to citizenship rights. It should also be noted that the grounds for this recognition had already been laid much earlier.[4] To date, out of 192 member-states in the United Nations, more than 150 have signed the Declaration indicating that most states wish to be associated with human rights even if few have succeeded in fulfilling all the terms in the Declaration (Weiss, Forsythe, Coate, & Pease, 2010).

The most controversial aspect of the Declaration remains the paradox concerning citizenship and human rights. On one hand, the Declaration, signed by member nation-states comprising the United Nations, indicates that the decision to adhere to human rights still rests with the authority of the state. On the other hand, acceptance of the Declaration is itself an indication by the state that the administration of rights concerning the individual no longer rests solely with the state and thus represents an acknowledgment by the state that it must transfer some of the authority it previously monopolized to international governing bodies in the global sphere. This conflict between how much authority concerning the rights of the individual should be withheld by the state and how much of this should be granted to intergovernmental organizations to which it is accountable remains highly controversial to this day.[5] Despite this, nation-states increasingly value membership in the international community and in this second later wave of globalization, coercion, expansion, and military force, which were primary instruments of state power in the nineteenth century, have given way to economic instruments, competition, and cooperation (Held, McGrew, Goldblatt, & Perraton, 1999). The implication therefore, is that as international exchange and cooperation increases, global consciousness becomes heightened and human rights will increasingly take precedence over citizenship rights.

Education for Global Citizenship

The category of global citizenship precipitated by the Second World War privileges human over nationalistic citizenship rights. In this sense, global citizenship shares a similarity with world and cosmopolitan citizenship in its belief that contemporary citizenship can no longer be defined in relation to the nation-state alone and that there is a need to transcend nationalistic citizenship through the category of the human. At the same time, there are key differences among the terms "world," "global," and "cosmopolitan" citizenship. In his extensive research on citizenship, Heater describes world citizenship as that involving "multiple citizenships" based on the principles of cosmopolitanism (2002, p. 181) and involving feelings of "universal identity" and "universal morality" (1999, p. 137). While in these examples, Heater equates world citizenship with cosmopolitanism and universal identity, in his earlier works, he (1990) conflates education for world citizenship with education for international understanding and global education. Although in his later work, he (2004) mentions that the labels "world," "global," and "cosmopolitan" cannot be synonymous with each other, he does not clearly distinguish these terms and instead uses them interchangeably in the rest of his book. In what follows, I seek to distinguish the subtle differences among these configurations of citizenship.

The central question in this section is how global citizenship is different from world citizenship. Here, I argue that the primary difference has to do with perception. This concerns whether the earth is perceived as a world or as a globe. One way to distinguish this more clearly is to examine the etymology of the terms "globe" and "world." The word "globe" is derived from the Latin *globus* and originally carried two meanings: "a bowl or sphere, any round thing" and "a lump or clod of earth" (Lemon, 1783, p. 264). From the fifteenth to the nineteenth centuries, the first idea of a sphere was given priority and linked to a mathematical term denoting "a solid body exactly round, contained under one surface in the middle of which is a point from whence all right lines drawn to the surface are equal to one another" (Scott, 1755, p. 574). In the early twentieth century, "globe" was still defined as a sphere but its secondary definition had expanded so that sphere and earth became connected, and "globe" also meant "a sphere on which is a representation of the geography of the earth and of the heavens" (Fernald, 1906, p. 206). Today, it is this secondary definition that has become the dominant meaning associated with "globe."[6] One current dictionary describes "globe" as the sense of planet Earth or a three-dimensional map (Harper, 2011). In this case, "globe" represents Earth in the context of the universe whereas "world" represents bounded time and territorial space in the context of Earth. In the first sense of the term, "world" is defined in relation to a "course of time" (Wedgwood & Atkinson, 1872, p. 737), "the course of man's life, of man's experience" (Shipley, 1945, p. 393), or more specifically, "the age of man" (Ayto, 2005, p. 550). In the second sense of the term, "world" is connected to "a division of things belonging to the earth" (Fernald, 1906, p. 517) or more specifically, "the physical or material world, the earth; the land comprising the physical world" including the kingdoms, dominions, realms that constitute it (McSparran & Price-Wilkin, 2001).

These linguistic distinctions between "globe" and "world" are reflective of deeper conceptual differences concerning the way the earth is to be perceived. A world paradigm conceives the way man organizes, categorizes, and divides the earth he or she inhabits in terms of time and space and how these components interrelate. This was the primary orientation of the League of Nations which was a federation of nation-states that regarded themselves as units within a collective organization. As Darren O'Byrne (2003) observes, world citizenship operates within a systems framework that particularly reinscribes the nation-state. In this sense, education for world citizenship involves an examination of component parts of the world so that, for example, a world paradigm to teaching literature would center on particular historical periods, geographical locations, or thematic concerns. What follows is a movement from part to whole or from an inward to outward perspective as observed in intertextual approaches in its comparative methodology. Here, the goal is to attain an understanding of how concerns in one nation-state relate to other nation-states, the eventual goal being to attain a holistic view of the world community.

While a world paradigm involves the movement from part to whole, a global paradigm is the opposite in its movement from whole to part. It begins by emphasizing what O'Byrne (2003) terms "globality" or "an orientation to the world as a whole" (p. 86) regardless of geographic boundaries. This is similar to William Gaudelli's (2011) notion of "global seeing" that seeks more transnational ways of seeing that transcend the superficial consumptive style of tourist-like seeing. He distinguishes global seeing from a flattened form of seeing that transforms three-dimensional reality into two.

Extending Gaudelli's notion of seeing, I use the metaphors of a world map and a globe to distinguish world-oriented and global-oriented seeing. World-oriented seeing is akin to the way a map is flattened on a wall and countries are categorized by boundary divisions. This is opposed to global-oriented seeing which is what I term a kind of spherical seeing of the human. This connotes two significant ideas. First, the globe is perceived as a whole so that before one perceives it as comprising nations or countries, its spherical nature ensures that it is first perceived as a planet in the universe. Thus, education that emphasizes spherical seeing of the human prioritizes students' consciousness of themselves as citizens of the human race first followed by citizens of their nation or community. This means that engagement with global issues concerning the environment, human rights, terrorism, and so on takes precedence in the curriculum and such engagement aims to develop in students "transnational imaginaries" in order that they comprehend their moral obligations to humanity (Gough, 2000).

Second, in spherical seeing, the point of reference constantly changes as observed in that at any point when the globe stops spinning, a new point of reference emerges. It also becomes evident that this point of reference is limited so that, for example, when one looks at Australia on the globe, one has to shift one's position to locate the United States. In other words, consciousness of the limitation of one point of reference leads to a search for multiple points of reference. Similarly, education for global citizenship encourages a disposition of multi-referential curiosity that ensures that perception and frames of reference are never fixed but, instead, fluid and shifting. As discussed in the previous chapter, one of the problems with the approach Goethe took toward the study of non-European literature was that these texts were studied from the privileged reference point of the West. What was primarily absent was Goethe's reflexive examination of his own Eurocentric lens employed to critique foreign culture and its cultural texts.

The two ideas concerning holistic and fluid approaches toward the global essentially imply that spherical seeing entails deconstructing the myth of authenticity. As Gareth Griffiths (1995) notes, claims to authenticity are often appealed to by indigenous and colonized groups as a recuperative strategy but these only lead to fetishizing representations of the "authentic" that consequently construct a privileged hierarchy within particular racial or ethnic communities. The result is that one tribe, culture, or group is deemed more "authentic" than another and the complexities of cultural differences are erased. The lesson following the Nazi program of genocide during the Second World War has only reiterated the dangers of subscribing to such purist myths.

The Conceptual Formation of a Global Pedagogical Paradigm

The Introduction of Global Education in Schools

Essentially, the goal of education for global citizenship emphasizes the promotion of spherical ways of seeing oriented toward understanding the human and defending human rights. In the United States, this goal became embedded in the movement of global education in the 1960s and was increasingly incorporated into school curricula toward the end of the decade (Frey & Whitehead, 2009; Marshall, 2009). Gaudelli (2003) observes that global education emerged as a response to the dissatisfaction with world study that tended to be organized according to discrete subdisciplines such as world history, world cultures, and world geography. Within each subdiscipline, content tended to be organized according to a nation-state perspective, for example, American History or Geography of East Asia.

Global education therefore sought to provide a more interdisciplinary, integrated perspective.[7] The goal of promoting spherical ways of seeing the human was translated into educative practices aimed at developing global awareness of common human problems and at empowering students to improve and shape their world. This idea of empowering students as active citizens has been envisioned in a number of ways. Martin Albrow (1997) uses the term "performative citizenship" and states that "global citizenship is world citizenship focused on the future of the globe" (p. 177). Here, Albrow emphasizes a future-oriented, positivistic stance in which individuals work collectively through coordinating and networking on a global scale to confront issues facing the planet. Other terms such as "Pragmatic globality" (O'Byrne, 2003) and the "Global Reformer" (Falk, 1993) emphasize practical actions that individuals can take to affect changes in the world. In order to affect changes, the student has to be empowered to act in the world. This would involve developing global literacies in students such as equipping them to be critical thinkers able to evaluate the cultural, economic, and political systems impacting the world and preparing students to be globally competitive by equipping them to critically engage with multiple forms of literacies (cultural, digital, economic, linguistic, multimodal, etc.).[8] In relation to literature education, empowerment was a core aspect in various movements that contributed to a global pedagogical paradigm.

The Concept of Empowerment in Disciplinary Movements

Unlike a world paradigm that posits a belief that the teaching of literature cultivates collective taste leading to the collective improvement of society, a global paradigm perceives that the good of teaching literature is in its capacity to empower the individual to act. More specifically, empowerment occurs on two levels. On one level, empowerment involves equipping students to think critically about texts rather than be passive consumers of texts and on another level, empowerment involves helping students to think ethically by seeing the world more fully or, in other words, by being more globally conscious. In relation to the former, the new criticism movement was significant in emphasizing discriminatory sensibilities in students while in relation to the latter, the cultural studies movement served to broaden the scope of literary analysis.

New Criticism and the Communicative Turn. During this second later wave of globalization, the discipline of literature in Britain and the United

States shifted toward an emphasis on communication. The force that facilitated this communicative turn was the movement of new criticism that began in the 1920s and 1930s with the works of British scholars such as I. A. Richards and T. S. Eliot and later in the 1940s by American scholars Cleanth Brooks, John Crowe Ransom, William K. Wimsatt, and Monroe Beardsley. New criticism's pedagogical approach, centered on a close reading of texts, was first applied in American high schools in the 1940s. By the 1960s and 1970s, it had become the standard in both schools and colleges (Applebee, 1974; Murfin & Ray, 2008). Broadly, new criticism arose as a reaction to empiricist-idealist views of the world in which man is viewed as the source of all meaning and therefore, in order to understand the text's meaning, one would need to probe the intentions and mind of the author. The new critics argue that the text rather than the author or reader is the focus of literary criticism. To base one's interpretation on the authorial intention of the work is to commit intentional fallacy, while to base one's interpretation on one's subjective responses to the work is to commit affective fallacy (Wimsatt & Beardsley, 1946/2001a, 1949/2001b). Literary criticism, argues Cleanth Brooks (1947/2001), should be neither biographical, historical, nor subjective. Rather, like science, it should be objective, precise, and analytical. Graff (2007) notes that the new critics' insistence on the disinterested ahistorical close reading of texts ironically masked an interested agenda that was essentially the aim of establishing greater methodological rigor by associating literature pedagogy with a science of communication. This was crucial given that, during this period, literary criticism sought to become a respectable discipline in the face of stiff competition with the sciences (Eagleton, 1996).

Arguably the most influential new critic was I. A. Richards whose method of practical criticism not only helped operationalize new criticism's theories, it enabled the study of literature to become closely attached to the study of communication or, more specifically, a scientific study of the way language works. This attention to the communicative aspect was largely due to a reaction toward the rise of a global media age. Richards was explicitly concerned about the threat of mass culture and the infusion of all kinds of media texts from newspapers and magazines to television that were eroding the discriminatory powers of the public. Hence, Richards (1924/2004) defines criticism as "the endeavor to discriminate between experiences and evaluate them" (p. viii). What we observe is that though criticism remains the privileged method in literature education inherited from the discipline of

English literature when it was institutionalized in the late eighteenth century, it loses its association with taste. Instead of taste, criticism is now associated with discrimination. At the same time, this break between criticism and taste also implies another break — that between criticism and the beautiful in its association with taste. Richards specifically seeks to demystify the concept of the beautiful as a mystical, inherent property in literary texts. This, he claims, is a delusion, since it is not the property of the beautiful but the experience of it that qualifies one to make the claim that a text is beautiful. By valorizing the reader's experience with the text, Richards (1924/2004) can then make the case that criticism is a branch of psychology so that "critical remarks are merely a branch of psychological remarks and that no special ethical or metaphysical ideas need be introduced to explain value" (p. 18). Richards (1924/2004) then proceeds to state that "the two pillars upon which a theory of criticism must rest are an account of value and an account of communication" (p. 20). In relation to the first pillar, Richards argues that any critical statement judging whether a literary work is good or bad should be based on a purely psychological account, that is, how the text's constructed nature affects particular responses in the reader. The text and its effects are central here and the good critic is one who can discriminate the value of literary works based on a close analysis of the text's effects on the reader. In order to acquire such discrimination, it is necessary to move the focus of literary analysis away from an ontological study of what is inherently pleasing or beautiful in a literary work of art to analyzing how language functions in the text. This forms the second pillar to Richards' (1929) theory of criticism:

> My suggestion is that it is not enough to learn a language (or several languages), as a man may inherit a business, but we must learn too, how it works. And by "learning how it works," I do not mean studying its rules of syntax or its grammar, or wandering about in its lexicography — two inquiries that have hitherto diverted attention from the central issue. I mean by "learning how it works," study of the kinds of meaning that language handles, their connection with one another, their inferences; in brief, the psychology of the speech-situation. (p. 318)

Thus, an analysis of the literary text becomes an objective, scientific, and psychological analysis of communication in four key aspects that Richards highlights: (1) sense (the sense of what the author is saying through the text), (2) feeling (the author's attitude toward what he or she is saying), (3) tone (the author's attitude toward the listener or reader), and (4) intention (the author's purpose as conveyed through the text). Criticism's former ties to taste and the beautiful are now disrupted so that criticism is now tied to discrimination. An analysis of the text is then an exercise in developing one's sensitivity to the art of communication via an understanding of the operations of language. In the context of the age of communication, mass media, and the information revolution, criticism's ties to discrimination is grounded on a belief that students would be empowered as they develop the capacity to discriminate and critically evaluate all kinds of texts in multiple modalities within the global flow of information.

Cultural Studies and the Cultural Turn. Another aspect of empowerment is related to the development of a sense of global consciousness in students so that they are able to grasp the multilayered and multidimensional complexities of the world. In his writings on criticism, Richards is exclusively concerned with poetry though ironically, by positioning literary analysis under the category of communication studies, he has served to remove poetry from its privileged generic status so that, as he himself (1929) states at the beginning of *Practical Criticism*, "poetry itself is a mode of communication. What it communicates and how it does so and the worth of what is communicated form the subject-matter of criticism" (p. 10). In this sense, Richards is indicating that the literary text is one out of many other cultural texts aimed at promoting communication in the public and global spheres. In so doing, he contributes to the second movement in literature education during this period: the cultural turn.

Generally, cultural critics may be divided into two camps. On one end are critics who adopt a negative attitude toward the study of culture and cultural texts. This is most clearly observed in the position of F. R. Leavis. His book *Culture and the Environment*, published with Denys Thompson in 1964, was written specifically for English teachers and was used as a textbook in schools. The first paragraph of the book (1964) begins as follows:

Many teachers of English who have become interested in the possibilities of training taste and sensibility must have been troubled by accompanying doubts. What effect can such training have against the multitudinous counter-influences — films, newspapers, advertising — indeed, the whole world outside the classroom? (p. 1)

In the above paragraph, Leavis already makes clear that criticism centered on taste is no longer enough. He reiterates this latter point in his call for a shift toward criticism centered on discrimination. Yet, this is a discrimination that is defensive in nature, since it is meant to counter the influence of the media. Leavis' disdain toward mass culture is clear. He calls technology the great agent of the destruction of culture and accuses mass production of a general lowering of cultural standards. To guard against the dumbing down of culture, he proposes to apply Richards' method of practical criticism to an analysis of popular culture texts such as advertisements and popular fiction. In this sense, Leavis is returning to the Arnoldian dichotomy between high culture as the spiritual standard to be protected and mass culture which is associated with materialism, irrationality, and anarchy.

In stark contrast to Leavis and situated on the opposite camp are cultural critics who adopt a more positive attitude toward the study of culture. This may be observed in the work of the Centre for Contemporary Cultural Studies (CCCS) at the University of Birmingham. Prominent scholars include Raymond Williams and Richard Hoggart who were central to initiating British cultural studies in the 1950s. These writers essentially extended the reductive practice of traditional Marxism, with its overemphasis on class and capital, to studying culture, ideology, language, and the symbolic (Hall, 1992). Unlike Leavis, these writers sought a more democratic commitment to the study of culture. This was a form of cultural studies established on the notion that culture is reflective of the individual's inhabitation in the world and was specifically centered on providing a fuller and deeper understanding of the everyman and the everyday. Such an understanding inevitably contributes to a consciousness of the complex and multifaceted realities of the global world.

The everyman, a term popularized by a late fifteenth-century medieval morality play of the same title, represents the common individual who is at the center of both Hoggart's and Williams's work. Hoggart, who founded the CCCS, published his (1957) seminal work titled *The Uses of Literacy*, which provides an account of working class life and how "genuine class culture is being eroded in favor of the mass opinion, the mass recreational product, and the generalized emotional response" (p. 311). Here, Hoggart echoes Leavis' concerns about the damaging effects of the mass media and describes them as "anti-life" (p. 308) in their corruption of moral values and in their promotion of materialistic consumer culture. In this environment, an education centered on developing discriminatory powers in students is thereby the vital antidote. The main difference, however, is whereas Leavis shows a disdain for the ordinary, common citizen, viewing him or her as defenseless and easily duped by mass media, Hoggart seeks to understand this category of the everyman. Perhaps the tendency to celebrate and romanticize the everyman stems from the fact that Hoggart, as well as Williams, grew up in working-class environments and taught working-class groups in university adult education classes for many years before getting jobs in English departments at prestigious universities. Nevertheless, the significance of their work is in the deconstruction of stereotypes concerning the everyman. For example, Hoggart invites us to reconsider popular stereotypes propagated by the media in which the working class is portrayed as uneducated and unthinking as well as prone to uncontrolled gratification of their sexual appetites. Instead, Hoggart reveals the complexities and contradictions inherent in this class. He discusses how the intimate, the sensory, and the personal are highly valued among this group. Though they may not be interested in grand theories or movements, they are deeply invested in the local and the personal and are immersed in developing close personal relationships. All this has contributed to their acute sensitivity toward analyzing reality and reading people that may be even more perceptive than the insights of an educated bookish intellectual who filters his or her interpretation of reality through books and high theory. The everyman is therefore a complex figure who daily maneuvers loyalty and duty to home and community amid the broader global influence of the mass media which he or she at times succumbs to while at other times resists and rejects.

In a similar vein, Williams cautions against the masses = working and lower middle class = mob equation. "There are in fact no masses," Williams (1958) notes, "there are only ways of seeing people as masses" (p. 300). What is needed is therefore a broadening of one's vision that involves an attunement toward global spherical seeing that first acknowledges seeing as an imperialistic act of categorizing, interpreting, and fixing the other. In other words, to see is to engage in stereotyping whereas spherical seeing insists that one does not remain locked into one mode of seeing the other. This then involves deep cultural understandings premised on what Williams (1958) terms "an equality of being" (p. 338) so that spherical seeing must be centered on the recognition that all human beings are equally rational beings.

Such a vision necessarily converts the category of masses as irrational mob to the category of rational human beings. Williams goes on to say that this eventually leads to the development of a "common culture" or a solidarity grounded on respect, cooperation, and a vision of collective development.

Belief in the good of spherical seeing established on the principal commitment to understanding the everyman must necessarily entail a commitment to an understanding of the everyday, or, more specifically, the everyday realities and lived experiences in which the everyman inhabits. This forms the primary basis of empowerment, since the individual cannot be empowered to act in the world if he or she is first not conscious of the vast spectrum of life itself. This is a key point Williams (1958) emphasizes throughout *Culture and Society: 1780–1950*. A study of culture can no longer be limited to specific kinds of products accorded with status but must essentially encompass "a whole way of life" (p. 325) involving the material, intellectual, and spiritual realities of human experience. It is then this holistic image that ultimately inspires the individual to act. Interestingly, perhaps we can trace the beginnings of the "death of literature" debate,[9] which I discussed in the introduction chapter, to this postwar period, since from I. A. Richards, F. R. Leavis, and on to Richard Hoggart and Raymond Williams, a central line of thought seems apparent in their arguments: literature can no longer retain its central, privileged status in the public sphere, since it is now one of many artifacts through which one can understand culture and, more precisely, the human being in all its fullness.

The Concept of Humanity of the Universal and Particular in Philosophical Contributions

While British cultural theorists Hoggart and Williams confine their discussion of culture at the societal level through their examinations of popular culture and the working class, the question is how an ethos based on the everyman and the everyday can be extended to the global sphere. In other words, how can concepts of the everyman and the everyday be combined with the concept of the everyone? During this second later wave of globalization, German cultural theorists sought to provide a philosophy of aesthetics (including literature). Here, the work of Theodor Adorno is particularly relevant given the intersection of ethics and aesthetics in his work. Adorno was part of a group of German intellectuals associated with the Institute for Social Research at the University of Frankfurt; this group later came to be known as the Frankfurt School (Storey, 2006). Based on Adorno's notion of "non-identity thinking," the everyone is not a universal category nor does it involve a morality grounded solely on the concept of universal humanity that, as I have argued, became attached to a world paradigm informing literature education. Instead, the everyone is a non-conceptual category involving a morality grounded on the concept of both a humanity of the universal and the particular. At the same time, how can that which is a concept be non-conceptual, how can the notion of the everyone be rooted in the universal and particular at the same time? The key to understanding this paradox may be found in the term "Negative Dialectics" which is also the title of Adorno's (1966/1973) book. Here, Adorno is critical of Hegelian dialectics in its reconciliation of thesis and antithesis with synthesis. Synthesis is a way of achieving unity in the face of difference and contradiction. In this sense, it is a positive dialectic. At the same time, synthesis, in its striving for unity and totality, imposes concepts on experiences of reality. These concepts are ways of bringing what we experience under our control by naming and giving an identity to it. Adorno argues for a disenchantment of the concept that is a way of troubling the concept by pointing to that which is beyond it or that which cannot be conceptualized, that is, the non-conceptual in the concept. In this way, Adorno calls for a negative dialectic that does not aim at synthesis. Instead, it aims to disrupt any kind of synthesis through striving at the non-conceptual.

Adorno (1966/1973) argues that this negation of synthesis can be achieved by privileging otherness over self. Adorno terms this the privileging of the object over the subject. The object in this sense is what is not the subject or what is the non-I. Take for instance, this statement, "I see you." In grammatical terms, "I" refers to the subject, "see" refers to the verb, and "you" refers to the object. In order for the subject "I" to grasp the object "you," "you" must be objectified and this occurs through the imposition of concepts, since the subject can never enter into the consciousness of the object. This occurs in everyday situations when we impose categories of gender, race, and class such as "woman," "black," "Hispanic," "middle class," "teenager," "disabled," and other labels on individuals we encounter. What Adorno is essentially arguing for is the recognition that the concept is insufficient because every entity is more than the concepts that are imposed on it. Hence, theories and philosophical inquiries can oftentimes be inhibiting when the diversity, complexity, and richness of experiences are turned into concepts and universals are imposed on the specific and the particular.[10] The point, therefore, is to aim not at theory or philosophy but at self-reflexive theorizing and philosophizing in which the emphasis is on a continued process and never-ending quest to trouble fixed theories and concepts. This then is the intention underlying non-identity thinking, which provides space for true diversity and equality by attempting to understand the individual beyond its imposed conceptual identity.

One could criticize this as a kind of relativistic thinking in which, since concepts are continually deconstructed and no concepts can be imposed, anything and everything is at the same time permissible. Yet, Adorno dismisses relativism to bourgeois individualism in which individual opinions are privileged and the subjective consciousness is prioritized instead of the object or the other. The only way to prevent non-identity thinking from becoming relativistic thinking is to privilege the object over the subject or to privilege otherness over the self. What this means is that non-identity thinking involves a principle of justice by guarding against the subject's desire to determine or impose definitions and concepts on the other as well as by guarding against the subject's tendencies to say whatever it wants about the object or the other. If the object or the other is primary, then the subject is bound by a sense of justice to understand the object or the other by constantly probing for the non-identical in the concept. Another way of saying this is that the non-identical is that which is the human in the object. This is the notion of the human in all its complexity and fullness that transcends any given or assigned identity. What this also means is that a global paradigm attempts to go beyond any kind of identity politics. For example, the English literature head of department in a Singapore high school, whom I had recently interviewed, mentioned that at secondary one and two levels (grades seven and eight), her school places a strong emphasis on the study of Singapore literature. While literature in Singapore has been written since the colonial period in the early nineteenth century, this category only emerged following the country's independence in 1965. The department head added that she believes this emphasis on Singapore literature is important because students will identify more with such texts and their local issues rather than with Western texts. While there is a case for the democratic inclusion of all kinds of literature (including Singapore literature) in the classroom, teachers also need to be aware that this category itself can breed exclusivity. The pitching of Singapore literature against British or American literature leads to a fixing of identities to categories of Singaporean, British, or American. What is then neglected is how the term "Singaporean" engages with rather than becomes defined in opposition to the West as well as how the meaning of Singaporean is always more than the concept itself. Thus, the reason why Singapore literature should be encouraged in a Singapore classroom should not be because students can identify with the Singaporean but so they can identify in order to dis-identify with this concept. When this subtle shift in mindset occurs, the classroom becomes an open space that allows for students to engage with Singapore literature alongside other world literature. What occurs too is that this removes the hegemony of the term "Singaporean" as an all-encompassing identity, since, other than being a Singaporean, the student may also be identified as third-generation Malay, Buddhist, Male, Social Media guru, and so on.

Adorno's non-identity thinking is especially thought-provoking for literature education in that it challenges educators to consider privileging the human over the citizen. This is a reversal of a world paradigm in which literary texts of specific nation-states are examined and compared in order to gain a deeper understanding of that which is universal in the human condition. Conversely, in a global paradigm, the human is examined first perhaps through global-political issues such as human rights before a particular category of literature such as Singapore literature is studied. What occurs is a reciprocal process involving the interrogation of the particular by the universal (such as when students become aware of the limitations of the term "Singaporean" in describing the identity of the human being) and the interrogation of the universal through the particular (such as identifying instances when human rights fail to account for particular circumstances).

In short, underlying non-identity thinking is an ethos of justice — one that seeks to do justice to the fullness of reality (O'Connor, 2004). What occurs in the constant probing at that which is non-identical and non-conceptual in the object or the other is the disintegration of universals and grand theories and a return to the particular. Take the example of recent attempts at imposing American democracy in Iraq following the removal of the dictator Saddam Hussein in 2006. In this case, American democracy has been universalized as a concept associated with freedom and imposed on this newly independent country. The question is whether such a concept can be troubled in order to encompass a broader notion of freedom that can account for the political, historical particularities of this newly independent country. For Adorno (1970/1997), artworks, including literary texts, provide a powerful platform where the particular can be valorized in order to problematize universal concepts. Their particularity is observed in that not only do artworks capture a specific moment in history, they also focus on particular events or characters that trouble generalizations. Artworks, in their incompleteness, evade any objectification to thought (Huhn, 2004). It is in this sense that artworks recognize the ungraspable nature of experience and reality that brings them closer to truth. Here, Adorno echoes Heidegger's (1950/1971a) claim that "Art is truth setting itself to work" (p. 38) that he made in *The Origin of the Work of Art*. Here, Heidegger links truth to the Greek word *aletheia* which refers to the unconcealedness of things. This is to say that the role of the artist is to un-conceal what is un-truth which, in this case, refers to truth that has not yet been uncovered. Heidegger (1927/1962) elaborates on the relation between art and truth with two other concepts. The first is the idea of knowing. Implicit in being-in-the-world is an awareness of temporality and therefore the human being becomes inevitably engaged in the world. Knowing is then an effect of his or her relation to the world and others in it. Related to this is the second idea of concern that stems from the human being's concern in the world and the responsibility he or she feels toward this knowing of the world. Both in Adorno and Heidegger then, we see a moral imperative that artworks, in probing truth and destabilizing fixed identities and concepts, do not aim at anarchy or relativism; instead they value freedom from the oppression of imposed theories and concepts. Artworks constantly push toward this freedom as they are propelled by principles of justice based on a concern and prioritization of the other.[11]

Part of Adorno's moral imperative grounding the artwork must be the event of the Holocaust. Adorno, whose father was an assimilated Jew living in Germany, was removed from his position at the Institute for Social Research in Frankfurt in 1933 when Hitler assumed power and was then forced into an eleven-year exile in the United States (Huhn, 2004). Adorno's (1967) famous dictum, "To write poetry after Auschwitz is barbaric" (p. 34), is based on his disillusionment with any claims that human civilization has progressed or that artworks have the power to make human beings morally better. Nazi Germany provided the prime example that within a culture immersed in high intellectual and artistic pursuits, the worst kind of barbaric acts could occur in the same breath. This explains why Adorno pushes for reflective and reflexive philosophizing rather than philosophy that aims at totalizing and fixed theories. Adorno (1966/1973) states, "When men are forbidden to think, their thinking sanctions what simply exists" (p. 85) and here we are reminded of Hannah Arendt's description of Adolf Otto Eichmann, the man who had meticulously organized the mass deportation of

Jews to the extermination camps during the Holocaust. Also writing in the 1960s, Arendt describes Eichmann as a medium-sized, middle-aged man with receding hair, ill-fitting teeth, and nearsighted eyes that led her to coin the phrase the "banality of evil." Yet, what was truly banal about Eichmann was his inability to think or, more specifically, "the total inability to look at anything or to think from the standpoint of somebody else" (Arendt, 1963/2003, p. 324).

The term "think" as used by Adorno and Arendt refers specifically to a kind of reflective and reflexive thinking in which the object or the other is prioritized over the subject. This forces the subject to think outside itself and through the lens of another. Like Adorno, Arendt suggests that this kind of thinking can be facilitated through literature. In her reflections on Eichmann's trial in Jerusalem, Arendt (1963/2003) references two occasions regarding Eichmann's apathy toward the literary. First, she notes that during the trial, Eichmann proudly proclaimed that he had read Adolf Bohm's *History of Zionism*, which was a considerable achievement to him, as he admitted to the court his reluctance to read anything except newspapers so that even his own father was distressed that Eichmann never read any books in the family library. Second, she describes how, while Eichmann was detained in Jerusalem, a police officer handed him the book *Lolita* for relaxation, which he rejected and returned after two days. Perhaps the point of these examples is Arendt's implicit suggestion that Eichmann had so surrounded himself with Nazi propaganda that his lack of engagement with other forms of literature ensured his very insular worldview.

Another similarity between Adorno and Arendt is their recognition of the dangers of totalitarianism. Referencing examples of imperialism, colonialism, and anti-Semitism, Arendt (1968) shows how these different forms of totalitarianism aim toward a reification of thought through the use of propaganda designed to mold and remold the minds of the public as well as a reification of thought through stripping the human of its essence and imposing concepts and categories such as "Jew," "homosexual," "Gypsy," and so on upon him or her. It is therefore not enough to prioritize object over subject or the other over the self, since, even in this prioritization, it is necessary to return to the particular that the object calls for in order to break and disrupt imposed concepts. For Adorno, one powerful arena in which the particular can disrupt the universal is with regard to the sufferings of others. This is a category that cannot be universalized, since suffering is an inherently personal and specific instance in history (Bernstein, 2006). More than historical or philosophical texts, literature, in its incompleteness and its provision of specific examples, offers a powerful space for reflections on suffering. Paradoxically, these particular instances continually aim toward an understanding of the universal in terms of the human. Yet, implicit in this gesture is a recognition that the human can never be grasped, since the moment a concept of the human is fixated, the particular must enter to release its hold. It is this negation of the particular disrupting the universal and the particular reaching toward a universal understanding of the human in all its diversity that represents this dynamic operation of the literary.

In summary, the goal of education for global citizenship encompassing spherical ways of seeing oriented toward understanding the human and defending human rights informed the development of a global paradigm in literature education. This involved replacing a world paradigm anchored on the goals of education for world citizenship as connected to concepts of collective taste and universal humanity with a global paradigm anchored on the goals of education for global citizenship as connected to concepts of empowerment and humanity of the universal and particular. The latter is grounded on a belief that the good of teaching literature is not so much that it facilitates students' moral contemplation of the Absolute or that it deepens his or her understanding of the universal human condition; rather, the good of teaching literature is in developing students' critical, ethical, and reflective capacities so that they may have a deeper understanding of the human in both the universal and the particular. The particular can be observed at all levels of society down to the ordinary experiences of the everyman; it can also be observed in all aspects of political, cultural, and social living of the everyday. Finally, in the push toward understanding the human through particular and specific realities, a more democratic and inclusive space is opened to embrace the everyone.

Applications of Global Approaches to Teaching Literature

The new critics, together with British and German cultural theorists, contributed to a global paradigm in literature pedagogy during the second later wave of globalization. The concept of humanity of the universal and particular is especially important in this paradigm in stressing the need to understand the object as universally human and particular at the same time. However, as mentioned previously, since the object is always external to the subject, it is always that which is non-I and hence objectified through the imposition of concepts and categories. One of the main tasks of education informed by a global paradigm is to then subjectivize the object, to turn the object into a subject or to turn the non-I into the I. Though this is an impossibility, it is nevertheless a goal to be strived for. Using both historical examples from this period as well as more recent examples, I want to explore four approaches to teaching literature informed by a global paradigm invested in subjectivizing the object.

The first approach addresses the concept of empowerment by aiming to equip students with discriminatory powers and with the capacity to produce cultural texts. This is achieved by forging a closer connection between the discipline of literary studies and the disciplines of media and cultural studies. This closer connection can occur in three main ways. The first way is to expand the scope of texts studied in the literature classroom to include media texts in a variety of modes such as words, images, and sounds as well as in a variety of genres such as film and radio. Historically, this has been occurring since the postwar period when, in what Braj Kachru (1992) has described as the Inner Circle of English nations[12] comprising countries such as Australia, Britain, Canada, and the United States, film and media texts became increasingly incorporated into English classes in the 1960s and 1970s. The second way involves the incorporation of media and cultural studies' emphasis on active critical engagement in literary studies.[13] For example, this would involve replacing new criticism's passive close reading of literary texts, especially poetry, with semiotic criticism's active close reading of all forms of textualities. The latter centers on equipping students to recognize linguistic, visual, gestural, and other semiotic signs in all forms of texts. At the same time, recognition is insufficient, since students also need to be equipped to critically interpret the constructed nature of texts. They can do this by analyzing concepts of representation, stereotypes, and bias in texts. These concepts were traditionally associated with cultural studies in Canada and media studies in the United States from the 1950s and have increasingly been introduced into literary studies especially after the 1970s as a result of numerous studies linking the mass media to violence such as the report by the Surgeon General's Scientific Advisory on Television and Social Behavior.[14] Despite their ties to media and cultural studies, educators have increasingly recognized their value to literature education in promoting active criticism. For example, teachers can facilitate students' analysis of a literary text's representation of a particular race, gender, or cultural group; they can encourage students to compare stereotypical representations in a literary text with the film version of this text; they can also draw students' attention to voices that are negated or absent in texts, thereby revealing the text's inherent bias. Activities such as these encourage students not to be mere passive appreciators and consumers of texts; instead, equipped with the tools of semiotic criticism as well as critical concepts such as representation, stereotypes, and bias that enable them to actively critique texts, students would be empowered to make discriminatory judgments about texts and to probe for the ideological bias underlying the text's construction. Finally, the third way is to incorporate a media and cultural studies' production component into literary studies. In order to promote more active engagements with texts, instead of passive consumption of texts, literature teachers have increasingly required students to produce original creative works such as a fictional work or a play script that are then counted as part of students' formal assessment.

The connection of literary studies to media and cultural studies contributes to empowering students with the capacity to critically formulate informed responses to texts as well as with the capacity to act (write, speak, produce) in ways that can promote the subjectification of the object. However, one challenge is how can the subject act for the object in ways that will not lead to a further objectification of the object? This leads to the next two approaches concerned with historicizing the object and de-representing the object that are based on the principle of understanding the object as universally human and particular at the same time.

The second approach involves historicizing of the object that occurs through negotiating the tension between the universal and the particular. To reach toward that which is fully human and fully particular in the object, one needs to begin by examining the object's historical relation to place. As Robert Livingston (2001) notes, globalization has resulted in an obsession with place as contingent in defining the individual's sense of identity so that place becomes reflective of a moral order. The question, therefore, is how can the object's location in a particular place be historicized and contextualized so that it is no longer a singular site that defines the object's identity but multiple, overlapping sites? The continual displacement of singular place as attached to the identity of the object contributes to ever-expanding circles of understanding that which is fully human in the object. Take the example of the proliferation of the study of non-Western national literatures in what Kachru (1992) describes as the Outer Circle of English nations as opposed to the Inner Circle as mentioned earlier. These are nations that have undergone periods of Western colonization such as India, the Philippines, and Singapore so that English is regarded as an official language even though their citizens are generally non-native speakers of English. There have tended to be two responses toward English literature once formerly colonized nations gained independence. One response is to marginalize English literature in the curriculum by separating it from English language. In Singapore, the ruling People's Action Party, which came into power in 1959 following the withdrawal of the British, sought to institute a system of public education that would promote nationalism. At the same time, it remained cautious against prioritizing any of the vernacular languages given the multiracial mix of the nation. Thus, it instituted the policy of bilingualism that became compulsory for all students in 1966. The policy stipulated that English was to be the first language of the country and students were to learn a second language in their mother tongue. Meanwhile, English literature was relegated a less significant position. Similarly, in India, English language was emphasized while English literature was marginalized following its independence from British rule in 1947. While the government had initially recommended that English be replaced with Hindi as the official language of the country in 1956, anti-Hindi riots resulted in a reversal of this policy. An Official Language (Amendment) Act passed in 1967 decreed that English would continue as an associate official language (Kapoor, 2008). The significant position of English in India may be observed in that it remains the privileged medium of instruction in colleges, which also means that schools that provide English medium education are at an advantage over those that emphasize education through the medium of vernacular languages (Ramanathan, 2005).[15] This polarization of English language and English literature demonstrates that English is no longer seen as a threatening colonial language but as a neutral language that bridges different racial and ethnic communities. English is also perceived as the language of economic progress that provides access to the wealth and knowledge of the West. English literature, on the other hand, is viewed as problematic given its historical roots in Britain's civilizing mission of colonizing cultures. The consequence is that while English language is valued in formerly colonized countries, English literature is paradoxically devalued.

Aside from the marginalization of English literature, a second response is to create new categories of literatures in English. I have mentioned the emergence of Singapore literature as a new category included for study in English literature courses in Singapore schools. Another example is the category of commonwealth literature that was introduced to school and university literature courses as a way of coming to terms with colonial history and its after-effects. On one hand, the emergence of commonwealth literature represented the act of the Empire writing back so that there was now a space in which the formerly colonized object could be historicized and understood in relation and in conversation with other formerly colonized objects in the commonwealth. The teaching of this new category of commonwealth literature also meant that a space would now be provided for the unique cultural and literary traditions of these nations to be reimagined and rearticulated. However, the creation of counter-canons can problematically re-emphasize the hegemony of the canon as an anchor to which the identity of counter-canons may be defined. As Ruth Vinz (2000) reminds us, the inclusion of other canons does not necessarily disrupt traditional Western ideological interpretive practices; what may be more productive instead is to conceive of literary texts as not organized into discrete categories but as a spider web of stories in dialogue with other stories. Additionally, a category such as commonwealth literature conflates African, Australian, Canadian, Indian, West Indian, and other writing as equally postcolonial and ignores the uneven relations of power between the metropolitan countries and less economically advanced counties (Niranjana, 1992). The point, however, is not to fully reject counter-canons, since these provide spaces to articulate new historicized understandings of the other, but to instead recognize the inherent tendencies toward replacing one universalizing scheme of identifying and naming otherness with other equally totalizing systems. It is therefore historicizing in its continuous tense as an ongoing process of contextualizing the object that is crucial. Thus, for example, in teaching commonwealth literature, one might draw attention to the category of Singapore literature; in teaching Singapore literature, one might draw attention to the category of Straits-Chinese literature that emerged during the colonial period of the early nineteenth century; in the category of Straits-Chinese literature, one might draw attention to modern literature of China up to the seventeenth century that subsequently informed the writings of the Straits-Chinese as they emigrated from China to Southeast Asia from the fifteenth century onward or the category of early Malayan literature, since many of the Straits-Chinese men intermarried with Malay women in the communities they settled in and so on. Essentially, the location of histories within histories is an ongoing process of understanding the object as constituted within a dynamic space of overlapping histories. Eventually, one comes to the point when nation and place disappear so that it is the notion of the human transcending histories and geographical spaces that becomes more and more visible.

The process of historicizing the object also points to a third approach, which involves the conscious attempt to de-represent the object. Any attempt to represent and re-present the object is an attempt to fixate history and objectify a singular universalizing identity on the object which then necessitates a de-representation of the object by highlighting the particular that destabilizes the grounds of the universal. As mentioned previously, tendencies toward a global paradigm emerged during the second later wave of globalization. These tendencies became more fully realized toward the late twentieth century as the category of global literature emerged. In theorizing what the globalizing of literary studies involves, Rey Chow (2001) provides an insightful comment about Derrida's stereotyping of the Chinese language as an ideographic rather than a phonetic language. Citing scholars who discuss the common misreading of Chinese as an ideographic language, Chow argues that Derrida is complicit in circulating an oriental stereotype that is then used as a foundation for his arguments against logocentrism that he attributes to the West. Therefore, the paradox is that in attempting to deconstruct Western systems of power, Derrida himself reverts to East and West essentialisms. What Chow argues for is the strategy of deconstructing stereotypes that must lie at the heart of globalizing literary studies.

> Although stereotypes are not necessarily visual in the physical sense, the act of stereotyping is always implicated by visuality by virtue of the fact that the other is imagined as and transformed into a (sur)face, a sheer exterior deprived of historical depth. (p. 73)

The critical reading of stereotypes or, in other words, reading against representations, which Chow demonstrates in her text aims at something deeper that can only be located in a continuing process of historicizing. Here too, we observe how the terms "stereotype" and "representation" are part of the tool of ideological analysis imported from the disciplines of media and cultural studies. De-representation or the breaking of stereotypes occurs through the provision of particular instances that challenge universalizing concepts and categories. This is what Shu-mei Shih (2004) describes as "the granting of universality to the exceptional particular" (p. 27). She cites the example of Gao Xinjian who was awarded the Nobel Prize in literature. The response was great indignation by the government and scholarly community in China, as they regarded Gao an inauthentic representation of China, since he wrote his major literary works in Chinese, while living in exile in France, which were then published in Taiwan. Gao is the exceptional particular that breaks the stereotypical notion of what it means to represent an authentic Chinese voice. Similarly in the teaching of literature, teachers can lead students to identify the exceptional particular, whether this may lie in specific characters or events depicted in the literary texts, and how this interrogates imposed universalisms.

Paradoxically, the ongoing process of pushing toward the exceptional particular results in a return to an as yet unknown universal: that which transcends space-time or history in characterizing the human. For example, if I say the object of my study x breaks the stereotypical concepts imposed on him or her, then I am also subscribing to the implication of difference as a fundamental aspect of humanity. This points to the fourth approach, which is a consciousness of the global that teachers can highlight in the classroom. This can involve centering the study of literatures from around the world on an understanding of the human as opposed to citizenship; demystifying myths of globalization such as cultural homogenization by pointing out specific examples through literary texts where cultural diversity, community, or individual uniqueness exist; and linking the literary text to contemporary real-world global concerns about the economy, environment, terrorism, disease, mass media, and so forth. Global consciousness can also be facilitated by the strategy of encouraging spherical seeing through shifting frames of reference as previously discussed. In a description of how literature is used to teach global education, a high school language arts teacher in Ohio describes how she begins her class by getting students to think about the meaning of humanism and how humanists are concerned about the condition of all human beings no matter where they live (Bender-Slack, 2002). Using this as a lens, she then has her students examine concepts underlying the United Nations' Universal Declaration of Human Rights relating these to questions of ethics and human responsibility in literary texts such as *Brave New World* by Aldous Huxley and the poem "Hollow Men" by T. S. Eliot. In the next part of her lesson, students are asked to conduct research on these same issues, particularly human rights violations, occurring in other countries. While the teacher reports that her students came away horrified at the kinds of violations going on and that this then demonstrated their sensitivity to the importance of respecting the rights of humans to be different, there is of course the danger that human rights can become another totalizing frame that students use to read other countries and cultures. However, what seems most helpful in this teacher's program is her intention to raise her students' consciousness of themselves as being global citizens before being American citizens. Having established this as a broad principle, she then has her class analyze questions of ethics and human rights in Western literature, followed by the literature of other countries. What would be helpful following this is to encourage students to adopt shifting frames of reference. For example, she mentions how her students discussed police brutality in Mexico. What would happen if literary and non-literary texts depicting violations of human rights in Mexico were placed in conversation with such texts focusing on human rights violations in Britain or the United States? How would a Mexican respond to questions of human rights in these countries? The point in such an exercise would be to get students to not just examine an issue from multiple perspectives but also to shift from a subject to object analysis to an object to subject analysis. This means taking a serious commitment to both questions: what do I think of the other as well as what the other thinks of me.

Another example involving the application of shifting frames of reference is the film *Flags of Our Fathers*, directed by Clint Eastwood in 2006, which describes the capture of the Japanese island of Iwo Jima during the Second World War from the perspective of the American military. This movie was accompanied by a second one, also directed by Eastwood, titled *Letters from Iwo Jima* which describes the war from the perspective of the Japanese army that defended the island. By releasing these two films together, Eastwood challenges audiences to interpret the war of Iwo Jima from both the perspective of the Americans and Japanese and to look at how each side interpreted the other. What occurs is that the "enemy" becomes humanized and subjectivized rather than an abstract category of evil. In some ways, Goethe, in his world literature paradigm, had promoted this way of studying literatures from around the world. That is, he believed that world literature should consist of reciprocal criticism among countries and he himself admitted to gaining new insights about his own work through reading reviews published in French journals (Strich, 1949). However, Goethe's exclusive concern with the opinions of Europe, particularly France, on German literature, meant that such an idea never truly acquired a global scope. A curriculum that pushes students to think about how other foreign nations, even those categorized as enemy nations, view their own as well as other dominant nations, promotes a broader consciousness of citizenship tied to the human rather than the nation-state.

In summary, what I have attempted to explore in this chapter is the question of how a global paradigm informing the teaching of literature was aimed at propagating the goals of education for global citizenship that was connected to concepts of empowerment and humanity of the universal and particular. I have suggested four approaches based on the principle of subjectivizing the object. Toward the late twentieth century, this principle has become even more significant, particularly given the intensification of globalization and the disintegration of the nation-state. The key challenge for literature pedagogy is to consider what new roles it needs to play in confronting the escalation of global forces aimed at objectifying the other to such extremes that the other becomes demonized and spiritualized as observed in polarizing tendencies of fundamentalist and anti-fundamentalist movements in the world today. How can approaches to teaching literature not be conceived from a solely materialist subject-object position but from a position that can also account for that which is in the realm of the extraterritorial and the extramaterial?

CHAPTER FIVE

Cosmopolitan Approaches to Teaching Literature

The scene of contention occurs when Victor Frankenstein, the scientist and protagonist of Mary Shelley's famed novel, is confronted by the monster he has created. The monster now demands that Victor create a female companion. "Shall each man ... find a wife for his bosom, and each beast have his mate, and I be alone?" the monster cries. Yet, Victor refuses to give in, his argument being that this would result in another demonic creature of his own making let loose upon the earth. A student stands up and asks his classmates to examine the moral reasoning behind Victor's argument. Citing various passages from the text, the student argues that Victor does not understand the monster's plight and constantly reverts to the logic of science. It is a moral argument based on scientific rationality rather than empathy for the monster's plight. After making his argument, the student sits down and another student now stands up to rebut him. "What we must understand," the student states, "is that Victor has an obligation to society not to create such monsters." He then points out the text's allusion to the creation story, where Eve tempts Adam, to show how the female species has been associated with evil and the fall of man. This allusion is contained in Victor's fear of creating another female species because this may possibly contribute to a second original sin. The discussion continues for another half an hour.

The fifteen students in this grade ten class have been divided into two groups. The first half of the group is arranged in an inner circle while the second half is arranged in an outer circle. Throughout the class, the teacher stands outside both circles and interjects only occasionally to remind the class of the objective of the lesson. This she has done at the beginning of the class by introducing students to the principles of Socratic questioning. The point is for students to raise good critical questions about the text by probing assumptions, questioning the evidence given by others, raising other questions from questions raised, and so on. By focusing on questions, the teacher wants her students to approach this classical literary work not as an artifact to be passively appreciated; instead, she wants her students to actively question the construction of the text, particularly the way its philosophical and religious arguments are framed.

As students warm up to this culture of questioning the text and questioning the question, an exciting discussion takes place on the issue of the creator's obligation to the larger society. One student argues that the creator also has an obligation to acknowledge what he has created. Another student adds that by differentiating the creator's obligation to his society from his obligation to his created being or monster, it assumes that the creator is different from the monster when, in fact, both exhibit a similar degree of violence toward the other. This leads off to a tangent as students think about how God is different from and similar to a human being. What becomes clear is that by the end of this class on Gothic literature, students have not engaged in detail with areas typically associated with literary analysis: plot (an understanding of what the story is about), character (an analysis of the characters' relationships and motivations), style (devices that contribute to the aesthetics of the text), and author (the intentions of the writer). While these four areas continue to be given emphasis in high school literature assessments, it is not the focus of this literature class where the boundaries of engagements with literature and philosophy are blurred so that while students grapple with issues suggested by the literary text, these become entry points for them to discuss sin (religion), moral rights and obligation (ethics), God and man (metaphysics), and the limits of science and knowledge (epistemology). At the end of the class, the teacher asks the outer circle to assess the quality of questions and responses provided by the inner circle. The rubric she gives the outer circle to help them in their peer assessment is interestingly based on the distinction between dialogue and debate in which the emphasis is on the former rather than the latter. While a dialogue is collaborative and aims to provide multiple viewpoints on an issue, a debate is oppositional and aims at a singular viewpoint; while a dialogue calls for a suspension of one's belief and an open-minded attitude, a debate calls for a full investment of one's belief and a close-minded attitude. The teacher assigns a specific student in the outer circle the task of assessing another student in the inner circle by providing qualitative rather than quantitative feedback on the extent to which a student's response and questions promote dialogue, probe assumptions, extend perspectives, and foster an openness toward further philosophical exploration.

The above was a lesson I observed as part of my research in the spring of 2011 at a high-performing secondary school in Singapore. It provides an example of a cosmopolitan approach to teaching literature that involves first, the use of the literary text as an entry point to ethical, philosophical, and religious discussions about the relationship among human beings, their world, and their universe, and second, the teacher's adoption of the distanced stance of a facilitator as opposed to approaches predominant in the late eighteenth century in which the teacher was the main source students turned to for an explication of the text. More contemporary approaches encourage students to formulate their own arguments about issues raised in the text and the notion of the literary text as a self-enclosed entity to be appreciated for its own sake is replaced with the notion of the literary text as a polysemous entity containing multiple meanings. Thus, interpretation should privilege ambiguity and any suggestion of closure or fixing of meaning is to be regarded with skepticism and deconstructed in order to expose the text's ideological operations.

Historically, one of the factors contributing to a cosmopolitan paradigm to teaching literature was the introduction of literary theory in the universities which provided the platform for students to grapple with philosophical-religious questions. In the United States, this occurred from the 1970s when literature departments introduced Derrida and Foucault among others and established the subdiscipline of literary theory. Literature professors began to introduce philosophical readings alongside literary texts and students began writing theses and dissertations on philosophical topics (Bernheimer, 1995; Rorty, 2006). As literary theory became more pervasive in universities, schools were also pressured to move away from text-centered approaches that paid over-attention to the formal properties of the text at the expense of its underlying humanistic, philosophical, and existential concerns. For example, in 1983, deans of twelve Pennsylvania colleges issued a statement titled "What We Expect" to policymakers and school administrators in which they made clear the sort of training they wished their incoming freshmen to have in various courses including literature. One of their key points was that "Literature must be studied in the contexts of personal experience, history, philosophy, psychology, economics, sociology, religion and ethics, the natural sciences, and the arts" (Gruenberg, 1986, p. 31). As literature teachers grew increasingly dissatisfied with new criticism,[1] a range of influential scholarly articles emerged in the 1970s and 1980s advocating poststructuralist criticism, particularly reader-response criticism. David Bleich (1975) made the case for including subjective-experience in interpretation so that interpretation would not be limited to the aesthetic features of the text but could also include discussions about the text's philosophical concerns. Robert Probst (1981) advocated the use of reader-response in the teaching of literature in schools to promote a culture of questioning in the classroom, to encourage students' self-examination and self-reflection, and to promote deeper explorations of the historical and cultural concerns in the text. Similarly, in an edited collection of articles, Alan Purves (1972) argued that reader-response's student-centered approach provides democratic spaces for philosophical discussions about human nature raised in the text. Such philosophical discussions, according to George Hillocks and Larry Ludlow (1984), represent higher-order forms of literary interpretation. Based in part on an observation of secondary students' responses to fiction, Hillocks and Ludlow devised a taxonomy of skills that teachers could develop through questions posed to students. While lower levels of the taxonomy involved questions focusing on textual details or character analysis, higher levels involved questions focusing on more abstract analysis such as "author generalization" questions that require students to engage with the author's philosophical concerns about the nature of the human condition.

Even though poststructuralist movements influenced more student-centered and dialogic literature teaching practices, its impact in schools was more evident in terms of literature pedagogy. Meanwhile, a bulk of literature teachers remained unaware of developments in literary theory occurring in the universities. In the early 1990s, a nationwide survey of schools with reputations for excellent literature programs in the United States revealed that 72 percent of the teachers reported little or no familiarity with literary theory (Applebee, 1993). Despite this, various scholars have been promoting more rigorous engagements with theory. For example, Kathleen McCormick (1994) argues that reader-oriented pedagogy that was popularized in schools in the 1970s and 1980s was ironically text-centered and failed to include political and ideological criticism of both the position of the reader and the production of the text. The importance of literature education in grappling with theories (such as poststructuralism, postmodernism, and feminism) is also a point advanced by Deborah Appleman (2009) who argues that this is necessary in order to provide a repertoire of critical ways of seeing and interpreting the world. She bases her arguments on key events such as September 11, the war in Iraq, and the Columbine shootings that occurred at the turn of the twenty-first century; these demonstrate that, more than ever, we are living in an increasingly ideological world where the need for a cosmopolitan paradigm to teaching literature is all the more pertinent to develop philosophical reflective capacities in students.

The Third Wave of Globalization and Education for Cosmopolitan Citizenship

The Rise of Global Mobility

The 1970s and 1980s witnessed massive global movements toward democracy so that in more than thirty countries in Asia, Europe, and Latin America, democratic systems replaced authoritarian regimes. Huntington (1991) terms this the third wave of democracy and describes key changes that occurred during this period. In Europe, military-led dictatorships in Greece, Portugal, and Spain were replaced with civilian governments. This also occurred in Argentina, Bolivia, Ecuador, and Peru among others. The period also witnessed the final phase of European colonization which saw the emergence of newly independent countries with some degree of democracy in parts of Africa (e.g., Algeria and Senegal) and the Middle East (e.g., Egypt and Jordan). Most importantly, by the end of the 1980s, the communist system collapsed and countries such as Czechoslovakia, East Germany, Hungary, Romania, and the Soviet Union embraced democracy. Even post-Mao China, though still a communist country, recognized the backwardness of socialist policies and, from 1972, introduced various reforms that resulted in the creation of democratic spaces within authoritarian rule. Examples of these spaces are the Special Economic Zones (SEZs) in cities such as Shenzhen and Xiamen as well as Special Administrative Regions (SARs) such as Hong Kong, Macao, and Taiwan. Aihwa Ong (2006) describes how these spaces represent exceptions to political rule in China so that SEZs are marketed as open cities with few bureaucratic rules and are designed to attract overseas investors who enjoy a high degree of autonomy while SARs, many of which operate on democratic systems, possess their own independent political institutions and judiciaries.

By 1989, these massive movements led political theorist Francis Fukuyama to famously proclaim the end of history. Fukuyama (2006) is not claiming that the world or history can no longer progress or improve. What he is arguing for is essentially the end of history as the end of ideological wars, since the crisis of communism has signaled clearly that liberal democracy is the most valid ideological system because it accords recognition in the form of individual freedom (liberty) and popular sovereignty (democracy).[2] Essentially, the dominance of liberal democracy created a climate favorable to global interchange and exchanges. By the 1980s, concepts such as global, globality, globalism, and globalization dominated intellectual discourse, and though most scholars acknowledge that globalization is not a singular condition but a multilayered, overlapping, fluid phenomenon lacking in any precise definition or unified theory (Held, McGrew, Goldblatt, & Perraton, 1999; O'Byrne, 2003), the one commonality has to do with globalization's innate mobility, and this can be observed in its three sub-phenomena: economic, technological, and cultural globalization.

Theories of economic globalization subscribe to the view that capital is the primary driver of globalization since it is propelled by the need to expand surplus or profits, thereby leading to the constant search for new markets. With the spread and dominance of neoliberalism since the 1980s, which involves minimal state involvement and subscription to a belief that unconstrained market forces will provide the greatest benefits to society, the late twentieth century has been described as the highest and most advanced stage of capitalist imperialism (Berberoglu, 2003; Scholte, 2005). Neoliberalism facilitates the mobility of capital as well as the production and distribution of goods and services as companies increasingly tend to locate factories where labor costs are lower. Mobility is also precipitated by the rise of a transnational capitalist class that moves flexibly wherever regional offices are established and their essential lack of allegiance serves to erode the authority of the nation-state (Tabb, 2009).

Theories of economic globalization often converge with theories of technological globalization as observed in the conjoining of these two forces in terms such as "digital economy" and "techno-capitalism" (Kellner, 2002). During this third wave of globalization, knowledge has overtaken labor as the most important form of global capital in industrialized nations so that these nations are best described as operating on a "knowledge economy" fueled by "knowledge capitalism." These terms originate from various policy documents by the OECD and World Bank in the 1990s[3] that describe the strong dependence on production, distribution, and use of knowledge in industrialized "post-Fordist" nations that privilege market flexibility, competition, and innovation particularly in technology (Brown & Lauder, 1996). At the same time, the spread of knowledge points to the increasing mobility of information as it is exchanged in cyberspace where time and place have become immaterial. Mobility of information and the rise of a networked society also serve as push-factors for technological innovation that is crucial in maintaining efficiency so that information may be transacted quickly, securely, and in an unhindered manner (Kellner, 2002).

As a result of economic and technological mobility, a third sub-phenomenon of globalization has emerged, that of cultural globalization. Cultural globalization describes the exchange of knowledge, capital, and products or services among people and groups around the world. Such exchanges are dependent on physical mobility whether this takes the form of tourists, internet users, or even diasporic communities and asylum seekers. The result is a kind of transplanetary connectivity involving the creation of a transnational or global imagination as a result of these real or virtual exchanges (Scholte, 2005).

Extraterritorial Actors and Spaces

By this time, it may be overstating the obvious point that the consequence of mobility inherent in economic, technological, and cultural globalization is the erosion of the authority of the nation-state in managing its citizens. More than any other period in history, the imagined identities of individuals and communities can no longer be solely defined by the nation-state, since the authority once conferred upon it has been increasingly dispersed to various actors occupying what can be described as extraterritorial spaces. The extraterritorial is the space where power is wielded by actors that are not tied to any physical sovereign territory and this can be observed at many different levels. On a more overt level, extraterritorial political actors include intergovernmental organizations (IGOs). In addition to the United Nations, discussed in the previous chapter, the period from the late 1960s onward saw the formation of new IGOs, such as the OECD. Many of these were interregional in nature such as the Association of Southeast Asian Nations (ASEAN), the African Union, and the Asia-Pacific Economic Cooperation (APEC). Previously formed IGOs also expanded as observed in the doubling of membership in the European Union in the 1970s from its original six to a total of twenty-seven members at present. Other examples include non-governmental organizations (NGOs) such as Amnesty International, founded in 1961, to defend human rights and Greenpeace, founded in 1971, to address global environmental concerns. These extraterritorial actors play a significant role in the creation of multilayered systems of governance occurring at the global and regional levels, where policies, agreements, and treatises affect political and economic practices at the level of the nation-state, compromising its sovereignty as a result.

On a more quasi-overt level, extraterritorial actors that have become increasingly influential are multinational corporations (MNCs) and transnational corporations (TNCs). The 1970s saw the rise of predominantly American, European, and Japanese corporations particularly in manufacturing industries. Masao Miyoshi (1993) notes a subtle difference between MNCs and TNCs. The degree of mobility is more evident in the case of TNCs as compared to MNCs. Whereas TNCs are not tied to any nation-state, MNCs continue to retain their headquarters in a home nation. However, both MNCs and TNCs are similar in that their offices are spread across the world, which enables them to oversee the marketing, distribution, and management of products. The quasi-overt nature of these corporations lies in the fact that they employ post-Fordist methods of production that allow factories to be set up in countries where labor costs are low and where there are fewer political and economic barriers (Miyoshi, 1993). This means that the products are oftentimes assembled from different parts of the world so that they can no longer be tied to a single country of origin. Aspects of the manufacturing process may even be outsourced to local private companies so that in the end, the consumer is unaware of the vast networks of corporate relations underlying each product. Their identification of the product becomes tied superficially to the company's brand rather than to any physical territory. At the same time, these corporations, particularly TNCs, have sufficient economic and political clout to influence governments to compromise on the territorial sovereignty of nation-states. One example can be observed in U.S. relations with Afghanistan, whose location in the Central Asian region offers a strategic site for transnational corporations to tap into the vast oil and gas reserves in the area. Critics have claimed that in 1996, when the Taliban came into power in Afghanistan, the U.S. government supported it partly to secure an oil pipeline for the American transnational corporation UNOCAL that would cut across Afghanistan and Pakistan (Stabile & Kumar, 2005). Thus, it remained silent when the Taliban began its oppressive assault on the Afghan people, particularly its women. Following the September 11 attacks, the United States invaded Afghanistan in 2001 with the rationale of dismantling the terrorist organization, Al Qaeda. However, various critics have again pointed to the development of a trans-Afghanistan oil and gas pipeline as a significant incentive behind the intervention, especially since, shortly after the invasion, an agreement was signed with the Afghan government to commence the construction of this pipeline (Berberoglu, 2003).

Aside from overt and quasi-overt levels, extraterritorial spaces can also operate on a covert level. This is particularly evident in relation to two problems — migration and terrorism — associated with the intensification of global mobility in the late twentieth century. Globalization has led to extreme categories of classes with the transnational elite class on one end and the transnational refugee on the other. Unlike the former, the latter category is comprised of individuals driven out of their nation-states by force as a result of war, poverty, or lack of employment or individuals who have left their nation-state in the hope of a better life. Technological and cultural globalizations have especially facilitated the movements of refugees not only by making traveling easier but also by initiating a "migration of dreams" (Nassar, 2010, p. 14) that occurs when the mass media projects images of the good life of those living in prosperous, economically advanced nations. As a result of such exposure, individuals from less advanced nations begin to imagine what it would be like to live in these other nations. In other words, before migration becomes a reality, it must first occur in the imagination. At the same time, increasing numbers of mobile migrants have also led to another global extremity. On one hand, globalization has led to the liberalization of borders particularly in relation to the lowering of barriers to free trade; on the other hand, globalization has also led to the erection and increasing surveillance of physical borders resulting in the insulation of nation-states from the influx of immigrants, refugees, and asylum seekers. Wendy Brown (2010) provides an interesting study of the recent phenomenon of walling as a result of global interconnectedness. The examples are numerous and include the construction of a U.S.-Mexico border to curb the flow of drugs and immigrants; the security fence in Israel constructed along the West Bank to keep Palestinians away; barriers erected in India to deter refugees from Bangladesh, Burma, and Pakistan; electric fences constructed in Botswana along its border with Zimbabwe; walls between Egypt and Gaza, Saudi Arabia and Yemen, Brazil and Paraguay, and Iraq and Kuwait among others. One senses that borders and the walling of nation-states have almost become the political paranoia of the twenty-first century. As Brown (2010) observes, the paradox of walling is that states claim to promote a free and open society on one hand but argue that this can only occur by insulating society from negative outside influences. Further, even as the state's authority is being eroded by external global forces, states continue to persist in retaining some form of authority by attempting to convince their citizens that they can still protect them from the potential invasion and pollution of the "other." This argument is premised on the notion of the state as the divine protector versus the corrupting other as a demonized figure.

Increasingly in the late twentieth century, states also turned to extraterritorial spaces that function as borders. One example is Christmas Island, located between Indonesia and Australia, which houses the Australian Immigration Reception and Processing Center. Individuals, particularly from parts of Asia seeking asylum in Australia, are sent to this center for "processing." What is interesting is that Christmas Island is technically on Australian soil but is considered an administered territory that has no state government. It also falls outside Australia's migration zone which essentially means that the government does not have to adhere to any international legal obligations concerning claims to asylum. Asylum seekers who are sent to this island are detained in conditions with prison-like characteristics and denied any rights as well as prevented from accessing any legal or health services (Amnesty International, 2009). On one hand, this gives the state flexibility in dealing with immigrants as well as relieves it from responsibility. At the same time, while the state continues to display its protective policing function, it ironically projects a dilution of this authority. This is evident in recent trends in which detention facilities, once the jurisdiction of the state, are increasingly outsourced to private companies. At present, detention facilities and services have reaped huge profits for these companies which have turned into multinational industries. One problem is that these companies, in their attempts to be cost-efficient, have resorted to providing only basic services to detainees and, in worst cases, have attempted to keep detainees for longer periods (Bacon, 2005).

Like Christmas Island, Guantánamo Bay is another example of an extraterritorial space. It is more controversial because, while Christmas Island functions to address the problem of migration, Guantánamo functions to address the problem of terrorism. Since 2002, Guantánamo has been used as a camp in which Taliban and alleged Al Qaeda members are imprisoned and interrogated. What is interesting is that Guantánamo Bay is technically on Cuban soil and falls under Cuban sovereignty. At the same time, the Bay falls under the control of the United States. Historically, since 1903, the Bay was occupied by U.S. military following its victory in the Spanish-American War. Under a contractual agreement, Cuba agreed to lease the Bay to the United States, which held the right to withhold consent to terminating the agreement; this occurred when Cuba informed the United States that it wanted to end its contractual obligations. Since then, Cuba has considered the U.S. occupation of Guantánamo Bay as illegal (de Zayas, 2003). To the United States, however, Guantánamo provides a strategic extrajudicial, extraterritorial location because, though it is on Cuban soil, Cuban law does not apply. Also, though the United States has territorial control of the Bay, American law does not apply because Cuba technically has sovereignty over the whole island (Kaplan, 2005). In short, Guantánamo represents a place where law is suspended, where prisoners are denied any rights or legal representation, and where the U.S. government is not obligated by state or international law to observe regulations prohibiting the inhumane treatment and torture of the prisoners.

The stateless refugee or asylum seeker finding him- or herself in places like Christmas Island and the terrorist confined to detainment camps such as Guantánamo Bay have little recourse but to appeal to human rights that represent a form of extraterritorial law transcending particular nation-state laws and agreed upon at the international level. As discussed in the previous chapter, human rights came to the foreground following the end of the Second World War. During the latter part of the twentieth century, however, human rights has been increasingly problematized. One question concerns how human rights can be implemented in practical terms in extraterritorial spaces where individuals have no legal rights of representation and it is not clear which legitimate body can adequately represent the stateless subject. Another question concerns a more powerful extraterritorial force that more potently threatens to override the extraterritorial laws of human rights. This concerns religion, and a good example may be observed when, following the September 11 attacks, international law and human rights were disregarded in favor of militarism. When, in 2009, President Barack Obama ordered the closure of the detention camp following international criticisms of the military's abusive and degrading treatment of prisoners, this plan was obstructed, notably by Republicans who argued that it would lead to the release of dangerous prisoners and would mean having these prisoners transferred for trial on U.S. soil (Yasui, 2011). Within this paranoia, one can discern the repeated theme of the state acting as a theological force bent on keeping the other outside its territorial boundaries. Such a move is reiterated by political rhetoric such as the "war on terror" framed within a logic of good versus evil, us versus the enemy. Within this logic, revenge and torture are permissible, since the enemy can be dehumanized and depicted as belonging to the "axis of evil," a term used by former American president George W. Bush to describe countries involved in developing weapons of mass destruction and funding terrorist groups. Bush classified Iran, Iraq, and North Korea as belonging to this category; this list later extended to include Cuba, Syria, Libya, and Sudan. Even the term "terrorist" itself connotes a moral connotation linked with religious fanaticism, irrationality, and violence (Nassar, 2010).

In the United States especially, the focus on terrorism has primarily centered on Islamic groups. Yet, the lines between the West and Islamist terrorists can oftentimes be blurred so that both sides often engage similar methods. On one hand, Islamist terrorists, while decrying the harmful effects of Western capitalism, have themselves utilized sophisticated methods of technology to achieve their ends (Pasha, 2004), such as in 2008 when terrorists who attacked Mumbai utilized GPS navigation devices, satellite telephones, and social networking. On the other hand, the West, particularly the United States, while accusing terrorist groups of barbarism and irrationality, have themselves utilized methods of terrorism. This includes the adoption of a similar logic of vengeance through violence (such as Bush's vow to retaliate by attacking countries that supported terrorists who conducted the September 11 attacks), roguish behavior that contravenes international laws and codes (such as the U.S. decision to invade Iraq despite opposition from a majority of members-states such as China, France, Germany, and Russia in the United Nations Security Council),[4] the deliberate killings of civilians in Iraq and Afghanistan,[5] and the use of torture and rape on suspected terrorists detained in Abu Ghraib and other prison camps. Underlying both the language and methods of terrorists and their accusers is therefore the oldest and most powerful extraterritorial force: religion. This is a force that has a more significant global influence than transnational governments, organizations, and corporations; it also has more powerful pragmatic implications compared to human rights as religion is capable of fueling individuals and communities in diverse places to participate in holy wars, crusades, and jihads to the contravention of international laws and basic rights of humanity.

While religion had been relegated to the private sphere from the sixteenth century with the emergence of a modern and secular age (Taylor, 2007), the late twentieth century has witnessed renewed calls for more serious engagements with religion and ethics in discourses occurring in the public sphere given the rise of fundamentalism and terrorism. Various scholars have called for a "return of the sacred" in the social sciences (Ebaugh, 2002), "a return to religion" in philosophy (Derrida & Vattimo, 1996), a "return to ethics" (Butler, 2000), a consideration of real and imaginary ethics (Eagleton, 2009), as well as a reemphasis on "cosmopolitan ethics" (Walkowitz, 2009). It is this last category that is especially interesting because, as I will demonstrate, cosmopolitanism at its heart grapples with issues of extraterritoriality concerning displaced subjects as well as religious resurgence.

Education for Cosmopolitan Citizenship

Since the 1990s, cosmopolitanism has become a buzzword in fields such as cultural anthropology, education, international relations, philosophy, and political science. Here, I want to focus specifically on cosmopolitanism's relation to extraterritoriality and its implications for education. Historically, aspects of cosmopolitanism may be located as far back as the Hindu *Upanishads*, Confucius' *Analects*, and the Socratic dialogues (Hansen, 2011). The term itself emerged with Diogenes the Cynic (404–323 BC) who set up his home in the marketplace to demonstrate his rejection of material comfort (Nussbaum, 1997). Diogenes primarily proclaimed his affinity with humanity and thus rejected the status of a *politēs*, a citizen, in favor of a *kosmopolitēs*, a citizen of the cosmos or universe (Heater, 2002). The Stoic philosophers later integrated Diogenes' cosmopolitan concept into their own worldview in which human beings, the material world, and cosmic nature were regarded as one. Thus, they conceived citizenship as being tied to the cosmos rather than the material world or the state, which meant that whether one was an emperor or a slave, one was a citizen of a universal city governed by divine laws of nature (Brown, 1992). Although it is common for contemporary scholars to translate *kosmopolitēs* as citizen of the world, the idea of *kosmopolitēs* envisioned by the Stoics as citizen of the cosmos or universe connotes both a material and transcendental quality to the notion of cosmopolitanism. If, as I will proceed to argue, cosmopolitanism is an orientation grounded on extraterritorial aspirations, then this latter definition may be more appropriate. To understand why, I will elaborate on the connection between cosmopolitan orientation and extraterritorial aspirations.

Cosmopolitanism is a complex term that may be manifested in political, cultural, and economic projects. One commonality underlying these different articulations is the view of cosmopolitanism as a perspective that is invested in the other. That is, it recognizes one's affiliation to a community or nation while at the same time, it demonstrates commitment toward the notion of a common humanity transcending territorial boundaries (Lu, 2000). Cosmopolitanism has been described broadly by various scholars as an attitude demonstrated by a willingness to engage the other (Mehta, 2000), an orientation that allows one to learn from rather than merely tolerate the other (Hansen, 2011), a normative response to the excesses of globalization (Cheah, 2006), an existential orientation concerning being in the world (Tagore, 2008), a movement toward reattachment, multiple attachments, or attachment at a distance (Robbins, 1998), and a sensitivity toward empathizing with others (Nussbaum, 1997). The terms "attitude," "response," "movement," and "sensitivity" may be encapsulated under the broad category of orientation, since what these terms share is the sense in which one is directed and turned toward the other. Such an orientation addresses the question of how one can best relate to others different from oneself.

A cosmopolitan orientation is anchored on extraterritorial aspirations even though one may be a "cosmopolitan patriot" or "rooted cosmopolitan" attached to one's home while being open to other cultures (Appiah, 1998, p. 91). It is also this connection between cosmopolitanism and extraterritoriality that has allowed some theorists to draw on the connection between cosmopolitanism and capital which, by its extramaterial nature, is inherently extraterritorial. The cosmopolitan nature of capital was elaborated by Marx and Engels (1848/2006) who argue that "the bourgeoisie has through its exploitation of the world market given a cosmopolitan character to production and consumption in every country" (p. 45). The bourgeoisie, in contemporary terms, is the elite cosmopolitan who traverses the globe, exhibits worldly sophistication, forges global networks for the purposes of trade and profit-making, and may even have superficial material expertise of other cultures. Variations of cosmopolitan citizenship in the form of multiple citizenship (Heater, 2004) or flexible citizenship (Ong, 1999) promote the view of globally mobile transnational citizens, which runs the risk of aligning itself with goals that support global corporate elitism (Calhoun, 2002). Other theorizations of cosmopolitanism focus on providing a more hybrid and complex picture concerning individuals' engagements at the material level of culture. Here, the connection between cosmopolitanism and extraterritoriality has to do with the movement between one's familiar social territory of the community or nation and the broader, more abstract extraterritorial space of the universe or cosmos. This movement implies first that differences, rather than uniformity within one's familiar territory, are privileged. Unlike an older form of cosmopolitanism that emerged in the eighteenth century, otherwise known as universalism, which proposed the formation of a uniform enlightened culture while minimizing differences between cultures and nations, contemporary theorizations of cosmopolitanism tend to appreciate the distinctiveness of local communal and national traditions (Williams, 2007). For example, rather than advocate the end of the nation in favor of world government, some scholars argue that cosmopolitanism cannot be antithetical to the nation because the nation has been the site for shared historical experiences and distinctive cultural expressions of collective history (Robotham, 2005). While affirming cultural expressions within the territory of the local and familiar, a second movement occurs in relation to the extraterritorial universe. Here, extraterritoriality involves an abstract commitment to the human race as a whole. This involves a kind of planetary vision akin to the moment when one is looking at Earth from a space shuttle; one then begins to get a sense of Earth as situated within the larger universe and of people as essentially human beings inhabiting Earth. At this level, questions such as why do I exist, who created the universe, what occurs after death all contain a metaphysical quality. If a cosmopolitan orientation concerns the question of how one can relate to others different from oneself, then at a deeper level, it must also engage with different cosmological belief systems inscribed within such questions.

The movement between territorial familiarity and extraterritoriality implies the coexistence between affinity to the local and affiliation to the human race as a whole (Scheffler, 1999; Williams, 2007). This is a dynamic movement that is aspirational in its aims to balance between what David Hansen (2011) terms a "reflective openness to the new with reflective loyalty to the known" (p. 1) where I have argued that reflective openness must necessarily engage with material cultures as well as extraterritorial cosmological questions. What this suggests is that a cosmopolitan paradigm can be conceived as a four-dimensional way of seeing the world where the cosmos represents the fourth dimension. In previous chapters, I have described how a world paradigm is akin to two-dimensional mapping, such as when a map is flattened on a wall and countries are categorized by boundary divisions. I then use the metaphor of three-dimensional spherical seeing to describe a global paradigm in which the world is perceived as a whole and, like a sphere that turns, the point of reference constantly changes. What connects world and global paradigms is the emphasis on materiality that refers to human inhabitation within the space of material earth. This parallels Heidegger's (1927/1962) notion of being-in-the-world in which "Dasein [being] itself is 'spatial' with regard to its Being-in-the-world" (p. 138). In other words, these are ontological perspectives concerned with how being is bound up with the intelligibility of the world[6] and how being's dwelling in the space of the earth enables it to form connections with other beings and entities (such as nature) encountered within this space. What distinguishes a cosmopolitan paradigm from these two paradigms is that though such a paradigm grapples with the materiality of the earth, it contains a fourth dimension concerning that which is extramaterial, extraterritorial, and in the domain of the cosmological.

The idea of the fourth dimension has been of great interest in fields of cultural studies, mathematics, mysticism, religion, and science. In physics, the idea of a four-dimensional reality came to light in 1920 from Albert Einstein's work on relativity in which time as the fourth dimension is no longer separate from the three dimensions of space (Hawking & Mlodinow, 2010). In theology, the fourth dimension is the extraterrestrial realm involving heaven, hell, angels, demons, God, and Satan. In science fiction, questions about the fourth dimension were posed in a nineteenth-century satirical novel about Victorian society titled *Flatland* by Edwin Abbott (1884/1983). The narrator of the story is a square who lives in Flatland with other two-dimensional geometric lines and shapes. In the story, the square tries to convince his people of the existence of a third dimension. Later on, he is visited by a three-dimensional sphere who introduces him to the world of Spaceland whereupon the square begins to imagine the existence of a fourth dimension. To live in such a world, one would have to be a hyperbeing equipped with godlike qualities of omnipresence, omniscience, and with the power to move through two- and three-dimensional spaces as well as the power to move back and forth through time (Pickover, 1999).

The Conceptual Formation of a Cosmopolitan Pedagogical Paradigm

The Inclusion of a Cosmopolitan Paradigm in Education

Across a wide range of fields, the fourth dimension has been variously imagined and theorized, and while all this seems speculative, education for cosmopolitan citizenship can aspire toward four-dimensionality in three main ways. The first way is to emphasize interspatial engagements particularly in relation to identity and disciplinary knowledge. Teachers can begin by familiarizing students with their own traditions and culture while encouraging a despatalizing education in which notions of nation and culture as bounded and homogenous concepts tied to space are problematized. This can then lead to a non-spatalizing education where the emphasis is on having students recognize themselves as interrelated beings affiliated not just to the territorial space of nation and community but also to the human race as a whole. Interspatiality can also occur as educators facilitate interdisciplinary learning so that students learn to recognize connections among varied disciplinary fields such as geography, history, literature, music, politics, and science (Lingard, Nixon, & Ranson, 2008). The second way is to promote time-shifting so that as students examine global issues in the present and speculate on the future, this is complemented with a commitment to a historical analysis of the past. Teachers can encourage students to fluidly weave among future, present, and the past through classroom explorations of concepts. The point is for students to develop capacities to not merely see the other but also to see the other in as many rich and multifaceted ways as possible. Here, teachers can tap into students' imaginations, especially since the imagination operates interspatiality and intertemporally, so that students, in order to imagine and see from the perspective of others, must be well acquainted with the significant histories of different communities in order to consider their present and future. Finally, the third way is for students to engage in cosmological questions. Through such extraterritorial speculations and imaginings, students become open to the notion of the fourth dimension, a reality that transcends the material world. It is here that literature offers a powerful tool, since, more than any art form, it provides access to the consciousness and belief systems of another person or community (Choo, in press; Donald 2007; Jollimore & Barrios, 2006). Ultimately, education for cosmopolitan citizenship should not seek to impose a universal belief system, since this runs the risk of becoming hegemonic and imperialistic while overlooking distinctions among different belief systems (Dallmayr, 2003). Instead, such an education centers on an appreciation of differentiated values with the goal of opening democratic spaces for understandings and dialogues with others who hold different philosophical-religious beliefs.

The Concept of Responsible Engagement in Disciplinary Movements

Unlike world and global paradigms to teaching literature, a cosmopolitan paradigm values literature education not for improving collective taste (according to a world paradigm) or for empowerment (according to a global paradigm); instead, a cosmopolitan paradigm places a stronger accent on responsible engagement. This means that the point of exposing students to literary texts from around the world is twofold. First, it is to facilitate a greater awareness of extraterritoriality, particularly with regard to entities that are extraterritorial either in a general sense of individuals outside one's familiar territorial space or in a more specific sense of individuals belonging to extraterritorial, extrajudicial zones. Second, it is to facilitate a greater engagement with extraterritorial ideas concerning philosophical and religious belief systems. Consequently, the goal is that such engagements should lead to a stronger, more active commitment to supporting or helping these individuals and to deepening understanding of different belief systems. In relation to literature education, two important movements were catalytic to emphasizing this concept of responsible engagement: the reader-response movement that gained momentum in the 1960s and the 1970s in the United States and the critical literacy movement that came to prominence particularly in Australia in the 1990s.

Reader-response and Active Engagement. In the case of the first movement, reader-response critics essentially challenged new criticism's insistence on a disinterested evaluation of the literary text by arguing that meaning occurs through the reader's transaction with the text (Rosenblatt, 1994/1978), through the reader's act of filling in gaps in the text based on prior dispositions and experiences (Iser, 1972), and through the reader's interpretation of the text as colored by his or her interpretive community (Fish, 1980). Reader-response had a powerful influence on the teaching of literature in the United States, but rather than dethroning new criticism, contemporary literature teaching approaches tend to advocate a balance of both. For example, a 1970s survey of literature education in ten countries found that the three English-speaking countries included — Britain, New

Zealand, and the United States — emphasized expressing response to a variety of texts including both canonical and contemporary popular culture texts as well as critical reading and the use of critical terminology in literature syllabi (Purves, 1973). In other words, from this period, both reader-response and new criticism were and continue to be dominant approaches to teaching literature in these countries. Even in high-stakes literature assessments, it is common to find questions that fuse new criticism and reader-response such as questions requiring students to provide an informed response to the text, that is, a personal response based on a close analysis of the formal structures of the text.

The reader-response movement was a significant precursor to shaping a cosmopolitan paradigm to teaching literature even though its emphasis was on active rather than responsible engagement of the reader. Louise Rosenblatt, a scholar writing in this tradition who had an immense influence on the teaching of literature in schools, provides a convincing theory about the relationship between reader and text in the form of a transaction. This is a better description than interaction she (1988/2004) argues because interaction assumes discrete elements coming into contact with each other whereas transaction connotes the notion that the subject, the object, and the relationship between them are all part of one process with each element conditioning and being conditioned by the other. Essentially, transaction involves active engagement occurring at three levels. The first is at the level of the reader and the text. As the reader approaches the text, he or she engages actively with it. On one hand, the text provides the verbal symbols and interpretive codes to guide the reader into making sense of it; on the other hand, the reader brings to the text his or her store of memories, acquired knowledge, and past experiences. The second is at the level of the author and the reader. The author, in writing the text, transacts with an imagined or implied reader just as the reader transacts with the implied author of the text (Rosenblatt, 1988/2004). A literary text, by its very existence, calls for active engagement and communication from an author who yearns to share his or her insights about the world with the reader and who, through the act of writing, invites the reader to enter into conversation. The third is at a social level. Rosenblatt (1938/1995) envisions the literature classroom as a space for sharing personal responses. In this public space, students are pushed to move away from mere impressionism or emotionalism, since, before their peers, they must justify their responses. The process of dialogue and discussion also facilitates self-reflexivity as students become aware of the limitations of their own views as they listen to others. In this public space, engagement with literature does not involve only exchanges of facts, information, and knowledge that the student obtains from reading, or what Rosenblatt (1978/1994) terms "efferent reading." Instead, engagement also involves an exchange of feelings, attitudes, and ideas arising from the student's response to the text, or what she terms "aesthetic reading." Aesthetic reading essentially taps into the affective domain, involving feelings, sensations, and experiences, that then leads to personal rather than impersonal, committed rather than detached, responses to what is read. Rosenblatt's theory of transaction placed new importance on active engagement in literature education. No longer were teachers to encourage their students to be passive decoders who would approach texts in objective, distanced postures in order to analyze their formal properties; instead, they were to encourage students to relate to the text, to bring their emotions and experiences into the text, and to negotiate these responses with rational arguments based on evidence from the text. In so doing, space was provided in the classroom for students to respond to the text with feelings such as sympathy and compassion, which are basic emotions essential to commitment and engagement.

Through the work of scholars such as Rosenblatt, the reader-response movement was important in facilitating a cosmopolitan paradigm in literature education by providing space for subjectivity to coexist with objectivity. However, one of its shortcomings was its overemphasis on the reader to the exclusion of that which is non-I; this is the other who may be the object of the text is but who is left out of the transaction between the reader and the text. In other words, reader-response stressed active engagement to the neglect of responsible engagement. What seems typically forgotten is that when Rosenblatt first theorized a significant role for the reader in the transaction process, she had grounded this on the prioritization of the other. In the first chapter of *Literature as Exploration*, one of her earlier works, Rosenblatt (1938/1995) discusses how student responses to literature involve questions of right or wrong, justifiable or unjustifiable actions and so on. All these necessarily require students to consider the values and belief system of the other.

> The teaching of literature inevitably involves the conscious and unconscious reinforcement of ethical attitudes. It is practically impossible to treat any novel or drama, or indeed any literary work

of art, in a vital manner without confronting some problem of ethics and without speaking out of the context of some social philosophy. (p. 16)

What Rosenblatt argues is that literature education promotes engagements with various moral and philosophical value systems in the world. Thus, one of the core aims of literature education is to lead to an understanding and appreciation of these different systems, particularly those that are different from one's own. Rosenblatt (1938/1995) seems to suggest an other-centric view when she argues how, through studying literature, students "can gain heightened sensitivity to the needs and problems of those remote from him in temperament, in space or in social environment [and] can develop a greater imaginative capacity to grasp the meaning of abstract laws or political and social theories for actual human lives" (p. 261). Within the same moment, Rosenblatt reverts to a reader-centric argument as she begins to list the various reasons why the study of literature is pleasurable, for example, in allowing students to escape, to understand themselves better, and to vicariously experience other realities that one is curious about. These are reasons that essentially address the needs of the reader (the subject or the I) rather than the other (the object or the non-I). Such reasons leave out the possibility of studying literature in order to face the harsh realities of trauma and conflict, to meet the needs of other people, and to vicariously experience other realities that one may not be curious about and may in fact be antagonistic toward. Rosenblatt (1978/1994, 1938/1995) utilizes the metaphor of an electric circuit to describe the transaction between the reader and the text but once again, this is a two-way closed circuit that leaves out any considerations regarding the other.

More recent scholars have gone beyond the limitations of a subject or reader-centric perspective and thus have contributed to an other-centric cosmopolitan paradigm. The latter prioritizes responsible engagement in which, embedded in the notion of response, must be the idea of responsibility to the other. One such scholar is Nussbaum (1997, 2010) who argues that literature promotes the narrative imagination, thereby allowing one to step into the shoes and perceive the world through the eyes of others. This would help one understand how present and historical circumstances shape their needs. When cultivated, she argues, a narrative imagination leads to habits of empathy, sympathetic responsiveness to the needs of others, and its outcome will be demonstrated in an intense concern for the fate of others. Essentially, literature education informed by a cosmopolitan paradigm would involve a three-way engagement (as opposed to a two-way transaction) among the text, the reader, and the other which forms the apex as shown in figure 5.1.

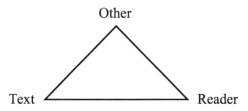

Figure 5.1. Literature education informed by an other-centric cosmopolitan paradigm

An ideal author may write for an implied reader in mind but his or her foremost concern is with the other. It is precisely a moral issue or cause concerning the other that beckons the author to communicate with the reader, which then distinguishes him or her from one who, in pursuit of wealth or fame, writes only for the reader or caters his or her writing to the target audience. Similarly, an ideal reader engages with the text with the needs of the other rather than his or her own needs prioritized. To push this idea a little further, one wonders how a literature curriculum would be designed if its goals involved having students read not for pleasure but from a sense of obligation and responsibility to others. How would this affect the literary texts chosen for study if the idea was not simply to choose texts that students can relate to or connect with personally but to choose texts that can help them become more conscious and committed to helping others, even others whom they may have been conditioned to dislike? Take for instance the book *Literature from the "Axis of Evil"* (Mason, Felman, & Schnee, 2006) which contains literature from so-called enemy nations belonging to this category (Iran, Iraq, North Korea, etc.) as previously described. The American editors who compiled this anthology aim to address the abstraction of this category that obliterates the distinctiveness of individuals living in these countries who daily face the realities of political oppression, poverty, and war. At the same time, the question is whether teachers and students from Western capitalist nations would be open to engaging with such literature. Essentially, an other-centric literature curriculum is one that may be intentionally discomforting rather than pleasurable. As Nussbaum (1997) nicely puts it, such a curriculum promotes "a kind of exile — from the comfort of local truths, from the warm nestling feeling of loyalties, from the absorbing drama of pride in oneself and one's own" (p. 11). The goal is to promote responsible engagement and commitment so that students see themselves as deeply interconnected with other worlds and can imaginatively partake in the suffering of others.

Critical Literacy and an Ethos of Liberation. Aside from reader-response, a second key movement focusing on critical literacy functioned as a precursor to a cosmopolitan paradigm in literature education. Critical literacy came to prominence in schools in the 1990s and its foundations can be traced to the work of Paulo Freire, who was powerfully inspirational in calling for a pedagogy that "makes oppression and its causes objects of reflection by the oppressed [so that] from that reflection will come their necessary engagement in the struggle for their liberation" (Freire, 1970, p. 30). In this spirit, various scholars in the United States have called for culturally responsive curriculum, teaching, and pedagogy (Gay, 2010; Ladson-Billings, 1994; Nieto, 2003; Sealey-Ruiz, 2007). Often aligned with the aims of multicultural education, these approaches seek to empower minority, low-achieving students by explicitly valorizing and sensitizing both teachers and students to issues of identity politics. While critical literacy in the United States has tended to focus more specifically on race, critical literacy in Australia encompasses a broader domain of culture and society. Critical literacy education attempts to go beyond equipping students with skills to decode texts and, instead, aims to equip students with the capacity to analyze texts by examining their relations to fields of social, cultural, and economic power (Luke 2000; Luke & Elkins, 2002). Students thereby become aware of the constructed nature of texts and develop the capacity to critique the ideologies embedded in these texts.

Broadly, critical literacy facilitates a cosmopolitan paradigm in literature education by decentering both the text and the reader. On one level, critical literacy seeks to challenge the authority of texts (literary and non-literary) that are viewed as ideologically constructed within the economic constraints of the market and serving the political aims of particular social classes and groups (Apple, 1993; McLaren & Lankshear, 1993). On another level, critical literacy also seeks to challenge the authority of the reader, whose rational, autonomous subjectivity has become questionable. Such a view is grounded on various poststructuralist theorists who demonstrate how individuals are determined by their immersion in systems of power. For example, the notion of the autonomous individual has been questioned by

Jacques Lacan (1957/2001b) in his argument that individuals are born into preexisting language systems that are already ideological in nature. Roland Barthes (1971/2001), Jonathan Culler (1983), and other poststructuralists have developed this idea to show how individuals' thoughts and behavior are governed by cultural codes determined by language. Other Marxist philosophers such as Louis Althusser (1968/2004) show how these codes are part of a larger ideology of those in power who, through ideological state apparatuses such as education and law, naturalize expected codes of conduct and behavior to "enslave the minds of others by dominating their imaginations" (p. 295).

The decentering of text and reader has led to a recentering on the other. Thus, critical literacy emphasizes responsible engagement by focusing on processes that liberate the other from oppression. Here, the other is specifically a category referring to groups that are oppressed, marginalized, victimized, and dispossessed. Various scholars have turned to literature as a platform for developing critical-ethical capacities in students so that they may interrogate lived social, political realities as they are exposed to diverse contemporary and historical texts that reveal multiple conflicting histories, cultures, and political and religious beliefs (Berlin, 1993; Luke, 2000). In other words, through literature education, responsible engagement occurs not through the actual emancipation of oppressed groups but through the transformation of students' thinking and their perceptions of the other. As students grapple with the ways in which language operates through texts to reinscribe social inequality and power differentiation, this naturally leads to ethical-philosophical reflection about the possibilities for a fairer, more democratic world. Thus, the teaching of literature provides that exploratory space for discussions about class, gender, race, and religion that then encourages students to become "(other)wise" (Vinz et al., 2000).

The critical literacy movement in schools served as an important precursor to a cosmopolitan paradigm in literature education by enlarging the space of transaction and shifting the focus away from text and reader to the other. However, one of its shortcomings was its emphasis on reading the other in relation to material (economic, social, political) inequalities. In other words, critical literacy grounded on an ethos of liberation aimed to connect ethical criticism with political criticism. What this neglected was the question of how ethical criticism can also connect with criticism of the extrapolitical, extramaterial, and extraterritorial. More recently, various scholars have sought to address this gap. In theorizing a new model for comparative literature, Spivak (2003) has conceptualized planetarity as a way to consider how the comparative study of literature can grapple with transnationalism. Planetarity provides an entry point through which we can begin to imagine ourselves as a species or a collective race in the universe. Spivak argues for "the planet to overwrite the globe" (p. 72) so that the world is not perceived according to borders and divisions but as a whole and, more importantly, this holistic view provides access to a consciousness of otherness:

> To be human is to be intended toward the other. We provide for ourselves transcendental figuration of what we think is the origin of this animating gift: mother, nation, god, nature. These are the names of alterity, some more radical than others. Planet-thought opens up to embrace an inexhaustible taxonomy of such names, including but not identical with the whole range of human universals: aboriginal animism as well as the spectral white mythology of postrational science. If we imagine ourselves as planetary subjects rather than global agents, planetary creatures rather than global entities, alterity remains underived from us; it is not our dialectical negation, it contains us as much as it flings away. And thus to think of it is already to transgress, for, in spite of our forays into what we metaphorize, differently, as outer and inner space, what is above and beyond our reach is not continuous with us as it is not, indeed specifically discontinuous. We must persistently educate ourselves into this peculiar mindset. (p. 73)

Spivak suggests that planetarity directs one toward thinking about alterity in existential terms that involves grappling with belief systems, even primordial ones, that address questions such as why do we exist, how did we come to exist, and what or whom do we exist for. Elsewhere, she (2006) argues that "to be human is to be intended toward exteriority" (p. 107) and here we observe planetarity's overlaps with cosmopolitan concerns with the extraterritorial. In short, a cosmopolitan paradigm is driven toward teaching literature for the planet which then unsettles the authority of the territory in defining categories for literary engagement (Dimock, 2001). A cosmopolitan paradigm calls for a posture of openness toward engagement with the extraterritorial; these are deep-seated, primordial impulses inherent in every culture, community, and individual. It is then in this openness that a desire for responsible engagement with the other can be located. This distinguishes cosmopolitan approaches to teaching literature from approaches informed by critical literacy. The latter emphasizes the active engagement of students grounded on an ethos of liberation. At the same time, this ethos is propelled by a negative, defensive critical attitude toward texts and readers as observed in critical literacy's alliance with poststructuralist and postmodernist skepticism or "incredulity toward all metanarratives" (Lyotard, 1979/1999, p. xxiv). Conversely, cosmopolitan approaches replace criticism grounded on hostility with criticism established on principles of friendship[7] or affinity with the other as a fellow member of the human race.

The Concept of Alterity in Philosophical Contributions

During the latter part of the twentieth century, key scholars theorizing a philosophy of literature have also been concerned with how aesthetics (including literature) can account for responsible engagements with extraterritorial entities and beliefs. One of these more influential scholars is Emmanuel Levinas, a Lithuanian Jewish philosopher whose family was murdered during the Holocaust and who was himself imprisoned by the Nazis in a labor camp. His most important works were published from 1969 to the 1990s and include both philosophical writings as well as religious writings concerning Judaism and the Talmud. In both of these writings, Levinas (1961/1969) demonstrates that "being is exteriority" (p. 290) which means that the existence of being already precludes transcendence beyond itself. Thus, Levinas' ethics is grounded on alterity or otherness, that is, being has always been relational and called to move beyond itself, beyond its own subjectivity, toward otherness. While it is beyond the scope of this section to discuss Levinas' complex and expansive thinking, I want to focus on a synthesis of his two major arguments that have significantly contributed to a cosmopolitan perspective: ethics as first philosophy and ethics as first theology.

Beginning with Aristotle through Descartes, Husserl, and Heidegger, Levinas (1984/1989a) criticizes major Western philosophers for their overconcern with ontological questions about being instead of with that which transcends being: being's engagement with the other. He then seeks to overturn Western philosophical tradition by arguing for ethics as first philosophy. That is, the goal of philosophical reflection should be grounded not on understanding the meaning of the self, subjectivity, or being but understanding being's ethical response to the other as observed when he (1995/1999) states:

> When I speak of first philosophy, I am referring to a philosophy of dialogue that cannot not be an ethics. Even the philosophy that questions the meaning of being does so on the basis of the encounter with the other. (p. 97)

First philosophy is philosophy that prioritizes the encounter with the other via dialogue which then determines language and philosophical reflection. Yet, this encounter between the I (subject) and the you (the other) is not one of equal reciprocity. Levinas (1995/1999) argues that it is an asymmetrical relationship established on a radical inequality in which the I is obligated and responsible to the other. This obligation entails an intense, unwavering commitment. "When you have encountered a human being," Levinas (1995/1999) says, "you cannot drop him. Most often we do so, saying 'I have done all I could!' We haven't done anything!" (p. 106). This is what it means to think and live in the shoes of the other person whose consciousness invades our own and to whom we must fully respond. In *Otherwise Than Being*, Levinas (1974/1998) continues to describe this obligation in very strong language. For example, he states that we are "ordered toward the face of the other" (p. 11), that ethics "requires this hold" toward the other (p. 44), that "escaping responsibility" is an impossibility (p. 14). Levinas goes so far as to say that our ethical responsibility effects a "burning for the other" (p. 50), a continual "exposedness to the other" (p. 50) and "culminates in a for another, a suffering for his suffering" (p. 18). In the end, the subject is left vulnerable and in "hostage" to the other (p. 117).

In many ways, Levinas' theorization of human obligation overlaps with Adorno's (as was discussed in the previous chapter). Not only were both deeply affected by the Holocaust, both describe the other as that which transcends objectification. For example, the everyone, or what Adorno describes as that abstract non-conceptual force of the other, is similar to Levinas' concept of face, an abstract force of the other that calls for our response. Perhaps the main distinction is that, on one hand, Adorno proposes that the act of responding to the other entails a subjectivizing of the other or taking the perspective of the other to understand fully its historical, material embeddedness in the world; on the other hand, Levinas calls us to go beyond a materialist understanding of the other. Such understanding contains an intense religiosity that perceives otherness or alterity in both the historical, material world as well as the extraterritorial cosmos. In other worlds, Levinas appeals to two overlapping notions of alterity. The first is the other in its concrete manifestation in the material world such as strangers we meet every day and proximate others such as our family or immediate community. The second is the extraterritorial other that is an abstract category referring to the larger community of fellow human beings that is beyond phenomenology and ontology. One is consciously aware of the living presence of the other but the other remains extramaterial and ungraspable because it cannot be fully known, possessed, or entered into discourse. It is what Derrida, in his (1967/1978) reading of Levinas' earlier works, describes as "a community of non-presence and therefore of non-phenomenality" (p. 91). Where does this intense religiosity toward the other, this sense of being held hostage to the other, come from? Our concern for the other touches on the affect involving emotions such as sympathy, affinity, and passion for the other that cannot be fully rationalized. This affect represents a deep-seated desire that pushes us to respond to the other but at the same time, it stems from a source that is beyond the other. Levinas (1975/1987) uses the terms "Other," "Infinite," and "God" to describe the force that is at the heart of our affections toward the other.

> Ethics is not a moment of being; it is otherwise and better than being, the very possibility of the beyond. In this ethical reversal, in this reference of the Desirable to the Non-desirable, in this strange mission that orders the approach to the other (autrui), God is drawn out of objectivity, presence, and being. He is neither an object nor an interlocutor. His absolute remoteness, his transcendence, turns into my responsibility — non-erotic par excellence — for the other (autrui). (p. 165)

That which is the Infinite Other cannot be objectified, cannot be fully known but its force penetrates into being's very core and does not allow being to retreat into itself, to exist only for itself. In this sense, it breaks into subjectivity and calls subjectivity to transcend itself into responsible engagements with the other (Peperzak, 1996). The voice of the Other is therefore exhibited in moral imperatives calling us to respond to the other (Lingis, 1998). Yet, it is precisely this religiosity, this subconscious consciousness of an Other that accounts for ethics and moral obligation toward others in the social community. In short, Levinas replaces Adorno's bipartite relation between the subject (I) and the object (the non-I) with a tripartite relation concerning the subject, the object (the other), and the Other (conceptions of God in the articulation of religion and religious beliefs).

Levinas' designation of the Other as Infinite differs from the notion of Absolute adopted by eighteenth-century German philosophers such as Hegel and Schelling as discussed in chapter two. The Infinite cannot be absolutely comprehensible; we can only see glimpses and traces of it through our ethical response to the other. This notion that the revelation of the Infinite occurs through our ethical response to the other forms the primary argument Levinas uses to criticize theological traditions. Theology, emphasizing abstract and metaphysical theorizations of God, draws attention to itself and its conceptions of God while neglecting to emphasize ethical engagements with the other (Purcell, 2006). Levinas himself modeled an approach to grappling with theology as director of a Jewish teacher-training institute in Paris. One of his former students describes how Levinas would encourage his class to engage with philosophers such as Nietzsche, Plato, and Socrates and literary writers such as Proust and Tolstoy alongside biblical and Jewish texts (Chalier & Bouganim, 2008). These engagements were meant not to lead students away from Judaism but to enrich their understanding of Judaism by opening a space for students to think about their religion in relation to the various ideas and descriptions of human life in the secular world. What Levinas aimed at was to shift theology from its self-absorption in abstract ideas about God, its insulated focus on Hebrew language and texts, toward relating theology to the secular public sphere of human belief systems and human concerns. The question was how theology can more intentionally engage the other and thus he proposed ethics as first theology (Purcell, 2006). In other words, God cannot be separate from ethical concerns and the nature of God can only be glimpsed through our ethical responsibility to the other and through our pursuit of acts of justice.

Both ethics as first philosophy and ethics as first theology also imply that in relation to literature education, ethics must be prioritized. First, the argument that ethics is first philosophy implies that literature education that facilitates philosophical reflections of literary works should privilege not a revelation about the self, the aesthetics of the literary work, nor the processes of literary creation, but responsible engagement with the other. Further grounds for this can be observed in the very nature of the literary work that contains an inherent alterity. This is primarily because literary texts operate through language whether linguistic or symbolic. Since language presumes an address to the other, literary texts already presuppose alterity or an encounter with the other (Levinas, 1972/2006, 1995/1999). Hence, literature education brings to consciousness this inherent alterity in literary texts.

Second, the argument that ethics is first theology, premised on the point that the Infinite cannot be completely objectified in aesthetic forms, raises the question of how literature education can provide space for the entry of the Infinite. One way is for teachers to promote interpretations of texts that aim not at closure but at openness in which questions lead to more questions instead of a conclusion. At the same time, these further questions are raised not for the thrill of asking more questions. The fact that the Infinite Other cannot be entirely known draws our attention to our obligations to the other and it is in this sense that ethical response to the other becomes the end goal in literature education. The ungraspable force of the Infinite bears itself in the form of a trace through language (Levinas, 1974/1998). Yet, its force resists any form of objectification in the literary work. This means then that the literary work, as well as all artworks in general, do not reflect truth about reality. This is the argument Levinas (1948/1989b) makes when he states that artworks represent non-truth and, rather than disclosing truth, it is "the very event of obscuring, a descent of the night, an invasion of shadow" (p. 132). The artwork is referred to as a shadow, a simulacrum of reality because it seeks to subject the multifaceted nature of reality and moral obligations into concrete symbolic forms and cultural codes. What is important to note here is how such an argument counters previously dominant accounts of artworks, such as the Heideggerian materialist view that the artwork is "truth setting itself to work" (Heidegger, 1950/1971a, p. 45) since it manifests being's interestedness in the world. Heidegger (1950/1971b) argues, "To write poetry is measure-taking, understood in the strict sense of the word, by which man first receives the measure for the breadth of his being" (p. 219). In other words, artworks open a way to unconceal truth about being's involvement in the world so that being obtains a revelation of itself. Conversely, Levinas argues that artworks conceal truth by seeking to concretize conceptions of the other and it is the force from the Infinite Other that ruptures such objectifications and pushes for the subject's ethical response to the other. Yet aesthetic education, including literature education, is called not to focus on the Infinite Other, since to do this would lead to objectifications of the Other, but to focus on concrete and responsible engagements with the other.

It is then the task of literature education to develop a deeper understanding of what exactly ethical response entails. Indeed, it is this privileging of ethics that is Levinas' key contribution to a cosmopolitan paradigm to teaching literature. What this suggests is that teachers can use literary texts as an entry point to exploring questions of alterity such as who is "othered" in the text, what are our obligations toward the other, and how should we respond ethically toward the other.

Applications of Cosmopolitan Approaches to Teaching Literature

Various movements involving forces of globalization, disciplinary changes, and philosophical contributions provide a glimpse of the ethos characteristic of a cosmopolitan paradigm to teaching literature. This is a paradigm aimed at the goal of education for cosmopolitan citizenship as tied to concepts of responsible engagement and alterity. Each of these concepts responds to the notion of extraterritoriality. Throughout this chapter, the extraterritorial has been discussed at many levels including the mobile elite, transnational governments, and corporations. Of particular interest is the extraterritorial other who is displaced, such as the refugee, the immigrant, and the asylum seeker. More broadly, the extraterritorial other refers to the fraternity of human beings, and extraterritorial consciousness is a consciousness of the human race as a species in the wider universe or cosmos. In this section, I want to propose three cosmopolitan approaches to teaching literature that consider ways to engage with extraterritoriality.

The first approach proposes that one powerful way in which literature as a discipline can engage with the extraterritorial at these different levels is through its closer alliance with the disciplines of philosophy and religion. Levinas' argument concerning ethics as first philosophy and ethics as first theology suggests a tripartite relationship among ethics, philosophy, and religion. Such a relationship compels us to reimagine literature education as a space that can accommodate explorations of the different conceptions of alterity through integrating both philosophical and religious reflections. Here, teachers can facilitate cosmopolitan thinking directed toward an understanding of alterity in both its material and transcendental contexts. The former explores philosophical questions in which the literary text forms an entry point to considerations of oppression, marginalization, and victimization of the other in the world while the latter explores how the other's behavior or actions are historically determined by his or her religious beliefs concerning the Infinite Other.

One avenue in which literature education can provide space for philosophical-religious questions is to broaden the kinds of questions assessed. Take for example literature examination questions provided from the Assessment and Qualifications Alliance (AQA), one of the largest accreditation bodies in Britain. The AQA administers the high-stakes General Certificate Advanced Level English Literature paper to graduating high school students. In the 2010 and 2011 papers, these three questions were asked based on Mary Shelley's *Frankenstein*:

- To what extent do you agree with the view that, in *Frankenstein*, Mary Shelley is exploring the dark side of the human psyche? (2010, January, p. 3)
- To what extent do you agree with the view that the humans in *Frankenstein* are more monstrous than the "Monster"? (2010, June, p. 3)
- "Mary Shelley presents *Frankenstein* as fearing his own sexuality and even as having repressed sexual feelings towards his mother." What are your reactions to this view? (2011, January, p. 3)

From the above, one may note that the questions fall into two categories: author analysis and character analysis. The first and last questions require the students to consider how the author explores human psychology or how she constructs the monster as sexually repressed. These are author analysis questions that differ from the second question which is a character analysis question requiring students to compare humans with the monster in the text. While the aim of author analysis questions is to have students appreciate the aesthetic design of the text, the aim of the character analysis question is to have students gain a deeper understanding of human motivation and human nature that may then lead to a better understanding of self. Simply put, author and character analysis questions valorize aesthetics in the context of the materiality of the text as well as an understanding of self, other, and human nature in the material world. Absent from these are questions concerning how the aesthetics of the text reveal deeper concerns about that which is extramaterial and how understandings of other and self are embedded in an understanding of the extraterritorial cosmos. Some examples of how students used *Frankenstein* as a platform to discuss metaphysical, existential, and religious questions have been given in the introduction to this chapter. Here, I want to show how each of these three questions in the AQA assessments can be further extended to promote philosophical-religious reflection such as the following:

- If Shelley is exploring the dark side of the human psyche in *Frankenstein*, then what is she suggesting about the limits of free will? To what extent can we claim that free will is free? Discuss with reference to one or more philosophical or religious belief systems concerning the concept of free will.
- In *Frankenstein*, Shelley suggests that humans are as monstrous as the monster. Yet it is through the human that the monster is created, just as it is believed that God created humans. Compare two philosophical or religious belief systems on their positions regarding the origins of concepts such as monster, evil, or sin.
- What are the author's beliefs concerning the relationship between man and God, the created and the Creator? To what extent do these beliefs conform to or challenge pre-Victorian Christian beliefs? By referencing one or two other philosophical or religious belief systems, show how they are similar or dissimilar from this worldview.

If literature education aims at facilitating a fuller and deeper engagement with the other, then this should occur at both the material and extramaterial planes so that literature assessments and discussions provide space for author analysis, character analysis as well as philosophical and religious analysis. The latter inevitably draws literature education into an interdisciplinary relation with the disciplines of philosophy and religion in which the main challenge is how teachers can sensitively negotiate various religious beliefs that are intensely and personally held by students. There are also warranted fears of the secular classroom transforming into a space for proselytizing and conversion. Since the advent of modernity, religion has been relegated to the private sphere and, aside from religious schools, discussions falling in this domain have been forbidden in public schools. However, with the late twentieth century rise of fundamentalism and terrorism, coupled with increasing prejudice toward individuals subscribing to particular religions such as Islam or Hinduism, it is important that these issues are addressed in public education. The solution is not keeping such questions out of the classroom but to think of ways to promote democratic, inclusive, and non-threatening explorations of religious beliefs. Ultimately, this must be grounded on the prioritization of ethics involving a commitment toward responsibly engaging the other. While conversion is subject-oriented and seeks to transform the other to the self, responsible engagement is other-oriented and seeks to turn the self toward understanding the other. The classroom can provide a powerful space where hospitality is practiced both in action and in the imagination if teachers work to establish an other-centric culture in the classroom. Such a culture encourages in students a commitment toward understanding others, particularly those who are in the minority and those who hold different beliefs from themselves.

In order to facilitate an other-centric classroom culture, I propose a second approach to teaching literature that emphasizes responsible engagement with the other through the strategy of responsible interruptions. By using the term "interruptions," I imply that the task of the teacher and student is to look for moments where the literary text or criticism objectifies the other and then to resist closure in the interpretation of the other.[8] Only through a deliberate sensitizing of oneself to moments of interruption can one demonstrate what it means to hospitably embrace the other. Responsible interruptions involve a double gesture toward a consciousness of universal humanity and humanity of the particular. That is, it always pushes toward understanding the other as fellow human being, but the moment this is concretized in the form of a text, an interpretation, or a critical statement, it is then to be disrupted by pointing to the human being situated in particular events or instances. The particular then resists totalizing, universalizing notions of the other. Perhaps a good example of this paradoxical movement can be observed in relation to questions about human rights that have recently generated much attention in academia. In examining the paradox of universal human rights, Slavoj Žižek (2005) argues that human rights appear depoliticized but operate as an ideological tool for Western powers to intervene politically, economically, and culturally in third world countries in the name of human rights. Similarly, Alain Badiou (2002) describes how human rights can become a tool of oppression and justification of the status quo operating on consensus. This occurs when universalizing principles become established and employed. The enactment of human rights exemplifies totalitarian tendencies that subscribe to an "ethics of difference" in which the other is positioned as a victim to be protected by the state. This serves to maintain the privileged-marginalized power relations. Badiou (2002) reiterates the importance of returning to particular concrete instances or what he terms "events" to counter-balance universalizing tendencies in moral formulations such as human rights.[9] In criticizing universal human rights, Žižek and Badiou are not calling for its eradication. Rather, they remind us that the articulation of universal human rights must be kept as an open space that allows for ongoing processes of dialogue and negotiation concerning the articulation of the rights of individuals caught in particular situations. What Žižek and Badiou implicitly suggest is also the need to account for both human rights and human obligation. The latter concerns the obligations of states to victims of war, refugees, or asylum seekers denied any rights as well as the Levinasian notion of the obligation of all human subjects toward the other.

The conception of ethical responses to the human involves the complex maneuvering between the universal and the particular as well as between rights and obligation. One useful strategy is Jacques Rancière's (2004, 2010) emphasis on dissensus as opposed to consensus. While consensus aims to fill the gaps that universal human rights and obligation cannot account for and, in so doing, closes any space for discussion, dissensus opens space for the other to bring to awareness particular situations that challenge universalizing principles denying them the power they should have. However, the minute dissensus is addressed, it becomes consensus that then calls for an appeal to rights and obligations located in other particularities. Yet, in broadening the space of the universal to include new articulations of rights and obligations, other articulations in particular situations are excluded. This then provides new opportunities for dissensus.

The movement between dissensus and consensus parallels the operations of responsible interruptions. Literature provides the prime site for the dynamic application of responsible interruptions because literary language never captures the totality of meaning. Extending Ferdinand de Saussure's linguistic theory of the sign,[10] Derrida (1968/2004) demonstrates how literary language particularly lends itself to a transcendent reading in that it draws attention to what lies beyond the signifier, the form, and the language. The aesthetic force in literary language reminds us that its meaning is never fixed, since its signifier contains the trace of other signifiers in an endless play of signification so that meaning always points to something else.[11] Literary language itself, in its inherent postponement of fixity provides the very condition for the interruption of any determination of meaning. Literature education can offer a powerful space for responsible interruptions so that the moment an opinion has been reached about how the other is to be interpreted through the text, it becomes necessary to return to the language of the text and to question how its underlying literariness leads to new insights about the other. The scene of teaching at the introduction of this chapter gives an example of how literary Socratic discussions can function as one avenue to promote ongoing open dialogues. This ongoing gesture toward that something else, that something other than what literary forms can convey, is essentially at the heart of a cosmopolitan paradigm committed to a never-ending quest of understanding the other more fully, more deeply, and in more multidimensional ways.

Aside from pedagogical approaches, teachers can also be conscious about the kinds of literary texts introduced for study in the classroom. Here, I propose the third approach to teaching literature that can promote a consciousness of alterity through the use of transnational literature. The transnational phenomenon is more specifically an outcome of globalization's "time/space compression" (Bauman, 1998). That is, vast improvements in communication and transportation technology have become catalysts to promoting more rapid and fluid flows of people, goods, and services across the world and, as discussed previously, this has consequently challenged the autonomy of the nation-state. Thus, transnational literature seeks to reflect this globally interconnected world in three senses of its term: transgressing, transcending, and transforming. First, transnational literature explores how the concept of "nation" is transgressed through the intermingling of different communities, cultures, and belief systems. Rebecca Walkowitz (2006) gives the example of the novel of multiculturalism that examines clashes and mixings of different national and ethnic origins resulting in new collectivities such as Salman Rushdie's (1980) *Midnight Children* that explores cultural mix-ups as a consequence of colonialism. Another example is *Netherland* by Irish-born writer Joseph O'Neill (2008) which describes the experiences of a Dutch banker who, shortly after the September 11 attacks, decides to remain in New York while his British wife and son return to their home in London. In the process, he becomes acquainted with different immigrant communities, their clashes, and intermingling over cricket games.

Second, transnational literature studies how cultural mixings transform "authentic traditions" and individuals rooted in such traditions. Benjamin Barber (1996) uses the term "McWorld" to describe the uniform nature of cultural commodities (such as media images, fast food chains etc.) that have dominated global mindset and imaginaries. However, the threat of uniformity can have the opposite effect of propelling ethnic groups to hold even more strongly to their beliefs and values. This tension between the universal and local-particular remains a dominant theme in transnational literature. For example, Singaporean writer Claire Tham's (1990) short story "Lee" centers on a father who is rooted in his culture and faces the challenge of communicating with his daughter who has recently returned after eight years studying abroad. Another example is found in the poems of Scottish writer Edwin Morgan (2000) that move between reminiscences of concrete experiences in Glasgow with imaginative reflections about planet Earth and how other beings might view the human species.

Third, transnational literature examines transcendental ideas concerning the relation among subject, the other, and the Other as the Infinite or God. It examines how these different religious perceptions concerning the Other may come into the conflict. One example is the short story "The Management of Grief" by Bharati Mukherjee (1988). The story is set in the context of the Air India Flight 182 terrorist bombing in 1985. The plane, having left Montreal en route through London to New Delhi, explodes over Ireland killing 329 people including 280 Canadians, 27 British citizens, and 22 Indians. In terms of airspace and casualties, the attack transgresses national borders, even though its rationale seems highly localized, since it concerns Sikh militants disgruntled over the Indian government's assault on one of Sikhism's holiest temple. In one part of the story, the protagonist, Mrs Bhave, is approached by Judith Templeton, an appointee of the Canadian provincial government. Judith asks Mrs Bhave, a Hindu woman, to help her persuade a Sikh couple, whose sons were killed in the attack, to sign a release form so that a government trustee can oversee all their bills and send them a monthly pension. The couple refuses to sign the release form preferring to hope that their sons will return even though their lights, gas, and electricity will stop soon and they will be turned out of the house. Perhaps the strongest phrase in the entire story is when Judith stands to leave and thanks the couple for offering her tea. Mrs Bhave then tells the Sikh couple, "She thinks you are being very hospitable but she doesn't have the slightest idea what it means" (p. 445). Here we see a direct criticism of Judith who represents the state. In a superficial sense, the state, through Judith, believes it is showing hospitality to immigrant communities such as the Sikh couple in keeping with Canada's multicultural policies by offering them money and a trustee to manage their finances. However, this is an example of shallow cosmopolitanism, since hospitality entails a commitment to engaging with the other even to the extent of trying to understand the other's belief system. In attempting to manage the grief of the victim's families, Judith has failed to see how the couple's insistence that "God will provide, not government" (p. 445) stems from their faith rather than their stubborn refusal to face reality.

Teachers can introduce transnational literature to raise students' consciousness of the different levels of alterity within the tripartite subject-other-Other relation. This can involve three broad areas of discussion. The first concerns questions that deal with the relationship between the subject and that which is positioned as other in the text, such as the question, "How does the text construct the other and what is my relationship to him or her?" The second concerns questions that deal with the relationship between the other and his or her beliefs about the Other as demonstrated in the text, such as the question, "To what extent does the text reflect philosophical-religious beliefs of the other and how do these beliefs influence the actions of the other?" Finally, the third concerns questions that deal with the relationship between the subject and his or her own beliefs that shape the interpretation of the text, such as the question, "What are my own philosophical-religious beliefs that lead me to interpret the other in particular ways?" The above questions are essentially aimed at promoting extraterritorial engagements in the classroom so that students become sensitized to the philosophical-religious beliefs implicitly held by that which is "othered" in the text as well as their own beliefs that color their interpretation of the other.

In summary, pedagogical approaches that integrate literature with philosophy and religion, that apply responsible interruptions in literary analysis, and that raise questions to explore alterity via transnational literary texts, are aimed at cultivating in students an imagination that is hospitable toward the other. Given an increasingly influential culture of individualism in the global sphere as a result of the spread of capitalism, liberalism, and democracy, such cosmopolitan-oriented approaches to teaching literature will become increasingly vital. At their core, these approaches reinforce the need for serious engagements with the other. This means going beyond superficial knowledge, readings, and acknowledgment of the other to involving a commitment to listening to the other, to learning about the other's historical past, and to perceiving the viewpoint of the other by probing the deeper philosophical-religious beliefs governing his or her worldview. It is in this spirit that the teaching of literature performs that significant role of replacing insularity with open-mindedness and self-absorption with accountability.

Conclusion: The Teaching of Literature and the Cultivation of a Hospitable Imagination

In tracing the historical evolution of literature education, I have discussed how, when English literature was first formally institutionalized as a subject within a system of mass education in Britain during the late eighteenth century, its goals were anchored on education for nationalistic citizenship. English literature served as an influential tool by the state to cultivate a civilized and disciplined citizenry, and concepts such as taste, the beautiful, morality, and the Absolute grounded the objectives of the curriculum and influenced the manner in which the subject was taught. In this context, the nation-state took over the function of moral guardian of the citizenry previously monopolized by the clergy and established the value system that citizens were to conform to. Education was then the ideological apparatus through which the state could enact its hegemonic influence over its citizens. Put another way, this nationalistic model of English literature education represents a nation-state model of values education.

One of the problems with a nation-state model of values education is that engagements with values and explorations of identity are conveyed in superficial, didactic ways with little room for student inquiry and exploration. It is essentially reflective of a Fordist paradigm of public education which, in contrast to a post-Fordist paradigm, emphasizes order, standardization, and an attitude of docility (Brown & Lauder, 1996). Perhaps it is the philosopher Michel Foucault (1995) who has most comprehensively described how, when this Fordist paradigm emerged during the late eighteenth century, it was governed by the invisible power of the state that served to mold and police citizens through everyday regiments and mundane regulations. Such power sought to discipline students into subservience through a system of rewards and punishments; through various forms of classifications such as subjects and classes; through the introduction of progression in learning and hierarchy among the student body such as seniors and juniors; and through the imposition of supervision and surveillance of students. More importantly, in this paradigm, teachers were positioned as mere ideologues of the state by reinforcing state objectives and a morality of obedience via a scripted curriculum and pedagogical approaches emphasizing reproduction and didacticism.

Increasingly, a transnational model of values education is vital in a progressively globalized world in which there can no longer be any more claims to a single, universally agreed-upon morality or value system. In other words, the nation-state can no longer maintain its authorial role in fashioning the individual's moral-ethical values. Increasingly, what we are witnessing is not merely a clash of cultures or civilizations[1] but rather a clash of value systems. This is an inevitable consequence of global mobility, whether this occurs physically as different communities and individuals (such as immigrants, refugees, asylum seekers, or individuals who choose to relocate) come into contact with each other or imaginatively as issues and concerns of different groups are transmitted via the internet and social networks leading to transnational forms of solidarity, activism, and citizenship (Falk, 1993). Zygmunt Bauman (1993) makes a distinction between modern and postmodern ethics. While a modernist moral paradigm preaches a universal, uncontested, and unambiguous set of values that is transmitted to individuals via institutional structures, he argues that "morality is incurably aporetic" (p. 12) and that "postmodernity [is] morality without ethical code" (p. 31).

At the same time, attempts by the nation-state to re-establish a universalizing value system are often met with controversy. Take for instance the case of banning the burqa in France. In 1989, three Muslim girls were expelled from their middle school after they refused to remove their headscarves. What followed was a series of public debates leading to the passing of a bill in 2011 banning the wearing of face veils in public places such as hospitals and schools. As the ban came into effect, it was met with protests by Muslim groups who felt stigmatized by this law. Part of the government's insistence on this ban is based on arguments grounded on three pillars of the French constitution: *liberté* (freedom), *egalité* (equality), and *fraternité* (citizenship). The wearing of the veil is therefore seen as counter to the egalitarian values of the state since it reinforces Muslim women's religious affiliation with Islam (Baquet, 2011). The ban is thus part of the government's strategy of reasserting universalism by promoting uniformity and equality as opposed to communalism where individuals subscribe to the values of their own particular ethnic groups instead of the values of the nation as a whole. However, various scholars have argued that the ban ironically runs counter to the concept of equality. For example, not only does the ban limit religious freedom, the argument that wearing the full veil is oppressive to women is a view espoused from a Western feminist perspective, which then reinscribes another level of inequality, since Western voices are essentially claiming to speak on behalf of Muslim women (Gal-Or, 2011). Further, the ban ignores the historicity of Muslim immigrant groups in France. For many Muslims, the veil and other forms of dressing represent an implicit social bond through the recognition of a shared experience of marginalization; paradoxically, by retaining a sense of personal affiliation with their community, this allows them to better assimilate in and open themselves to new, foreign, Western cultures (Hamel, 2002).

The controversy concerning the banning of the burqa in France once again illustrates the enormous difficulty facing the nation-state in justifying the imposition of any universal moral value system on behalf of its citizens. At the same time, without such a universal value system, there is the apparent threat of moral relativism. In order to address both the sense of a moral void and the danger of moral relativism, what is required is for education to shift from a focus on the transmission of values via codified language and texts to a focus on developing critical-ethical capacities. In this book, I have provided examples of how literature pedagogy can provide space for critical, ethical engagement of values beyond the directives of the nation-state by grappling with essential questions about what it means to be a world, global, or cosmopolitan citizen — as opposed to a nationalistic citizen — inhabiting the world. I have sought to theorize and provide a historical critique of these key paradigms to teaching literature. If there is one statement that can describe the essential intention underlying world, global, and cosmopolitan paradigms to teaching literature, it is to promote a hospitable imagination in order to engage the other fully. To engage the other fully, this does not mean that the teaching of literature should promote an unending, repetitive deconstruction of meaning for the pleasure of knowledge. Here, the pursuit of knowledge contributes to a kind of narcissistic self-pleasure and self-pride. Instead, hospitable ways of teaching literature prioritizes the other; they challenge us to think about how we can be accountable to multiple others in the world and how we can continually problematize the boundaries of openness toward the other.

Interestingly, during the late eighteenth century, which was the period that saw the attachment of sovereignty to the territorial nation-state leading to its strengthening and expansion as an ideal political model for the rest of the world (Opello & Rosow, 2004), it was Kant who provided one of the most convincing theorizations of hospitality in the public sphere. What is remarkable is that in the essay "Perpetual Peace," Kant connects political hospitality not within the nation-state (such as that concerning the way the state should treat its citizens) but to the broader notion of world citizenship. To Kant, the law of world citizenship must be grounded on hospitality as "the right of a stranger not to be treated as an enemy when he arrives in the land of another" (1795/1963, p.102). He elaborates that this implies the right of temporary rather than permanent visitation. While Kant conceived of hospitality beyond nation-state definitions and located in a vision of a fraternity of citizens in the world, this was later problematized by Derrida in the late twentieth century.

Derrida (2002) highlights how the Kantian notion of hospitality is conditional based on principles of temporary visitation and invitation that are incompatible with absolute hospitality. For example, when one is labeled "foreigner," "alien," "visitor," one is automatically distinguished from the host who assumes right of place and, correspondingly, a position of power. The host is granted authority to invite the visitor in, to impose conditions such as length of the visit or laws that determine his or her stay, and to label or name the visitor such as "friend" or "acquaintance" and in so doing, determine the parameters of the relations of power between host and visitor. Thus, hospitality risks protecting the limits of one's own borders while interrogating and depowering the other through a language of difference (Langmann, 2011). What Derrida is implying too is that hospitality enacted through the state and judiciary must be conditional, whereas absolute hospitality makes no claims on the visitor.[2] To illustrate this, Derrida gives the analogy of an unexpected stranger who arrives:

> If, in hospitality, one must say yes, welcome the coming, say the "welcome"; one must say yes, there where one does not wait, yes, there where one does not expect, nor await oneself to, the other, to let oneself be swept by the coming of the wholly other, the absolutely unforeseeable stranger, the uninvited visitor, the unexpected

visitation beyond welcoming apparatuses. If I welcome only what I welcome, what I am ready to welcome, and that I recognize in advance because I expect the coming of the hôte as invited, there is no hospitality. (p. 361)

Absolute hospitality entails an openness without conditions. At first, this thought seems too radical to be conceived, since, in making oneself vulnerable to an unknown other, it assumes an almost unthinking, naïve stance. By not imposing on the other, by not saying "I will welcome the other if . . . ," this assumes the other is rational and will not do violence to oneself or one's family, community, or nation. Perhaps this is why Derrida (2002) states that absolute hospitality is inconceivable, incomprehensible, yet it is that aspirational force. What Derrida's radical assertion causes us to consider is an awareness of the invisible boundaries that distinguish a family member such as a husband, wife, daughter, or son to whom we may say, "Come in to this house, which is your home, and in which everything belongs to you" from the stranger whom we show varying levels of distrust according to the restrictions we impose on him or her. What is needed, it seems, is a kind of planetary thinking in which our right to hold on to the materiality of things, objects, or property comes into question. Given a change of circumstance, might we not be in the position of the other? Further, how has the other been complicit in producing the very things we own? When we consider how a simple shirt may have been the work of millions of children aged four and above working in dismal conditions and long hours in factories in India, Pakistan, or Thailand for a meager pay, may we not say that the shirt belongs as much to them? When we consider how processed meat in the sandwiches we consume are driven by large-scale industrial farming and how, in countries such as Mexico, this has led to owners of small farms, some of whom have worked on their land for almost a hundred years, losing their land to governments and corporations, may we not say that they also own the food we have indirectly stolen from them? The point of these examples is not to promote guilt but accountability. While guilt directs attention to the self, accountability directs attention to the other by emphasizing how the self is integrally connected to the other. In this sense, the power of thinking hospitably in today's world is that it surfaces and disrupts the injustices of globalization, particularly in relation to the effects of capitalism.

What Derrida challenges us to consider is hospitality not as an act but an orientation containing an openness to the other without any limit. In relation to the teaching of literature, how can teachers encourage students to hospitably welcome and engage the other who cannot be entirely conceptualized so that interactions may even be risky? Perhaps it would involve permitting texts that cannot be easily understood such as texts written from a different language, from completely different traditions that provide space for engaging with unfamiliar or even non-existent concepts. What could happen then is that instead of the "host" text becoming a measure of the "foreign" text, the "foreign" text exerts influence over the "host" text, forcing us to re-examine how its language structures and codes lead to various conceptualizations of identity. Perhaps a curriculum aiming toward absolute hospitality would recognize that when affinity toward the human becomes concretized in the form of laws and duty, this ironically removes the sense of true welcome as Derrida (2002) argues, "If I welcome the other out of mere duty, unwillingly, against my natural inclination, and therefore without smiling, I am not welcoming him either" (p. 361). Thus, such a curriculum is propelled to begin by examining the concept of the "human" before "human rights" and particularly how, across history and cultures, attempts to concretize an understanding of the human always reveal that it exceeds language articulated in the form of rights, obligations, laws, and duties.

When Derrida (2002) argues that absolute hospitality involves letting "oneself be swept by the coming of the wholly other" (p. 361), he asks us to imagine the possibility that the other can overwhelm us by putting our politically and socially constructed identities into question. Yet, how is this possible? Perhaps it is only in moments of crisis when this may be glimpsed as observed when, in January 2012, sailors from an American navy ship rescued thirteen Iranian fishermen held hostage by Somali pirates in the Arabian Sea. In doing so, they momentarily ignored the intense political tensions between the two countries and the warning from the Iranian government that the United States should keep its ships out of the area. When the commander of the navy ship was asked why he chose to help the fishermen, he replied, "We saw a need and moved in to help people at sea who were in distress" (Cloud, 2012, para. 10). At the point of crisis, it is possible to forget our politically and socially assigned identities so that affinity to the other as human becomes possible.

The forgetting and blurring of assigned identities is also a key theme in Joseph Conrad's (1909) short story, "The Secret Sharer" which explores a moment of absolute hospitality when the distinction between self and other is blurred. Set in the gulf of Southeast Asia, the story revolves around a new captain who feels ostracized by his crew members. One night, he chances upon a mysterious stranger clinging to a ladder by the side of the ship. The stranger, he learns, has escaped from another vessel after he has been mistakenly accused of murdering a crew member during a violent sea storm. Realizing that the cold, impersonal force of the law will not do justice to this stranger, the captain brings him onboard the ship, hides him in his room, feeds, and clothes him. In attempting to help the stranger over the course of several weeks, an affinity develops between them and Conrad explores the psychological blurring of self and other when the captain begins to call this stranger his "other self" and "secret double." In one sense, absolute hospitality does not mean the loss of one's identity but the acquisition of a double self. In this case, by helping his double, the captain acquires a double vision of himself and his society when his perspective of the world is enlarged by that of the other.[3]

In these two examples, it is that compelling image of the other that becomes overwhelming, that momentarily throws one off-balance and causes one to become more conscious of something other than oneself. To be captivated by the other, caught in the gaze[4] of the other, perhaps this then is the significant role that world, global, and cosmopolitan approaches to teaching literature can play in pushing toward moments when absolute hospitality can be glimpsed or imagined. It is this captivation that interrupts and disrupts systems and language used to designate identities of power so that a greater consciousness of the human may be reached.

Notes

Chapter One. Introduction: Toward a Pedagogical Criticism
of Literature Education

1. See Gómez (1993). *Tales and Legends of Ancient Yucatan.*

2. In the first chapter of *A Secular Age*, Charles Taylor (2007) uses the contrast between 1500 and 2000 to discuss the conditions of belief in premodern and modern societies.

3. Although the term "literature education" encompasses the study of literature in all different languages, the focus of this study is specifically on English literature education.

4. Just as English literature was the most important subject in England in the late nineteenth century (Eagleton, 1996), Applebee (1974) describes how English, including the study of literature, had emerged as a major subject in schools by the 1890s and was essential to developing a common spirit of citizenship in the colony.

5. In the case of an "elective" subject, as opposed to a "full" subject, content is generally reduced by about half. In Singapore, students who opt for the full literature in English paper are assessed on paper 1 involving a close unseen analysis of poetry or prose as well as analysis of a prose text (such as a novel or a range of short stories) in addition to paper 2 involving an analysis of a drama text. Students who opt for the subject as an elective are only assessed on paper 1. Concerning the implications of the data, see Choo (2013) and Poon (2007).

6. Bloom is unapologetic about the elitist nature of literary study. In discussing literary criticism, he (1994) states, "Cultural criticism is another dismal social science but literary criticism, as an art, always was and always will be an elitist phenomenon. It was a mistake to believe that literary criticism could become a basis for democratic education or societal improvement" (p. 16).

7. Compare an earlier translation of the Socratic dialogues in which Socrates states, "We are not to be anxious about living, but about living well" (Plato, trans. 1897, Crito, 48b) with a later translation of the same passage that reads, "The most important thing is not life, but the good life" (Plato, trans. 2002, Crito, 48b).

8. The concept of education for citizenship has a long history predating the formation of the nation-state stretching all the way to the fifth century BC in Athens when the concept of the "citizen" originated and the third century BC in Rome when the establishment of the polis or the city-state meant that individuals no longer belonged to small disparate tribes but were part of larger political communities of about 50,000 members initially (Heater, 2004; Pocock, 1995). Derek Heater (2004) describes how education for citizenship in ancient Greece involved learning about citizenship obligations to the state, acquiring practical skills, and learning about the social, legal, and political rights of membership.

Chapter Two. Nationalistic Approaches to Teaching Literature

1. Brian Doyle (1989) discusses how, in the nineteenth century, teachers of English literature in schools were predominantly female and their quasi-maternal, semi-professional role meant that they occupied a lower-class status in society compared to male teachers who dominated colleges and universities. This also meant that English literature was deemed inferior to the Classics, since it was typically taught by female teachers.

2. The background to Dennis' attack on Pope originates from Pope himself who had earlier criticized Dennis for being unable to accept any criticism about his work. The tension between Pope and Dennis became so heated that the *Spectator* had to intervene to mediate the conflict. See Addison's (1711c) article in no. 253 of the *Spectator*.

3. Unlike Allison and Crawford, Guyer insists that Kant's analogy is unconvincing because the rationale of attunement is too weak to justify a demand for universal validity and the rationale of apprehension contradicts Kant's other philosophical principles governing aesthetics and morality. See Guyer (1997).

Chapter Three. World Approaches to Teaching Literature

1. See also Goethe's (1799/1986) essay "On Dilettantism" in which he attacks critics for their superficial interest in works of art as demonstrated in their reversion to established mechanical rules and models. Here, Goethe echoes early British periodical writers such as Addison (1714) who vocally condemned the shallow critic for lacking in taste and discernment.

2. There is, at present, no definitive history on how the study of world literature emerged in schools in the United States. Thus, in this section, my historical examples are taken from two important journals that provide insights into literature teaching in the early twentieth century — the *School Review* and *English Journal*. It is from these journals that one may get a sense of how world literature as a subject was constructed, taught, and experimented with.

Chapter Four. Global Approaches to Teaching Literature

1. In the 2011 NCTE Annual Convention, the session "Multicultural and Multidisciplinary Approaches to Literacy Learning" explores global literature in relation to culturally responsive learning (Laman & Mitchell, 2011). Similarly, in the session "Reading and Teaching Urban and Global Young Adult Literature," the panelists center on marginalized youth and how the teaching of global literature provides culturally inclusive forms of learning (Durand, Hinton-Johnson, Kumasi, & Thomas, 2011).

2. A difference between the LoN covenant and the UN charter was that in the event of an aggression of state A toward state B, the former provided for economic sanctions against the aggressor but did not specify the use of military force. Thus, member-states interpreted the covenant as indicating that there was no obligation for them to participate in any military enforcement action, which only served to create a weak and ineffective

system that eventually was powerless to prevent the outbreak of another global war. Conversely, the UN charter provides for both economic penalties as well as elaborate arrangements for the use of military force in the event of aggression including the discretion of the Security Council to activate armed forces from member-states under the control of the UN (Kolb, 2007; Potter, 1945; Thornton, 1956).

3. Naoko Shimazu (1998) has given a detailed analysis of the factors leading to rejection of the clause. For example, President Wilson's priority was to formalize and ensure the success of the LoN and to do this, it was imperative that he had the support of Britain. At the same time, Britain, having been persuaded by the Australian prime minister, who fervently defended the White Australia policy, turned against the inclusion of this clause.

4. There were three significant precursors to the recognition of universal human rights following the end of the Second World War. First, the American and French Revolutions of the eighteenth century introduced the concept of universal human rights; second, various transnational movements in the nineteenth century such as Marxism and the anti-slavery movement brought to light the struggles of the working class and contributed to a consciousness of the importance of defining rights beyond the confines of the state (Weiss, Forsythe, Coate, & Pease, 2010). Third, even though the LoN's covenant did not include a provision for racial equality, there were other instruments that detailed obligations of member-states to protect minority groups that later informed the writing of the Declaration (Burgers, 1992).

5. One recent example of this controversy is the first human rights review of Singapore conducted by the UN in September 24, 2011 (Chang, 2011a; Chang, 2011b). Following the eight-month review, the UN made several recommendations of which 52 were rejected by the government, a clear indicator that the state remains the decisive player where human rights are concerned. Since the state has traditionally been the custodian of the rights of the individual, it is not surprising that it would be reluctant to share this authority with a transnational human rights organization. A fundamental dilemma is that, at the transnational level, the individual as a human being has a basic right to life and liberty but what happens when his or her right to life and liberty encroaches on other citizens to whom the nation-state is accountable to?

6. Merriam-Webster dictionary (2003) defines "globe" as "a spherical representation of the earth, a celestial body, or the heavens" and the American Heritage dictionary defines it as "any body having the shape of a sphere, especially a representation of the earth or heavens in the form of a hollow ball" (Morris, 1978).

7. In the first and fourth chapters of the book *World Class Education*, Gaudelli (2003) gives an overview of the history of global education in the United States. He discusses some of the main tensions of global education such as accusations in the 1980s that the field was anti-American and undermining the national curriculum. He gives examples of more contemporary approaches to global education that balance a study of national and global issues.

8. See the New London Group's (1996) influential essay calling for a pedagogy of multiliteracies.

9. Debates concerning the decline of literature education in schools and colleges accelerated particularly toward the late twentieth century as observed in Alvin Kernan's (1990) book titled *The Death of Literature*. See Scholes (1998) for a discussion on the decline of literature education and Hall (1990) for an analysis of cultural studies' contribution to this decline.

10. See Thomas (1997) on his argument against the use of theory and its debilitating consequences in educational research.

11. See Sartre (1948/2001) who discusses the moral imperative in literature that is essentially the freedom from oppression.

12. Kachru (1992) has provided a useful sociolinguistic map of the global spread of English as an international language. His map consists of three concentric circles in which the first is termed the "Inner Circle" referring to countries such as Britain and the United States with traditional cultural and linguistic histories of English. The second is termed the "Outer Circle" referring to countries such as India and Singapore, where non-native varieties of English are spoken in regions that have passed through extended periods of colonization. The third is termed the "Expanding Circle" which includes countries such as China and Japan where English is regarded as a foreign language.

13. See Buckingham (1992) for a historical distinction between literary studies and the disciplines of media and cultural studies.

14. As a reaction to studies about the dangers of mass media, early courses in media and cultural studies were more reactionary in nature as observed in the way curriculum objectives emphasized terms such as "critical thinking" and "critical awareness" and were directed toward encouraging students to resist the influence of the media (Fedorov, 2008). More recent approaches have adopted a less reactionary stance and have focused instead on the development of discriminatory sensibilities in students.

15. See also Rajan's (1992) edited volume on the historical development of literary studies in India.

Chapter Five. Cosmopolitan Approaches to Teaching Literature

1. See John Clifford's (1979) description of how, as a high school literature teacher in the 1960s, he became disillusioned with new criticism and began to adopt reader-response centered approaches in his classroom. See also Charles Duke's (1977) argument about the necessity of students' direct involvement in the reading process as opposed to "divorced reading."

2. Various scholars have criticized Fukuyama for linking history with progress and modernity. Bruno Latour (1993) argues that modernity is based on Enlightenment distinctions among nature, society, and God and calls for non-modern thinking. By beginning with the premise that we have never been modern, that modernity has never begun, one is able to re-read history and get out of the trap of thinking about history as progressive or even as coming to a culminating point as Fukuyama argues. Like Latour, Albrow (1997) cautions against perceiving history as coming to an end, since this implicitly subscribes to a grand narrative of a progressive account of modernity. He

argues that history should be seen as a series of transformative epochal shifts in which the aggregate of global political events leads to overt social and cultural changes such as the Renaissance. The global would therefore be the dominant epoch of the present.

3. See OECD (1996, 2001) and World Bank (2003).

4. Former United Nations secretary-general Kofi Annan described the U.S.-led invasion of Iraq as an illegal act that contravened the UN charter ("Iraq war illegal, says Annan," 2004).

5. Video footages released by WikiLeaks have provided evidence of the deliberate killing of unarmed civilians by U.S. military in Iraq. See Thompson (2010).

6. See Dreyfus' (1991) discussion of spatiality as a function of being's existential concern in the world.

7. See Derrida's (2005) *The Politics of Friendship* in which he re-examines politics through the lens of friendship. Derrida argues that concepts like brother and fraternity are aspects of canonical friendship that have been historically fundamental to politics and political ideas such as sovereignty and power.

8. Levinas (1974/1998) pushes for such resistance when he distinguishes what he terms, "the saying" and "the said." The said is what has been culturally determined and through which language and cultural symbols are derived; the saying is what becomes subjected to the rules of cultural discourse but that resists this subjection at the same time.

9. Badiou (2002) criticizes Levinas for establishing his ethical philosophy on a response to the Infinite Other that bases ethics on religion. His aversion toward any hint of universalism or essentialism leads him to reject religion by locating his ethics on the ontological characteristic of the event or particular situations. Yet, Badiou ironically returns to discussing that which transcends the event.

10. The French linguist Ferdinand de Saussure (1972/1986) was highly influential in theorizing how meaning is caught up within a system of signs. Saussure argues that the linguistic sign consists of a signified (concept e.g., the idea of a tree) and signifier (sound pattern e.g., the word "tree"). His most important contribution was that the relationship between signified and signifier is arbitrary as a result of social conventions and that "in language there are only differences" (p. 118). Derrida would develop these ideas to theorize writing as undecidability in which meaning cannot be fixed.

11. See Spivak's (1997) elaboration about the trace of alterity in the structure of the sign in the introduction to Jacques Derrida's *Of Grammatology*. See also Barthes' (1977) discussion about the plurality of the text and how it defers any closure of the sign's meaning.

Chapter Six. Conclusion: The Teaching of Literature and the Cultivation of a Hospitable Imagination

1. The "Clash of the Civilizations" is part of the title of Huntington's (1997) book in which he argues for a need to foster understandings of the ideologies of various civilizations and advocates for a "multicivilizational character of global politics" (p. 21).

2. Derrida (2001) describes cities of refuge as a possible model of hospitality outside the nation-state. He gives the example of the International Parliament of Writers (IPW) which operates by establishing cities of refuge for writers forced into exile. Former presidents of the IPW include Salman Rushdie; Berlin, Paris, and Las Vegas are some examples of cities that have declared themselves refuge cities for such writers (Kelly, 2004). Essentially, the IPW nominates one writer per year and the city hosting the writer provides accommodation for his or her family, a modest living allowance, access to research facilities, and political-cultural platforms to discuss the writer's work openly. Cities of refuge allow the possibility for new solidarities to be formed outside the state's imposition of nationality and formal citizenship (Nyers, 2008) and so reimagines the possibility of citizenship and membership beyond the nation-state.

3. Hent de Vries (2010) describes the importance of having "double vision" or the ability to operate at more than one dimension — political, social, and transcendental. Also, Derrida (2008) talks about the notion of a "dissymmetry of the gaze" involving a de-centering of one's perspective as one is consumed by the gaze of the other.

4. The concept of the gaze has been widely theorized in the fields of philosophy and psychoanalysis — see Sartre (1943/2005) and Lacan (1949/2001a). In feminist and visual studies, the gaze has been used to describe the way the other becomes objectified in acts of seeing and interpretation — see Mulvey (1992). Norman Bryson (1988) argues that the gaze as an act of seeing is both social and political. The self who watches assumes it is at the center and in control of vision but unknowingly, its vision has been influenced by a network of signifiers and systems conditioning how it is to see. What is needed is then a de-centering of the self from the gaze.

Bibliography

Abbott, E. A. (1983). *Flatland: A romance of many dimensions*. New York: HarperCollins. (Original work published 1884)

Addison, J. (1710, April 27–April 29). *Tatler*, no. 165. Retrieved July 11, 2011, from http://www.gutenberg.org/files/31645/31645-h/31645-h.htm#No_165

———. (1711a, May 7.). *Spectator*, no. 58. Retrieved July 11, 2011, from http://www.gutenberg.org/files/12030/12030-h/12030-h/SV1/Spectator1.html#section53

———. (1711b, November 29). *Spectator*, no. 235. Retrieved July 11, 2011, from http://www.gutenberg.org/files/12030/12030-h/12030-h/SV2/Spectator2.html#section235

———. (1711c, December 20). *Spectator*, no. 253. Retrieved July 11, 2011, from http://www.gutenberg.org/files/12030/12030-h/12030-h/SV2/Spectator2.html#section253

———. (1714, September 10). *Spectator*, no. 592. Retrieved July 11, 2011, from http://www.gutenberg.org/files/12030/12030-h/12030-h/SV3/Spectator3.html#section592

Adorno, T. W. (1967). *Prisms* (S. Weber & W. Shierry, Trans.). Cambridge, MA: MIT Press.

———. (1973). *Negative dialectics* (E. B. Ashton, Trans.). London: Routledge. (Original work published 1966)

———. (1997). *Aesthetic theory* (G. Adorno & R. Tiedemann, Eds., & R. Hullot-Kentor, Trans.). Minneapolis, MN: University of Minnesota Press. (Original work published 1970)

Alberson, H. S. (1960). Nonwestern literature in the world literature program. In B. M. Haskell (Ed.), *The teaching of world literature: Proceedings of the conference at the University of Wisconsin, 1959* (pp. 45–52). Chapel Hill, NC: University of North Carolina Press.

Albrow, M. (1997). *The global age: State and society beyond modernity*. Stanford, CA: Stanford University Press.

Allison, H. E. (2001). *Kant's theory of taste: A reading of the* Critique of Aesthetic Judgment. Cambridge: Cambridge University Press.

Althusser, L. (2004). Ideology and ideological state apparatuses. In J. Rivkin & M. Ryan (Eds.), *Literary theory: An anthology* (2nd ed., pp. 693–702). Oxford: Blackwell. (Original work published 1968)

Amnesty International. (2009). *The history of Christmas Island*. Retrieved November 20, 2011, from http://www.amnesty.org.au/refugees/comments/20442/

Anderson, B. (2006). *Imagined communities: Reflections on the origin and spread of nationalism*. London: Verso.

Appiah, K. A. (1998). Cosmopolitan patriots. In P. Cheah & B. Robbins (Eds.), *Cosmopolitics: Thinking and feeling beyond the nation* (pp. 91–116). Minneapolis, MN: University of Minnesota Press.

Apple, M. W. (1993). Between moral regulation and democracy: The cultural contradictions of the text. In C. Lankshear & P. L. McLaren (Eds.), *Critical literacy: Politics, praxis and the postmodern* (pp. 193–216). Albany, NY: State University of New York Press.

———. (1999). *Power, meaning and identity: Essays in critical educational studies.* New York: Peter Lang.

———. (2004). *Ideology and curriculum* (3rd ed.). New York: Routledge.

Applebee, A. (1974). *Tradition and reform in the teaching of English: A history.* Urbana, IL: National Council of Teachers of English.

———. (1993). *Literature in the secondary school: Studies of curriculum and instruction in the United States.* Urbana, IL: National Council of Teachers of English.

Appleman, D. (2009). *Critical encounters in high school English: Teaching literary theory to adolescents* (2nd ed.). New York: Teachers College Press.

AQA. (2010, January). *General Certificate of Education Advanced Level examination — English Literature (Specification B) Unit 3: Texts and Genres.* Surrey, UK: Author.

———. (2010, June). *General Certificate of Education Advanced Level examination — English Literature (Specification B) Unit 3: Texts and Genres.* Surrey, UK: Author.

———. (2011, January). *General Certificate of Education Advanced Level examination — English Literature (Specification B) Unit 3: Texts and Genres.* Surrey, UK: Author.

Arendt, H. (1968). *The origins of totalitarianism.* Orlando, FL: Harcourt.

———. (2003). Eichmann in Jerusalem: A report on the banality of evil. In P. Baehr (Ed.), *The portable Hannah Arendt* (pp. 313–418). London: Penguin. (Original work published 1963)

Aristotle. (1985). *Nicomachean ethics* (T. Irwin, Trans.). Indianapolis, IN: Hackett.

Arnold, M. (1960). Common schools abroad. In F. Neiman (Ed.), *Essays, letters, and reviews by Matthew Arnold* (pp. 291–305). Cambridge, MA: Harvard University Press. (Original work published 1888)

———. (1993). *Culture and anarchy and other writings* (S. Collini, Ed.). Cambridge: Cambridge University Press. (Original work published 1861)

Auerbach, E. (1969). Philology and weltliteratur. *Centennial Review, 3*(1), 1–17.

Axson, S. (1906). The study of the history of English literature. *School Review, 14*(3), 164–177.

Ayto, J. (2005). *Word origins: The hidden histories of English words from A to Z.* London: A & C Black.

B. C. K. (1935). The Rook. *Rafflesian, 11*(2), 17.

Bacon, C. (2005). *The evolution of immigration detention in the UK: The involvement of private prison companies.* Refugee Studies Center, Working Paper No. 27. Oxford: University of Oxford.

Bacquet, S. (2011). Religious freedom in a secular society: An analysis of the French approach to manifestation of beliefs in the public sphere. Social Science Research Network. Retrieved January 14, 2012, from http://ssrn.com/abstract=1753229

Badiou, A. (2002). *Ethics: An essay on the understanding of evil* (P. Hallward, Trans.). New York: Verso.

Ballinger, G. J. (2002). Bridging the gap between A level and degree: Some observations on managing the transitional stage in the study of English Literature. *Arts & Humanities in Higher Education, 2*(1), 99–109.

Barber, B. R. (1996). *Jihad vs McWorld*. New York: Ballantine.

Barthes, R. (1977). The death of the author. In *Image-Music-Text* (S. Heath, Trans., pp. 142–148). New York: Hill & Wang.

————. (2001). From work to text. In V. B. Leitch (Ed.), *The Norton anthology of theory and criticism* (pp. 1470–1475). New York: W. W. Norton. (Original work published 1971)

Bauman, Z. (1993). *Postmodern ethics*. Malden, MA: Blackwell.

————. (1998). *Globalization: The human consequences*. New York: Columbia University Press.

Baumgarten, A. G. (2000). Prolegomena to Aesthetica. In C. Harrison & P. G. Wood (Eds.), *Art in theory 1648–1815: An anthology of changing ideas* (pp. 489–491). Malden, MA: Blackwell. (Original work published 1750)

Beiser, F. C. (1993). Introduction: Hegel and the problem of metaphysics. In F. C. Beiser (Ed.), *The Cambridge companion to Hegel* (pp. 1–24). Cambridge: Cambridge University Press.

Bender-Slack, D. (2002). Using literature to teach global education: A humanist approach. *English Journal, 91*(5), 70–75.

Bennett, W. J. (1984). *To reclaim a legacy: A report on the humanities in higher education*. Washington, DC: National Endowment for the Humanities.

Berberoglu, B. (2003). *Globalization of capital and the nation-state: Imperialism, class struggle, and the state in the age of global capitalism*. Oxford: Rowman & Littlefield.

Berlin, J. A. (1993). Literacy, pedagogy and English studies: Postmodern connections. In C. Lankshear & P. L. McLaren (Eds.), *Critical literacy: Politics, praxis and the postmodern* (pp. 247–269). Albany, NY: State University of New York Press.

Bernheimer, C. (Ed.). (1995). *Comparative literature in the age of multiculturalism*. Baltimore, MD: Johns Hopkins University Press.

Bernstein, J. M. (2006). Intact and fragmented bodies: Versions of ethics "after Auschwitz." *New German Critique, 33*(1), 31–52.

Blau, S. D. (2003). *The literature workshop: Teaching texts and their readers*. Portsmouth, NH: Heinemann.

Bleich, D. (1975). *Readings and feelings: An introduction to subjective criticism*. Urbana, IL: National Council of Teachers of English.

Bloom, H. (1994). An elegy for the canon. In H. Bloom, *The Western canon: The books and school of the ages* (pp. 15–42). New York: Penguin.

Bluett, J., Cockcroft, S., Harris, A., Hodgson, J., & Snapper, G. (2006). *The future of A-level English*. Sheffield, UK: National Association for the Teaching of English.

Board of Education. (1905). *The 1905 code of regulation for elementary schools*. London: Ministry of Education.

————. (1910). *Circular 753: The teaching of English in secondary schools*. London: Ministry of Education.

————. (1921). *The teaching of English in England, being the report of the departmental committee appointed by the president of the Board of Education to Great Britain.* London: Author.

Boerner, P. (Trans.). (2005). *Goethe.* London: Haus.

Bowers, C. A. (2003). Can critical pedagogy be greened? *Educational Studies, 34*(1) 11–21.

Brandes, G. (1899). On world literature. *University of Wisconsin.* Retrieved November 20, 2011, from http://global.wisc.edu/worldlit/readings/brandes-world-literature.pdf

Brock, P. (1984). Changes in the English syllabus in New South Wales, Australia: Can any American echoes be heard? *English Journal, 73*(3), 52–58.

Brooks, C. (2001). The well-wrought urn. In V. B. Leitch (Ed.), *The Norton anthology of theory and criticism* (pp. 1353–1365). New York: W. W. Norton. (Original work published 1947)

Brown, C. (1992). *International relations theory: New normative approaches.* New York: Columbia University Press.

Brown, P., & Lauder, H. (1996). Education, globalisation, and economic development. *Journal of Education Policy, 11*(1), 1–25.

Brown, W. (2010). *Walled states, waning sovereignty.* New York: Zone.

Bruner, J. S. (1961). The act of discovery. *Harvard Educational Review, 31*(1), 21–32.

————. (2006). *In search of pedagogy Vol. 1: The selected works of Jerome S. Bruner.* New York: Routledge.

Bryan, W. F. (1922). Review: An introductory study of world literature. *School Review, 30*(8), 627–628.

Bryson, N. (1988). The gaze in the expanded field. In H. Foster (Ed.), *Vision and visuality* (pp. 87–113). Seattle, WA: Bay.

Buckingham, D. (1992). English and media studies: Making the difference. *English Quarterly, 25*(2), 8–13.

Burgers, J. H. (1992). The road to San Francisco: The revival of the human rights idea in the twentieth century. *Human Rights Quarterly, 14*(4), 447–477.

Butler, J. (2000). Ethical ambivalence. In M. Garber, B. Hanssen, & R. Walkowitz (Eds.), *The turn to ethics* (pp. 15–28). New York: Routledge.

Calhoun, C. (2002). The class consciousness of frequent travelers: Toward a critique of actually existing cosmopolitanism. *South Atlantic Quarterly, 101*(4), 869–897.

Carter, M. (1948). The case for world literature. *School Review, 56*(7), 415–420.

Chace, W. M. (2009, Autumn). The decline of the English department. *American Scholar.* Retrieved December 20, 2012, from http://www.theamericanscholar.org/the-decline-of-the-english-department/

Chalier, C., & Bouganim, A. (2008). Emmanuel Levinas: School master and pedagogue. In D. Egéa-Kuehne (Ed.), *Levinas and education: At the intersection of faith and reason* (pp. 13–25). New York: Routledge.

Chandler, D. (1994). *The transmission model of communication.* Media and Communication Studies, Aberystwyth University. Retrieved November 20, 2011, from http://www.aber.ac.uk/media/Documents/short/trans.html

Chang, I. (1997). *The rape of Nanking: The forgotten Holocaust of World War II.* New York: Basic.

Chang, R. (2011a, September 22). UN completes S'pore human rights review. *Straits Times.*

——. (2011b, September 24). UN review of S'pore human rights ends: Govt agrees to ratify some conventions, but rejects other suggestions. *Straits Times.*

Cheah, P. (2006). *Inhuman conditions: On cosmopolitanism and human rights.* Cambridge, MA: Harvard University Press.

Choo, S. S. (2011). On literature's use(ful/less)ness: Reconceptualizing the literature curriculum in the age of globalization. *Journal of Curriculum Studies, 43*(1), 47–67.

——. (2013). Mapping the moral, political and aesthetic objectives of English literature education in Singapore: The period of colonisation and after. C. E. Loh, D. Yeo, & W. M. Liew. (Eds.), *Teaching literature in Singapore secondary schools* (pp. 6–19). Singapore: Pearson.

——. (in press). Cultivating a cosmopolitan consciousness: Returning to the moral grounds of aesthetic education. *Journal of Aesthetic Education.*

Chow, R. (2001). How (the) inscrutable Chinese led to globalized theory. *PMLA, 116*(1), 69–74.

Clifford, J. (1979). Transactional teaching and the literary experience. *English Journal, 68*(9), 36–39.

Cloud, D. S. (2012, January 7). U.S. Navy rescues Iran fishermen held by Somalia pirates. *Los Angeles Times.* Retrieved March 1, 2012, from
   http://articles.latimes.com/2012/jan/07/world/la-fg-us-iran-pirates-20120107

Cohen, P. (2009, February 24). In tough times, the Humanities must justify their worth. *New York Times.* Retrieved December 20, 2012, from
   http://www.nytimes.com/2009/02/25/books/25human.html

Collins, J. C. (1891). *The study of English literature: A plea for its recognition and organization at the universities.* London: Macmillan.

Conrad, J. (1909). The Secret Sharer. *Project Gutenberg.* Retrieved March 16, 2011, from
   http://www.gutenberg.org/files/220/220-h/220-h.htm

Cowan, B. W. (2004). Mr. Spectator and the coffeehouse public sphere. *Eighteenth-Century Studies, 37*(3), 345–366.

Crawford, D. W. (1974). *Kant's aesthetic theory.* Madison, WI: University of Wisconsin Press.

Culler, J. (1983). *The pursuit of signs: Semiotics, literature, deconstruction.* New York: Cornell University Press.

Curtis, P. (2009, April 28). Number taking GCSE in English literature falls. *Guardian.* Retrieved December 20, 2012, from
   http://www.guardian.co.uk/education/2009/apr/29/schools-english-literature-gcse-decline

Dallmayr, F. (2003). Cosmopolitanism: Moral and political. *Political Theory, 31*(3), 421–442.

Damrosch, D. (2003). *What is world literature?* Princeton, NJ: Princeton University Press.

——. (2009). *How to read world literature.* Sussex, UK: Wiley-Blackwell.

Damrosch, D., Melas, N., & Buthelezi, M. (Eds.). (2009). *The Princeton sourcebook in comparative literature: From the European Enlightenment to the global present.* Princeton, NJ: Princeton University Press.

de Saussure, F. (1986). *Course in general linguistics* (C. Bally & A. Sechehaye, Eds., & R. Harris, Trans.). Chicago: Open Court. (Original work published 1972) de Vries, H. (2010, April). *Secular faith: Sari Nusseibeh, Hannah Adrendt, and the politics of miracles.* Paper presented at the seminar on Myths of Secularism and the Sacred, Columbia University, New York.

de Zayas, A. (2003). The status of Guantánamo Bay and the status of the detainees. Douglas McK. Brown Lecture. Vancouver: University of British Columbia.

Delbanco, A. (1999, November 4). The decline and fall of literature. *New York Review of Books.* Retrieved December 20, 2012, from
http://www.nybooks.com/articles/archives/1999/nov/04/the-decline-and-fall-of-literature/

Dennis, J. (1704). The grounds of criticism in poetry. University of Toronto. Retrieved July 11, 2011, from https://tspace.library.utoronto.ca/html/1807/4350/displayprosef821.html

Derrida, J. (1978). *Writing and difference* (A. Blass, Trans.). London: Routledge. (Original work published 1967)

————. (2001). *On cosmopolitanism and forgiveness.* New York: Routledge.

————. (2002). Hospitality. In G. Anidjar (Ed.), *Acts of religion* (pp. 356–420). New York: Routledge.

————. (2004). Différance. In J. Rivkin, & M. Ryan (Eds.), *Literary theory: An anthology* (2nd ed., pp. 278–299). Oxford, UK: Blackwell Publishing. (Original work published 1968)

————. (2005). *The politics of friendship* (G. Collins, Trans.). New York: Verso.

————. (2008). Secrets of European responsibility. In *The gift of death* (D. Willis, Trans., 2nd ed., pp. 3–36). Chicago: University of Chicago Press.

Derrida, J., & Vattimo, G. (1996). *Religion.* Stanford, CA: Stanford University Press.

Dewey, J. (1902). *The child and the curriculum.* Chicago: University of Chicago Press.

————. (1915). *The school and society.* Chicago: University of Chicago Press.

————. (1938). *Experience and education.* New York: Macmillan.

————. (1939). *Theory of valuation.* Chicago: University of Chicago Press.

Dimock, W. C. (2001). Literature for the planet. *PMLA, 116*(1), 173–188.

Donald, J. (2007). Internationalisation, diversity and the humanities curriculum: Cosmopolitanism and multiculturalism revisited. *Journal of Philosophy of Education, 41*(3), 289–308.

Doyle, B. (1989). *English and Englishness.* London: Routledge.

Dreyfus, H. L. (1991). *Being-in-the-world: A commentary on Heidegger's Being and Time, Division I.* Cambridge, MA: MIT Press.

Dryden, J. (1679). The grounds of criticism in tragedy. In J. Dryden, *Troilus and Cressida or Truth Found Too Late: A Tragedy* (pp. 257–298). London: Strand.

Duke, C. R. (1977). The case of the divorced reader. *English Journal, 66*(2), 33–36.

Durand, S. E., Hinton-Johnson, K., Kumasi, K., & Thomas, E. E. (2011). *Reading and teaching urban and global young adult literature.* Paper presented at the National Council of Teachers of English Annual Convention, Chicago.

Eaglestone, R., & McEnvoy, S. (1999, November 29). A critical time for English. *Guardian.* Retrieved December 20, 2012, from
http://www.guardian.co.uk/education/1999/nov/30/schools.theguardian1

Eagleton, T. (1996). *Literary theory: An introduction* (2nd ed.). Malden, MA: Blackwell.

————. (2009). *The trouble with strangers: A study of ethics.* Malden, MA: Blackwell.

Ebaugh, H. R. (2002). Return of the sacred: Reintegrating religion in the social sciences. *Journal for the Scientific Study of Religion, 41*(3), 385–395.

Eckermann, J. P. (1998a). Wednesday, January 31, 1827. In J. K. Moorhead (Ed.), *Conversations of Goethe with Johann Peter Eckermann* (J. Oxenford, Trans., pp. 164–168). New York: Da Capo. (Original work published 1836)

———. (1998b). Early in March 1832. In J. K. Moorhead (Ed.), *Conversations of Goethe with Johann Peter Eckermann* (J. Oxenford, Trans., pp. 424–426). New York: Da Capo. (Original work published 1836)

———. (1998c). Tuesday, December 16, 1828. In J. K. Moorhead (Ed.), *Conversations of Goethe with Johann Peter Eckermann* (J. Oxenford, Trans., pp. 281–286). New York: Da Capo. (Original work published 1836)

Ekelund, B. G. (2002). "'The age of criticism'": Debating the decline of literature in the US, 1940–2000. *Poetics, 30,* 327–340.

Elliot, R. (1968). The unity of Kant's "Critique of Aesthetic Judgment." *British Journal of Aesthetics, 8*(3), 244–259.

Falk, R. (1993). The making of global citizenship. In J. Brecher, J. B. Childs, & J. Cutler (Eds.), *Global visions: Beyond the new world order* (pp. 39–52). Boston: South End.

Fedorov, A. (2008). Media education around the world: Brief History. *Acta Didactica Napocensia, 1*(2), 56–68.

Fernald, J. C. (1906). *The comprehensive standard dictionary of the English language, designed to give the orthography, pronunciation, meaning, and etymology of about 38,000 words and phrases in the speech and literature of the English-speaking peoples, 800 pictorial illustrati.* New York: Funk & Wagnalls.

Finney, G. (1997). Of walls and windows: What German studies and comparative literature can offer each other. *Comparative Literature, 49*(3), 259–266.

Fish, S. (1980). *Is there a text in this class? The authority of interpretive communities.* Cambridge, MA: Harvard University Press.

———. (2008). Will the humanities save us? *New York Times.* Retrieved, December 20, 2012, from http://opinionator.blogs.nytimes.com/2008/01/06/will-the-humanities-save-us/

Foucault, M. (1995). *Discipline and punish: The birth of the prison* (A. Sheridan, Trans.). New York: Vintage. (Original work published 1975)

Freire, P. (1970). *Pedagogy of the oppressed* (M. B. Ramos, Trans.). New York: Continuum.

Frey, C. J., & Whitehead, D. M. (2009). International education policies and the boundaries of global citizenship in the US. *Journal of Curriculum Studies, 41*(2), 269–290.

Fukuyama, F. (2006). *The end of history and the last man.* New York: Free Press.

Gal-Or, N. (2011). Is the law empowering or patronizing women? The dilemma in the French burqa decision as the tip of the secular law iceberg. *Religion and Human Rights, 6*(3), 315–333.

Garner, R. (2005, April 19). Scrap English literature A-level, teachers demand. *Independent,* p. 14.

Gaudelli, W. (2003). *World class: Teaching and learning in global times.* Mahwah, NJ: Lawrence Erlbaum.

———. (2011). Global seeing. *Teachers College Record, 113*(6), 1237–1254.

Gay, G. (2010). *Culturally responsive teaching: Theory, research, and practice* (2nd ed.). New York: Teachers College Press.

Giroux, H. (1988). *Teachers as intellectuals: Towards a critical pedagogy of learning.* Westport, CT: Bergin & Garvey.

————. (1989). Schooling as a form of cultural politics: Towards a pedagogy of and for difference. In H. A. Giroux & P. McLaren (Eds.), *Critical pedagogy, the state and cultural struggle* (pp. 125–151). Albany, NY: State University of New York Press.

————. (1998). Education in unsettling times: Public intellectuals and the promise of cultural studies. In D. Carlson & M. Apple (Eds.), *Power/Knowledge/Pedagogy: The meaning of democratic education in unsettling times* (pp. 41–60). Boulder, CO: Westview.

Globe. (2003). *Merriam-Webster dictionary.* Retrieved November 20, 2011, from http://www.merriam-webster.com/dictionary/globe

Goethe Bicentennial Foundation. (1950). The International Goethe Convocation. In A. Bergstraesser (Ed.), *Goethe and the modern age* (pp. ix–xii). Chicago: Henry Regnery.

Goethe, J. W. (1921a). The production of a national classic. In J. E. Spingarn (Ed.), *Goethe's literary essays* (pp. 83–88). New York: Harcourt, Brace. (Original work published 1795)

————. (1921b). Goethe's theory of a world literature. In J. E. Spingarn (Ed.), *Goethe's literary essays* (pp. 89–99). New York: Harcourt, Brace. (Original work published 1827)

————. (1921c). German literature in Goethe's youth. In J. E. Spingarn (Ed.), *Goethe's literary essays* (pp. 226–245). New York: Harcourt, Brace. (Original work published 1811–1814)

————. (1986). On dilettantism. In J. Gearey (Ed.), *Johann Wolfgang von Goethe: Essays on art and literature* (E. Nardoff & E. H. Nardoff, Trans., pp. 213–216). Princeton, NJ: Princeton University Press. (Original work published 1799)

Gómez, E. A. (1993). *Tales and legends of ancient Yucatan* (M. Shrimpton, Trans.). Yucatan, Mexico: Editorial Dante.

Gough, N. (2000). Locating curriculum studies in the global village. *Journal of Curriculum Studies, 32*(2), 239–342.

Graff, G. (2007). *Professing literature: An institutional history.* Chicago: University of Chicago Press.

Gravani, M. N. (2008). Academics and practitioners: Partners in generating knowledge. *Teacher and Teacher Education, 24*, 649–651.

Griffiths, G. (1995). The myth of authenticity. In B. Ashcroft, G. Griffiths, & H. Tiffin (Eds.), *The postcolonial studies reader* (pp. 237–241). New York: Routledge.

Gruenberg, A. T. (1986). Report from the institute: Notes on the teaching of literature. *English Journal, 75*(6), 30–32.

Guillory, J. (2002a). The very idea of pedagogy. *Profession,* 164–171.

————. (2002b). Literary study and the modern system of the disciplines. In A. Anderson & V. Joseph (Eds.), *Disciplinarity at the fin de siècle* (pp. 19–43). Princeton, NJ: Princeton University Press.

Guyer, P. (1997). *Kant and the claims of taste.* Cambridge: Cambridge University Press.

Habermas, J. (1991). *The structural transformation of the public sphere: An inquiry into a category of bourgeois society* (T. Burger, Trans.). Cambridge, MA: MIT Press.

Habermas, J. (1998). *The inclusion of the other: Studies in political theory* (C. Cronin & P. de Greiff, Eds. & C. Ciaran, Trans.). Cambridge, MA: MIT Press.

Hall, S. (1990, October). The emergence of cultural studies and the crisis of the humanities. *Humanities as Social Technology, 53*, 11–23.

———. (1992). Cultural studies and its theoretical legacies. In L. Grossberg et al. (Eds.), *Cultural studies* (pp. 277–286). London: Routledge.

Hamel, C. E. (2002). Muslim diaspora in Western Europe: The Islamic headscarf (Hijab), the media and Muslims' integration in France. *Citizenship Studies, 6*(3), 293–308.

Hammermeister, K. (2002). *The German aesthetic tradition.* Cambridge: Cambridge University Press.

Hansen, D. T. (2011). *The teacher and the world: A study of cosmopolitanism as education.* New York: Routledge.

Harper, D. (2011). Globe. *Online Etymology Dictionary.* Retrieved November 20, 2011, from http://www.etymonline.com/

Hawking, S. W., & Mlodinow, L. (2010). *The grand design.* New York: Bantam.

Heater, D. (1990). *Citizenship: The civic ideal in world history, politics and education.* London: Longman.

———. (1999). *What is citizenship?* Cambridge: Polity.

———. (2002). *World citizenship: Cosmopolitan thinking and its opponents.* London: Continuum.

———. (2004). *A history of education for citizenship.* London: Routledge.

Hegel, G. W. (1993). *Introductory lectures on aesthetics* (M. Inwood, Ed., & B. Bosanquet, Trans.). London: Penguin. (Original work given in a series of lectures between 1820 and 1829)

Heidegger, M. (1962). *Being and time* (J. Macquarrie & E. Robinson, Trans.). New York: Harper & Row. (Original work published 1927)

———. (1971a). The origin of the work of art. In *Poetry, language, thought* (A. Hofstadter, Trans., pp. 15–86). New York: HarperCollins. (Original work published 1950)

———. (1971b). ". . . Poetically man dwells . . . ." In *Poetry, language, thought* (A. Hofstadter, Trans., pp. 185–208). New York: HarperCollins. (Original work published 1950)

Held, D., McGrew, A., Goldblatt, D., & Perraton, J. (1999). *Global transformations: Politics, economics and culture.* Stanford, CA: Stanford University Press.

Heng, S. K. (2013). *Schools offering and annual cohorts taking full Literature at 'O' and 'N(A)' levels* (Parliamentary release February 7). Singapore: Ministry of Education.

Hill, H. C. (1925). Teaching English with the social studies. *School Review, 33*(4), 274–279.

Hillocks, G. J., & Ludlow, L. H. (1984). A taxonomy of skills in reading and interpreting fiction. *American Educational Research Journal, 21*(1), 7–24.

Hobson, E. G. (1917). Co-operation between ancient history and English. *School Review, 25*(7), 480–487.

Hoggart, R. (1957). *The uses of literacy: Aspects of working-class life.* New York: Penguin.

Holden, P. (2000). On the nation's margins: The social place of literature in Singapore. *Sojourn: Journal of Social Issues in Southeast Asia, 15*(1), 30–51.

Houlgate, S. (2009). Hegel's aesthetics. *Stanford Encyclopedia of Philosophy*. Retrieved November 20, 2011, from http://plato.stanford.edu/entries/hegel-aesthetics/

Huberman, M. (1993). The model of the independent artisan in teachers' professional relations. In J. W. Little & M. W. Mclaughlin (Eds.), *Teachers' work: Individuals, colleagues, context* (pp. 11–50). New York: Teachers College Press.

Huhn, T. (2004). *The Cambridge companion to Adorno*. Cambridge: Cambridge University Press.

Hunter, I. (1997). After English: Toward a less critical literacy. In S. Muspratt, A. Luke, &. P. Freebody (Eds.), *Constructing critical literacies* (pp. 315–334). St. Leonards, NSW: Allen & Unwin.

Huntington, S. P. (1991). *The third wave: Democratization in the late twentieth century*. Norman, OK: University of Oklahoma Press.

————. (1997). *The clash of civilizations and the remaking of world order*. New York: Touchstone.

Hutchins, R. M. (1950). Goethe and the unity of mankind. In A. Bergstraesser (Ed.), *Goethe and the Modern Age* (pp. 385–402). Chicago: Henry Regnery.

Iannone, C. (2005). Reading literature: Decline and fall? *Academic Questions*, Summer, 6–12.

Ikeda, S. (1996). World production. In T. K. Hopkins & I. Wallerstein, *The age of transition: Trajectory of the world-system, 1945–2025* (pp. 38–86). London: Zed.

Iraq war illegal, says Annan. (2004, September 16). *BBC News*. Retrieved November 20, 2011, from http://news.bbc.co.uk/2/hi/3661134.stm

Iser, W. (1972). The reading process: A phenomenological approach. In D. Lodge (Ed.), *Modern criticism and theory: A reader* (pp. 211–228). Essex, UK: Longman.

Jameson, F. (1982). The political unconscious: Narrative as a socially symbolic act. In V. B. Leitch (Ed.), *The Norton anthology of theory and criticism* (pp. 1937–1960). New York: W. W. Norton.

Jollimore, T., & Barrios, S. (2006). Creating cosmopolitans: The case for literature. *Studies in the Philosophy of Education, 25*(5), 363–383.

Kachru, B. B. (Ed.). (1992). *The other tongue: English across cultures*. Chicago: University of Illinois Press.

Kahn, R. (2009). Towards ecopedagogy: Weaving a broad-based pedagogy of liberation for animals, nature, and the oppressed people of the earth. In A. Darder, M. P. Baltodano, & R. D. Torres (Eds.), *The critical pedagogy reader* (2nd ed., pp. 522–540). New York: Routledge.

Kamenetsky, C. (1984). *Children's literature in Hitler's Germany*. Athens, OH: Ohio University Press.

Kant, I. (1963). Perpetual peace. In L. W. Beck (Ed.), *On history* (L. W. Beck, R. E. Anchor, & E. L. Fackenheim, Trans., pp. 85–135). New York: Macmillan. (Original work published 1795)

————. (1987). *Critique of judgment* (W. S. Pluhar, Trans.). Indianapolis, IN: Hackett. (Original work published 1790)

————. (1995). *Foundations of the metaphysics of morals* (2nd ed., L. W. Beck, Trans.). Upper Saddle River, NJ: Prentice-Hall. (Original work published 1785)

Kaplan, A. (2005). Where Is Guantánamo? *American Quarterly, 57*(3), 831–858.

Kapoor, R. (2008). *Understanding and interpreting English as a school discipline in postcolonial India*. Unpublished doctoral dissertation. Minneapolis, MN: University of Minnesota.

Kellner, D. (2002). Theorizing globalization. *Sociological Theory, 20*(3), 285–305.

Kelly, S. S. (2004). Derrida's Cities of Refuge: Toward a non-utopian utopia. *Contemporary Justice Review, 7*(4), 421–439.

Kennedy, M. M. (1997). The connection between research and practice. *Educational Researcher, 26*(4), 4–12.

————. (2002). Knowledge and teaching. *Teachers and Teaching: Theory and Practice, 8*(3), 355–370.

Kernan, A. (1990). *The death of literature*. New Haven, CT: Yale University Press.

Kincheloe, J. L. (2008). *Critical pedagogy* (2nd ed.). New York: Peter Lang.

Koch, H. E. (1922). The value of books recommended for high-school students in widening the geographical horizon. *School Review, 30*(3), 193–198.

Kolb, R. (2007). The eternal problem of collective security: From the League of Nations to the United Nations. *Refugee Survey Quarterly, 26*(4), 220–225.

Kooy, M. J. (2002). *Coleridge, Schiller and aesthetic education*. New York: Palgrave.

Kraut, R. (2010). Aristotle's ethics. *Stanford Encyclopedia of Philosophy*. Retrieved November 20, 2011, from http://plato.stanford.edu/entries/aristotle-ethics/

Kuhn, T. S. (1962). *The structure of scientific revolutions*. Chicago: University of Chicago Press.

Lacan, J. (2001a). The mirror stage as formative of the function of the I as revealed in psychoanalytic experience. In V. B. Leitch (Ed.), *The Norton anthology of theory and criticism* (pp. 1285–1290). New York: W. W. Norton. (Original work published 1949)

————. (2001b). The agency of the letter in the unconscious. In V. B. Leitch (Ed.), *The Norton anthology of theory and criticism* (pp. 1290–1302). New York: W. W. Norton. (Original work published 1957)

Ladson-Billings, G. (1994). *The dreamkeepers: Successful children of African American children*. San Francisco: Jossey-Bass.

Laman, T., & Mitchell, J. (2011). *Multicultural and multidisciplinary approaches to literacy learning*. Paper presented at the National Council of Teachers of English Annual Convention, Chicago.

Langmann, E. (2011). Representational and territorial economies in global citizenship education: Welcoming the other at the limit of cosmopolitan hospitality. *Globalisation, Societies and Education, 9*(3–4), 399–409.

Latour, B. (1993). *We have never been modern* (C. Porter, Trans.). Cambridge, MA: Harvard University Press.

Lave, J., & Wenger, E. (1991). *Situated learning: Legitimate peripheral participation*. Cambridge: Cambridge University Press.

Lawall, S. (1994). Introduction. In S. Lawall (Ed.), *Reading world literature: Theory, history, practice* (pp. 1–64). Austin, TX: University of Texas Press.

Leavis, F. R., & Thompson, D. (1964). *Culture and environment: The training of critical awareness*. London: Chatto & Windus.

Lemon, G. W. (1783). *English etymology; Or, a derivative dictionary of the English alphabet.* London: G. Robinson.

Levinas, E. (1969). *Totality and infinity: An essay on exteriority* (A. Lingis, Trans.). Pittsburgh, PA: Duquesne University Press. (Original work published 1961)

————. (1987). *God and philosophy. In collected philosophical papers* (A. Lingis, Trans., pp. 153–174). Hingham, MA: Martinus Nijhoff. (Original work published 1975)

————. (1989a). Ethics as first philosophy. In S. Hand (Ed. & Trans.), *The Levinas reader* (pp. 75–87). Oxford: Blackwell. (Original work published 1984)

————. (1989b). Reality and its shadow. In S. Hand (Ed. & Trans.), *The Levinas reader* (pp. 129–143). Oxford: Blackwell.(Original work published 1948)

————. (1998). *Otherwise than being of beyond essence* (A. Lingis, Trans.). Pittsburgh, PA: Duquesne University Press. (Original work published 1974)

————. (1999). *Alterity & transcendence* (M. B. Smith, Trans.). New York: Columbia University Press. (Original work published 1995)

————. (2006). *Humanism of the other* (N. Poller, Trans.). Urbana, IL: University of Illinois Press. (Original work published 1972)

Lewes, G. H. (1908). *The life and works of Goethe.* London: Temple.

Liew, W. M. (2012). Valuing the value(s) of literature. *Commentary, 21,* 57–71.

Lingard, B., Nixon, J., & Ranson, S. (2008). Remaking education for a globalized world: Policy and pedagogic possibilities. In *Transforming learning in schools and communities: The remaking of education for a cosmopolitan society* (pp. 3–36). New York: Continuum.

Lingis, A. (1998). Translator's introduction. In E. Levinas, *Otherwise than being or beyond essence* (pp. xvii–xvlv). Pittsburgh, PA: Duquesne University Press.

Literature a dying subject in schools. (2002, October 3). *Straits Times.*

Livingston, R. E. (2001). Glocal knowledges: Agency and place in literary studies. *PMLA, 116*(1), 145–157.

Lu, C. (2000). The one and many faces of cosmopolitanism. *Journal of Political Philosophy, 8*(2), 244–267.

Luke, A. (2000). Critical literacy in Australia: A matter of context and standpoint. *Journal of Adolescent & Adult Literacy, 43*(5), 448–461.

Luke, A., & Elkins, J. (2002). Towards a critical, worldly literacy. *Journal of Adolescent & Adult Literacy, 45*(8), 668–673.

Lyman, R. L. (1935). English in relation to three major curriculum trends. *School Review, 24*(3), 189–195.

————. (1936). English in relation to three major curriculum trends. *English Journal, 25*(3), 190–199.

Lyotard, J.-F. (1999). *The postmodern condition: A report on knowledge* (G. Bennington & B. Massumi, Trans.). Minneapolis, MN: University of Minnesota Press. (Original work published 1979)

Macaulay, T. B. (1835). Minute on Indian Education. *University of Santa Barbara.* Retrieved August 20, 2011, from
http://www.english.ucsb.edu/faculty/rraley/research/english/macaulay.html

MacMillan, M. (2003). *Paris 1919: Six months that changed the world.* New York: Random House.

Mahbubani, K. (2008). *The new Asian hemisphere: The irresistible shift of global power to the East.* New York: Public Affairs.

Manuel, J., & Brock, P. (2003). "W(h)ither the place of literature?": Two momentous reforms in the NSW senior secondary English curriculum. *English in Australia, 136,* 15–26.

Marshall, H. (2009). Educating the European citizen in the global age: Engaging with the postnational and identifying a research agenda. *Journal of Curriculum Studies, 41*(2), 247–267.

Marx, K., & Engels, F. (2006). *Manifesto of the communist party* (S. Moore, Trans.). New York: Cosimo. (Original work published 1848)

Maslen, G. (2008, February). Australia: Humanities face global crisis. *University World News.* Retrieved December 20, 2012, from http://www.universityworldnews.com/article.php?story=20080214155946443

Mason, A., Felman, D., & Schnee, S. (Eds.). (2006). *Literature from the "Axis of Evil": Writing from Iran, Iraq, North Korea and other enemy nations.* New York: Words Without Borders.

Masterman, M. (1970). The nature of a paradigm. In I. Lakatos & A. Musgrave (Eds.), *Criticism and the growth of knowledge* (pp. 59–90). Cambridge: Cambridge University Press.

McCormick, K. (1994). *The culture of reading and the teaching of English.* New York: Manchester University Press.

McGaw, B. (1996). *Their future: Options for reform of the higher school certificate.* Sydney: DTEC.

McLaren, P. L. (1989). On ideology and education: Critical pedagogy and the cultural politics of resistance. In H. A. Giroux & P. McLaren (Eds.), *Critical pedagogy, the state and cultural struggle* (pp. 174–202). Albany, NY: State University of New York Press.

————. (1999). *Schooling as ritual performance: Toward a political economy of educational symbols and gestures* (3rd ed.). London: Routledge.

McLaren, P. L., & Lankshear, C. (1993). Critical literacy and the postmodern turn. In C. Lankshear & P. L. McLaren (Eds.), *Critical literacy: Politics, praxis and the postmodern* (pp. 379–429). Albany, NY: State University of New York Press.

McLeod, D. W. (1937). *Syllabus of instruction.* Singapore: Raffles Institution.

McSparran, F., & Price-Wilkin, J. (Eds.). (2001). *Middle English compendium.* Ann Arbor, MI: University of Michigan Press.

Meade, R. A. (1937). Literature in the Virginia course. *English Journal, 26*(4), 302–307.

Meader, E. I. (1899). A high school course in English. *School Review, 7*(8), 473–477.

Mehta, P. B. (2000). Cosmopolitanism and the circle of reason. *Political Theory, 28*(5), 619–639.

Michael, I. (1987). *The teaching of English: From the sixteenth century to 1870.* Cambridge: Cambridge University Press.

Milner, A. (1996). *Literature, culture and society.* New York: New York University Press.

Miyoshi, M. (1993). A borderless world? From colonialism to transnationalism and the decline of the nation-state. *Critical Inquiry, 19*(4), 726–751.

Montessori, M. (1947). A new world and education. *Association Montessori Internationale.* Retrieved November 20, 2011, from http://www.montessori-ami.org/articles1/article04.htm

Moore, G. E. (1903). Principia ethica. *Fair use repository.* Retrieved November 20, 2011, from http://fair-use.org/g-e-moore/principia-ethica

Moretti, F. (2000). Conjectures on world literature. *New Left Review,* 1 (Jan/Feb), 54–68.

Morgan, E. (2000). *New selected poems.* Manchester, UK: Carcanet.

Morris, W. (Ed.). (1978). *The American heritage dictionary of the English language.* Boston: Houghton Mifflin.

Moulton, R. G. (1911). *World literature and its place in general culture.* New York: Macmillan.

Mukherjee, B. (1988). *The middleman and other stories.* New York: Grove.

Mulvey, L. (1992). Visual pleasure and narrative cinema. In M. Merck (Ed.), *The sexuality subject: A screen reader in sexuality* (pp. 22–34). New York: Routledge.

Murfin, R. C., & Ray, S. M. (2008). *Bedford glossary of critical and literary terms.* New York: Bedford St Martin's.

Myers, M. (1996). *Changing our minds: Negotiating English and literacy.* Urbana, IL: National Council of Teachers of English.

Nassar, J. R. (2010). *Globalization and terrorism: The migration of dreams and nightmares.* Lanham, MD: Rowman & Littlefield.

New London Group. (1996). A pedagogy of multiliteracies: Designing social futures. *Harvard Educational Review, 66*(1), 60–92.

Nieto, S. M. (2003). Profoundly multicultural questions. *Educational Leadership, 60*(4), 6–10.

Niranjana, T. (1992). "History, really beginning": The compulsions of post-colonial pedagogy. In R. S. Rajan (Ed.), *The lie of the land: English literary studies in India* (pp. 246–259). Oxford: Oxford University Press.

Nussbaum, M. C. (1997). *Cultivating humanity: A classical defence of reform in liberal education.* Cambridge, MA: Harvard University Press.

———. (2010). *Not for profit: Why democracy needs the humanities.* Princeton, NJ: Princeton University Press.

Nyers, P. (2008). Community without status: Non-status' migrants and cities of refuge. In D. Brydon & W. D. Coleman (Eds.), *Renegotiating community: Interdisciplinary perspectives, global contexts* (pp. 123–138). Vancouver: UBC Press.

O'Byrne, D. J. (2003). *The dimensions of global citizenship: Political identity beyond the nation-state.* London: Frank Cass.

O'Connor, B. (2004). *Adorno's negative dialectic: Philosophy and the possibility of critical rationality.* Cambridge, MA: MIT Press.

O'Neill, J. (2008). *Netherland.* New York: Vintage.

O'Rourke, K. H., & Williamson, J. G. (2002). When did globalisation begin? *European Review of Economic History,* (6), 23–50.

OECD. (1996). *The knowledge-based economy.* Paris: Author.

———. (2001). *Schooling for tomorrow: What schools for the future?* Paris: Author.

Office of Qualifications and Examinations Regulation (Ofqual). (2011). *Review of standards in GCE A level English literature: 2005 and 2009.* Coventry, UK: Author.

Ong, A. (1999). *Flexible citizenship: The cultural logics of transnationality.* Durham, NC: Duke University Press.

————. (2006). *Neoliberalism as exception: Mutations in citizenship and sovereignty.* Durham, NC: Duke University Press.

Opello, W. C., & Rosow, S. J. (2004). *The nation-state and global order: A historical introduction to contemporary politics* (2nd ed.). London: Lynne Rienner.

Palmer, D. J. (1965). *The rise of English studies: An account of the study of the English language and literature from its origins to the making of the Oxford English School.* Oxford: Oxford University Press.

Pasha, M. K. (2004). Globalization, Islam and resistance. In F. J. Lechner & J. Boli (Eds.), *The globalization reader* (2nd ed., pp. 330–334). Oxford: Blackwell.

Patey, D. L. (2005). The institution of criticism in the eighteenth century. In H. B. Nisbet & C. Rawson (Eds.), *Cambridge histories online* (pp. 3–31). Cambridge: Cambridge University Press.

Paton, G. (2009, April 29). Teenagers "shunning English literature" at school. *Telegraph.* Retrieved December 20, 2012, from http://www.telegraph.co.uk/education/educationnews/5237477/Teenagers-shunning-English-literature-at-school.html

Peperzak, A. T. (1996). Preface. In A. T. Peperzak, S. Critchlet, & R. Bernascont (Eds.), *Emmanuel Levinas: Basic philosophical writings* (pp. vii–xvi). Bloomington, IN: Indiana University Press.

Pickover, C. A. (1999). *Surfing through hyperspace: Understanding higher universes in six easy lessons.* Oxford: Oxford University Press.

Pine, L. (2010). *Education in Nazi Germany.* Oxford: Berg.

Pizer, J. (2006). *The idea of world literature: History and pedagogical practice.* Baton Rouge: Louisiana State University Press.

Plato. (1897). *Apology, Crito and Phaedo* (H. Cary, Trans.). Philadelphia: David McKay.

————. (2002). *Five dialogues: Euthyphro, Apology, Crito, Meno, Phaedo* (G. M. A. Grube, Trans., 2nd ed.). Indianapolis, IN: Hackett.

Pluhar, W. S. (1987). Introduction. In *Critique of Judgment* (W. S. Pluhar, Trans., pp. xxiii–cix). Indianapolis, IN: Hackett.

Pocock, J. G. (1995). The ideal of citizenship since classical times. In R. Beiner (Ed.), *Theorizing citizenship* (pp. 29–52). Albany, NY: State University of New York Press.

Poon, A. (2007). The politics of pragmatism: Some issues in the teaching of literature in Singapore. *Changing English, 14*(1), 51–59.

Pope, A. (1711). An essay on criticism. University of Toronto Libraries. Retrieved July 11, 2011, from http://rpo.library.utoronto.ca/poem/1634.html

Posnett, H. M. (1886). *Comparative literature.* London: Keagan Paul, Trench.

Potter, P. B. (1945). The United Nations Charter and the Covenant of the League of Nations. *American Journal of International Law, 39*(3), 546–551.

Probst, R. E. (1981). Response-based teaching of literature. *English Journal, 70*(7), 43–47.

Purcell, M. (2006). *Levinas and theology.* Cambridge: Cambridge University Press.

Purves, A. C. (Ed.). (1972). *How porcupines make love: Notes on a response-centered curriculum.* Lexington, MA: Xerox College.

Purves, A. C. (1973). *Literature education in ten countries: An empirical study.* New York: Halsted.

Raban-Bisby, B. (1995). The state of English in the state of England. In B. Raban-Bisby, G. Brooks, & S. Wolfendale (Eds.), *Developing language and literacy* (pp. 51–66). London: Trentham.

Rajan, R. S. (Ed.). (1992). *The lie of the land: English literary studies in India.* Oxford: Oxford University Press.

Ramanathan, V. (2005). *The English-vernacular divide: Postcolonial language politics and practice.* New York: Multilingual Matters.

Rancière, J. (2004). Who is the subject of the rights of man? *South Atlantic Quarterly, 103*(2–3), 297–310.

———. (2010). *Dissensus: On politics and aesthetics* (S. Corcoran, Ed. & Trans.). New York: Continuum.

Reigniting the spark of literature. (2013, March 3). *Straits Times*, p. 42.

Richards, I. A. (1929). *Practical criticism: A study of literary judgment.* New York: Harvest.

———. (2004). *Principles of literary criticism.* London: Routledge. (Original work published 1924)

Richardson, A. (1994). *Literature, education, and romanticism: Reading as social practice 1780–1832.* Cambridge: Cambridge University Press.

Robbins, B. (1998). Introduction, part I: Actually existing cosmopolitanism. In P. Cheah & B. Robbins (Eds.), *Cosmopolitics: Thinking and feeling beyond the nation* (pp. 1–19). Minneapolis, MN: University of Minnesota Press.

Robotham, D. (2005). Cosmopolitanism and planetary humanism: The strategic universalism of Paul Gilroy. *South Atlantic Quarterly, 104*(3), 561–582.

Rorty, R. (2006). Looking back at "literary theory." In H. Saussy (Ed.), *Comparative literature in an age of globalization* (pp. 63–67). Baltimore, MD: Johns Hopkins University Press.

Rosenblatt, L. M. (1994). *The reader, the text, the poem: The transactional theory of the literary work.* Cardondale, IL: Southern Illinois University Press. (Original work published 1978)

———. (1995). *Literature as exploration* (5th ed.). New York: Modern Language Association of America. (Original work published 1938)

———. (2004). The transactional theory of reading and writing. In R. B. Ruddell & N. J. Unrau (Eds.), *Theoretical models and processes of reading* (pp. 1363–1398). Newark, DE: International Reading Association. (Original work published 1988)

Ross, A. (2002). Citizenship education and curriculum theory. In D. Scott & H. Lawson (Eds.), *Citizenship, education and the curriculum* (pp. 45–62). Westport, CT: Greenwood.

Rushdie, S. (1980). *Midnight's children.* London: Penguin.

Sartre, J.-P. (2001). What is literature? In V. B. Leitch (Ed.), *The Norton anthology of theory and criticism* (B. Frechtman, Trans., pp. 1336–1349). New York: W. W. Norton. (Original work published 1948)

———. (2005). *Being and nothingness: An essay on phenomenological ontology* (H. E. Barnes, Trans.). New York: Philosophical library. (Original work published 1943)

Scheffler, S. (1999). Conceptions of cosmopolitanism. *Utilitas, 11*(3), 256–276.

Schelling, F. W. (1989). *The philosophy of art* (D. W. Stott, Ed. & Trans.). Minneapolis, MN: University of Minnesota Press. (Original work given in a series of lectures between 1801 and 1804)

Schiller, F. (2004). *On the aesthetic education of man.* Mineola, NY: Dover. (Original work published 1795)

Scholes, R. (1998). *The rise and fall of English: Reconstructing English as a discipline.* New Haven, CT: Yale University Press.

Scholte, J. A. (2005). *Globalization: A critical introduction* (2nd ed.). New York: Palgrave MacMillan.

Schwartz, S. H., & Bilsky, W. (1987). Towards a universal psychological structure of human values. *Journal of Personality and Social Psychology, 53*(3), 550–562.

Scott, J. N. (1755). *A new universal etymological English dictionary: Containing not only explanations of the words in the English language; . . . but also their etymologies from the ancient and modern languages: and accents directing to their proper pronunciation.* London: T. Osborne & J. Shipton; J. Hodges; R. Baldwin; W. Johnston, and J. Ward.

Sealey-Ruiz, Y. (2007). Wrapping the curriculum around their lives: Using a culturally relevant curriculum with African American adult women. *Adult Education Quarterly, 58*(1), 44–60.

Shannon, C. E., & Weaver, W. (1949). *A mathematical model of communication.* Urbana, IL: University of Illinois Press.

Shannon, T. R. (1996). *An introduction to the world-system perspective.* Boulder, CO: Westview.

Shayer, D. (1972). *The teaching of English in schools: 1900–1970.* London: Routledge.

Shepherd, E. E. (1937). The survey of world-literature. *English Journal, 26*(4), 337–338.

Shih, S. (2004). Global literature and the technologies of recognition. *PMLA, 119*(1), 16–30.

Shimazu, N. (1998). *Japan, race and equality: The racial equality proposal of 1919.* New York: Routledge.

Shipley, J. T. (1945). *Dictionary of word origins.* New York: Philosophical Library.

Smith, D. V. (1941). *Evaluating instruction in secondary school English: A report of a division of the New York Regents' inquiry into the character and cost of public education in New York State.* Chicago: National Council of Teachers of English.

Spivak, G. C. (1988). Can the subaltern speak? In C. Nelson & L. Grossberg (Eds.), *Marxism and the interpretation of culture* (pp. 271–316). London: Macmillan.

———. (1997). Translator's preface. In J. Derrida, *Of grammatology* (pp. ix–lxxxvii). Baltimore, MD: Johns Hopkins University Press.

———. (2003). *Death of a discipline.* New York: Columbia University Press.

———. (2006). World systems & the Creole. *Narrative, 14*(1), 102–112.

Stabile, C. A., & Kumar, D. (2005). Unveiling imperialism: Media, gender and the war on Afghanistan. *Media, Culture & Society, 27*(5), 765–782.

State Board of Education. (1934). *Tentative course of study for the core curriculum of Virginia secondary schools: Grade VIII.* Richmond, VA: Author.

Stolper, B. J. (1935). World-literature in the high school. *English Journal, 24*(6), 480–484.

Storey, J. (2006). *Cultural theory and popular culture: An introduction* (4th ed.). Essex, UK: Pearson.

Strich, F. (1949). *Goethe and world literature* (C. A. Sym, Trans.). New York: Hafner.

Tabb, W. K. (2009). Globalization today: At the borders of class and state theory. *Science & Society, 73*(1), 34–53.

Tagore, R. (1961). To teachers. In A. Chakravarty (Ed.), *A Tagore reader* (pp. 213–223). New York: MacMillan.

Tagore, S. (2008). Tagore's conception of cosmopolitanism: A reconstruction. *University of Toronto Quarterly, 77*(4), 1070–1084.

Talbert, J. E., & McLaughlin, M. W. (2002). Professional communities and the artisan model of teaching. *Teachers and Teaching: Theory and Practice, 8*(3), 325–343.

Taylor, C. (2007). *A secular age.* Cambridge, MA: Belknap.

Tham, C. (1990). *Fascist rock: Stories of rebellion.* Singapore: Times Books International.

Thomas, G. (1997). What's the use of theory? *Harvard Educational Review, 67*(1), 75–104.

Thompson, M. (2010, April 6). Combat video: The Pentagon springs a Wikileak. *Time.* Retrieved November 20, 2011, from
http://www.time.com/time/nation/article/0,8599,1978017,00.html

Thomsen, M. R. (2008). *Mapping world literature: International canonization and transnational literatures.* New York: Continuum.

Thornton, E. W. (1956). The United Nations' debt to the League of Nations. *Social Studies, 47*(5), 187–191.

Turnbull, C. M. (2009). *A history of modern Singapore: 1819–2005.* Singapore: NUS Press.

United Nations. (1948). *The Universal Declaration of Human Rights.* Retrieved November 20, 2011, from United Nations: http://www.un.org/en/documents/udhr/

Vinz, R. (2000). Cautions against canonizing an(other) literature. In R. Mahalingam & C. McCarthy (Eds.), *Multicultural curriculum: New directions for social theory, practice, and policy* (pp. 127–154). New York: Routledge.

Vinz, R., Gordon, E., Hamilton, G., LaMontagne, J., & Lundgren, B. (2000). *Becoming (other)wise: Enhancing critical reading perspectives.* Portland, ME: Calendar Islands.

Viswanathan, G. (1989). *Masks of conquest: Literary study and British rule in India.* New York: Columbia University Press.

————. (2002). Subjecting English and the question of representation. In A. Anderson & J. Valente (Eds.), *Disciplinarity at the fin de siècle* (pp. 177–195). Princeton, NJ: Princeton University Press.

Walkowitz, R. L. (2006). The location of literature: The transnational book and the migrant writer. *Contemporary Literature, 47*(4), 527–545.

————. (2009). The post-consensus novel: Minority culture, multiculturalism, and transnational comparison. In R. Caserio (Ed.), *The Cambridge companion to the twentieth- century English novel* (pp. 223–237). Cambridge: Cambridge University Press.

Wallerstein, I. (1974). *The modern world-system: Capitalist agriculture and the origins of the European world economy in the sixteenth century.* New York: Academic.

————. (1996). The global picture, 1945–90. In T. K. Hopkins & I. Wallerstein (Eds.), *The age of transition: Trajectory of the world-system, 1945–2025* (pp. 209–225). London: Zed.

————. (2004). *World-systems analysis: An introduction.* Durham, NC: Duke University Press.

————. (2011). *The modern world-system IV: Centrist liberalism triumphant, 1789–1914.* Los Angeles: University of California Press.

Walshe, R. D. (2008). It's time Australia reshaped English. *Illuminations: Journal of the Arts, English and Literacy Education Research Network, 1*(1), 19–26.

Wedgwood, H., & Atkinson, J. C. (1872). *A dictionary of English etymology.* London: Trübner.

Weiler, K. (1991). Freire and a feminist pedagogy of difference. *Harvard Educational Review, 61*(4), 449–474.

Weiss, T. G., Forsythe, D. P., Coate, R. A., & Pease, K.-K. (2010). *The United Nations and changing world politics.* Boulder, CO: Westview.

Wellek, R. (1963). The term and concept of literary criticism. In S. G. Nichols (Ed.), *Concepts of criticism* (pp. 21–36). New Haven, CT: Yale University Press.

Welton, J. (1906). *Principles and methods of teaching.* London: Clive.

Wicks, R. (1993). Hegel's aesthetics: An overview. In F. C. Beiser (Ed.), *The Cambridge companion to Hegel* (pp. 348–377). Cambridge: Cambridge University Press.

Wilder, T. (1950). World literature and the modern mind. In A. Bergstraesser (Ed.), *Goethe and the modern age* (pp. 213–224). Chicago: Henry Regnery.

Williams, L. B. (2007). Overcoming the "contagion of mimicry": The cosmopolitan nationalism and modernist history of Rabindranath Tagore and W. B. Yeats. *American Historical Review, 112*(1), 69–100.

Williams, R. (1958). *Culture and society: 1780–1950.* New York: Columbia University Press.

————. (1977). *Marxism and literature.* Oxford: Oxford University Press.

Wilson, W. (1918). 8 January, 1918: President Woodrow Wilson's Fourteen Points. *The Avalon Project: Documents in Law, History, and Diplomacy.* Retrieved November 20, 2011, from http://avalon.law.yale.edu/20th_century/wilson14.asp

Wimsatt, W. K., & Beardsley, M. C. (2001a). The intentional fallacy. In V. B. Leitch (Ed.), *The Norton anthology of theory and criticism* (pp. 1374–1387). New York: W. W. Norton. (Original work published 1946)

————. (2001b). The affective fallacy. In V. B. Leitch (Ed.), *The Norton anthology of theory and criticism* (pp. 1387–1403). New York: W. W. Norton. (Original work published 1949)

World Bank. (2003). *Lifelong learning in the global knowledge economy: Challenges for developing countries.* Washington, DC: Author.

Yasui, H. (2011, April 25). Guantánamo Bay Naval Base (Cuba). *New York Times.*

Žižek, S. (2005). Against human rights. *New Left Review, 34* (July–August), 115–131.

Index

GLOBAL
STUDIES IN
EDUCATION

A.C. (Tina) Besley, Michael A. Peters,
Cameron McCarthy, Fazal Rizvi
General Editors

Global Studies in Education is a book series that addresses the implications of the powerful dynamics associated with globalization for re-conceptualizing educational theory, policy and practice. The general orientation of the series is interdisciplinary. It welcomes conceptual, empirical and critical studies that explore the dynamics of the rapidly changing global processes, connectivities and imagination, and how these are reshaping issues of knowledge creation and management and economic and political institutions, leading to new social identities and cultural formations associated with education.

We are particularly interested in manuscripts that offer: a) new theoretical, and methodological, approaches to the study of globalization and its impact on education; b) ethnographic case studies or textual/discourse based analyses that examine the cultural identity experiences of youth and educators inside and outside of educational institutions; c) studies of education policy processes that address the impact and operation of global agencies and networks; d) analyses of the nature and scope of transnational flows of capital, people and ideas and how these are affecting educational processes; e) studies of shifts in knowledge and media formations, and how these point to new conceptions of educational processes; f) exploration of global economic, social and educational inequalities and social movements promoting ethical renewal.

For additional information about this series or for the submission of manuscripts, please contact one of the series editors:

A.C. (Tina) Besley: t.besley@waikato.ac.nz
Cameron McCarthy: cmccart1@illinois.edu
Michael A. Peters: mpeters@waikato.ac.nz
Fazal Rizvi: frizvi@unimelb.edu.au

To order other books in this series, please contact our Customer Service Department:
    (800) 770-LANG (within the U.S.)
    (212) 647-7706 (outside the U.S.)
    (212) 647-7707 FAX

Or browse online by series:
    www.peterlang.com